Future Agenda

Future Agenda
The World in 2020

Contents

Foreword

The Future Agenda programme provides an open forum for discussion about how to address the major challenges which society faces over the next ten years, offering the opportunity for all to share ideas and potential solutions so that ultimately we can together inspire change.

We began this discussion by identifying a range of issues that we believed were the most important for the next decade. We then invited a number of experts from academia and industry to offer an initial perspective which we published online and in booklet form. We have spent the past twelve months talking to other experts and professionals across a wide variety of fields and asked them to challenge that initial point of view and build the debate. Overall we have talked directly to more than 2,000 people across many countries, from Australia and New Zealand to China and India, Germany and Spain, the UK and the US. In addition many people have added their comments to our website or followed the debate on Twitter. We are grateful to all those who took part in this project and who were prepared to voice an opinion and challenge the status quo.

This book is the latest step in the journey and offers an overview of the discussions we have shared to date. The aim has been to articulate the complex challenges we face and understand how we can learn from the ways they are being addressed in different societies. On some occasions there has been heated debate, particularly over issues such as climate change and the future provision of healthcare, and in some instances the problems have seemed almost too intractable to manage but perseverance has paid off; the debate has moved on and opportunities have been identified.

We hope you will find something which will inspire you to question the status quo and consider the possibility of change. All those who have participated so far have had important things to say that should be of interest to anyone concerned with creating a sustainable future for us all.

Mobile technology can offer many benefits but I think the most significant contribution that the industry I work in can provide is the power to allow people to communicate. Never has a global conversation been more important: we hope that our contribution will be a stimulus to others to continue.

Vittorio Colao, CEO Vodafone Group

Preface

Like many innovations, the Future Agenda project began with a number of questions and a rough idea of how to answer them. We wanted to provide a forum for discussion of the most significant challenges we face as a society over the next ten years and think about ways in which collectively we can address them.

Over the following twelve months, this largely experimental activity built up momentum. We have identified the key challenges and probable changes that will occur across many different areas, and we have also explored some of the main arenas in which these changes will be played out. We have engaged with a global audience and tried to build a bridge between the traditionally separate areas of foresight and innovation. In short, we have created a global open foresight initiative.

Our aim for the Future Agenda programme is to provide a lens through which organisations can identify major innovation opportunities. Many informed people from over 150 countries have been involved in the discussions and their contribution has helped us to highlight the big issues for the next decade and identify where they will have most impact. We hope it has also provided them and the organisations they represent with new provocations and insights that will guide their activities in new directions and stimulate fresh thinking.

Why not global open foresight?

Taking the long view has never been easy. Faced with rapid technological advances, shifting political movements, rising economic powerhouses in Asia and societal change at a faster pace than ever previously experienced, it has become increasingly challenging. Identifying the big issues of the future, however, is key to ensuring the long-term sustainability of business and society. It is vital for organisations to see the future early so that they can both prepare for it and put plans in place to take advantage of it. Rather than rely on science fiction, international bodies such as the UN, NATO and the OECD have now established long-term projections on such issues as population growth, military power and economic development so that they have insights upon which they can make key strategic decisions.

At the same time, some commercial companies are also taking the long view. The Rand Corporation led the way in scenarios thinking and this technique was quickly developed by such companies as Shell whose global scenarios rapidly became the benchmark. Alongside these institutional views of the emerging landscape, numerous academic and non-profit organisations were founded, most notably the Institute for the Future (IFTF) in Palo Alto which is now over forty years old. Using a variety of different techniques, the success of these varied groups lay not actually in predicting the future but in differentiating between the possible and the probable. This led them, and their customers, towards making increasingly informed decisions that either reduced risk or increased opportunity, and made them better prepared in the face of unfolding events.

Over the past decade or so, governments and other companies have joined in. The UK runs a Foresight Horizon Scanning Centre; the government of Singapore enthusiastically engages scenario thinking; the World Economic Forum has a huge foresight programme; IBM runs a highly successful Global Innovation Outlook programme; Siemens has a dedicated Futures Group; Arup has a widely respected Foresight Team; Procter & Gamble has a Future Works group; Philips Design has a well-regarded personas approach to futures thinking; Nokia and Ericsson both run regular futures projects. Likewise, industry bodies have focused on specific issues such as materials supply, the impact of the digital world, health changes, and so on, and a plethora of commercial futures consultancies have been formed that provide their clients with services looking at both short-term and macro trends as well as offering more long-term foresight.

As a consequence of all this activity and partial sharing of summary insights by some of the above, one could argue that we are now more informed about the likely future than we have ever been. As such, the governments and companies involved should be making the right decisions, avoiding big surprises and making some pretty successful bets on the future. In some cases this is true: some countries were better prepared than others for the global financial crisis; the UN FAO has a clear view on the global actions required to rebalance food supply and demand; Apple proactively saw the business opportunity in what became iTunes; on the back of its 2004 Technology Futures programme, Shell has invested in second and third generation bio-fuels; as a key development from its 2005 Global Innovation Outlook, IBM launched its Water Management business in 2009; and, supported by insights from their Future Works group, the likes of P&G have been steering towards the convergence of healthcare and cosmetics. All of these successes are good news for the organisations involved, as they have acted on the insights that were available to them and made bold yet informed decisions.

However, one concern that some involved in these programmes have been sharing is whether they are missing something. Although they all developed programmes that look ahead five, ten or twenty years, and try to encompass a broad view of the future, many are run with a single-industry or single-issue focus. While many look at their sector and immediate adjacencies, only a few, such as Nokia's Wildcards programme, seek to encompass a wider scope. In addition, although they all have a clearer understanding about the future, the commercial and societal value is only gained from the decisions they take on the back of these insights. Insights into the state of the world in five or ten years can rarely be seen to be confidential as they are largely reflections of multiple views from outside the organisation. Lastly, while a few organisations such as the UN, OECD, Siemens, Shell, IBM and IFTF publish an edited view of how they see the next decade or so, most keep the raw data to themselves. As a result of this we wondered whether there was a way in which these organisations could better pool their views of the future. While there are a few online commercially focused communities, there was no open repository for everyone's views.

This led to us ask: Why can't we create a transparent vehicle through which the views of the future can be shared and built upon? Why can't we bring together perspectives from a broad range of areas to highlight commonalities? Why can't we take the principles of open innovation upstream into the world of foresight? Or to put it another way: *Why can't we create a global open foresight platform?* The technology is clearly available and, as we know and have worked with many of the organisations already seen as the leaders in the field, we should be able to bring all parties together. What is more, if we adopt the 'open' philosophy and so encourage everyone to use each other's insights, then everyone should be able to gain a wider, more informed view of the future and so be able to make better decisions.

How do we engage the unusual suspects?

One of the criticisms of many existing futures programmes is that they are full of the usual suspects – a group of experts whose views and opinions are seen as increasingly cross-linked. They contribute a lot as they are routinely consulted by businesses or invited to participate in cross-government and corporate initiatives, but they are all largely white, Anglo-Saxon, middle-aged, middle-class men. So, if we continue to engage primarily with these recognised experts, will we really get as clear a view of the future as we could? While it is important to have their views in the mix, should we not try to engage with a broader church? What we wanted was to get first-hand views from a far wider range of leading academics and industrialists with deep knowledge of specific topics. We wanted non-Western views from the countries that are probably the centres of action for the next decade. And we wished to engage the younger generation who will be leading the world forward. Another challenge was to bring all these varied views together. Hence our second question: *How can we engage the unusual suspects?* If we have a global platform and can work with the organisations and communities that connect directly to many stakeholders, then we should be able to bring together a wider range of views, from multiple countries, from a broad portfolio of backgrounds and with different views of the ways things are going.

The initial idea

Discussing these two questions with colleagues, we came to the conclusion that, given the technology, contacts and relationships in place, there was a good chance we could bring our idea to life.

We live in a world where increasingly ubiquitous connectivity means that over one-third of the world's population has access to the internet. Consequently, more of us are engaging in two-way dialogue through social networks and blogs and there are growing numbers of people around the world who actively engage in debate who could be encouraged to participate in an open programme that gave them something interesting to tackle. In addition, if we set the time horizon on 2020 rather than just 'the future', that would give us a solid point for discussion – one that not only extends sufficiently beyond the short-term horizon, so that we are not simply talking about how current trends will play out, but also one that is not so far out that we enter the world of science fiction, when films such as *Minority Report*, *Blade Runner* and *I, Robot* begin to influence the strands of debate.

We also thought that rather than starting with a blank sheet of paper – or, more accurately, just a series of questions on a blog – if we started with some points of view to challenge and build upon, we could get further and faster. People could build on the initial views, highlight the areas that they agree with and propose alternative positions to those that they disagreed with. At the same time, if all comments were openly accessible on the website from the start then anyone could use the insights straight away, without having to wait six months for the synthesis to be undertaken and shared. Lastly, if a well-known global organisation could be interested in becoming involved in this, to both better inform its view of the future and also act as a sponsor, but importantly not the client for a programme, then the chances of gaining traction in key communities would be increased.

So, after just a few weeks of discussions, the Future Agenda programme was born. A standard blog platform would be used, launching in September 2009, to encourage a three-month global debate on some of the big issues for the coming decade. We thought that we would have a multitude of different views from around the world by the end of the year and so be able to share a unique view of the world of 2020 at the start of 2010. Highly significantly, Vodafone Group, the global communications company, agreed to sponsor the programme and help build the momentum through its connections and networks in many of the countries in which it provides mobile services.

The kick-off

We started with fifty candidate topics and reduced them down to sixteen on the basis of them being unique, and so covering different areas, open for significant change over the next decade and also focused on subjects around which there would likely be differences of opinion, so making them ripe for debate. These sixteen topics were the future of authenticity, choice, cities, connectivity, currency, data, energy, food, health, identity, migration, money, transport, waste, water and work.

In August 2009, recognised experts in each topic from across the academic, commercial and government arenas were invited to answer a number of common questions on the future. These were then edited and put into a standard format to ease navigation and to ensure a common structure. A mix of experts kindly shared their personal views about the next decade. These were each grouped into four sections – namely, the global challenges, options and possibilities, the way forward, and impacts and implications. The intention from the start was not only to get views for each topic on what the future would be, but also to get perspectives on which way we should go, why and with what consequences.

At the beginning of October, all sixteen initial perspectives were added to the site, pdf files were created for sharing and the programme was launched with a host of people around the world invited to add their views to the mix. The response was very thought-provoking but somewhat unexpected. According to the Google analytics on the site, in the first few weeks there were over 4,000 hits from 128 countries. Interestingly, alongside the US and UK, the other top countries from which people were accessing the site were India and Egypt – well ahead of other European nations. In addition, other countries in the top twenty included Pakistan, the Philippines, Thailand, Indonesia, Singapore, Saudi Arabia and Vietnam, so clearly the audience was global and the programme was engaging a broad community. From a topic perspective, the most popular ones in terms of initial visits were food, health, authenticity, cities, connectivity and energy. The challenge was that only a hundred or so people were actually adding to the blog.

Future Agenda v2

Talking to a sample of people who had accessed the site, who were enthusiastic about the idea and who were keen to contribute revealed two pivotal insights: first, the initial perspectives were seen to be so authoritative that not many were ready to add alternative views and, second, even if they wanted to, few were actually willing to blog. Although individuals in academia, government and the corporate sector were all very keen to share their perspectives with the programme, doing so via a blog was culturally, commercially and politically difficult: civil servants are largely restricted from giving opinions in public; academics still largely prefer real debate to virtual discussion; and, although people in companies have views to share, if their employers have no ready-made specific perspective on a topic, then any comments from a .com email address would have to go for internal approval prior to sharing. The whole premise upon which we had based the programme – that people are ready to engage in online discussions – was clearly wrong. While lots of us are blogging, the media are talking about it and we are all meant to be comfortable in the Web 2.0

world, the programme was plainly pushing too hard against pre-existing constraints.

What was notable was how quickly people came up with suggestions as to how we could get around the problems.

- "Let me make my view anonymous" – therefore we took down any need to show who was adding comments to the blog and this started to build some momentum.

- "Give me a hard copy I can read on the train and I will send you my thoughts" – so we printed 4,000 copies of the initial perspectives. For such rich topics, people wanted to have a hard copy in their hands and we quickly started to get comments back, largely as email but even through the mail. One book came back to us covered in sticky notes!

- "Come and have a chat and I will tell you what I think" – this led to a pivotal change in approach. Rather than use the site as the primary means of insight gathering we would offer organisations half-day workshops to discuss specific topics conducted under Chatham House Rules and then share the views, tagged as 'workshop feedback'. In other words, stick with a more traditional vehicle for debate that people are used to, one that allows them to interact with others in the same space and so build on each other's views.

These suggestions changed the nature of the Future Agenda programme significantly – but not its philosophy or ambition. Rather than being simply a three-month online debate it became a global nine-month programme of around fifty workshops engaging over 2,000 people face to face. Some of these were within single organisations but many brought together different expertise from many different avenues. Some took place in corporate conference facilities, some in hotels and restaurants and others in village pubs – whatever worked best. In locations around the world, including both the expected (London, New York, Brussels, Sydney, Shanghai, Madrid, Rome, Barcelona, Mumbai, Delhi, Oxford, etc) as well as the unexpected (such as a village in Oxfordshire), groups of people from many cultures, of varied ages and with many different perspectives shared their views. Supported by comments fed back after around 21,000 downloads of the initial perspectives in 147 different countries, although not as originally designed, the Future Agenda programme became a platform for global open foresight that engaged the usual and the unusual suspects.

Programme outcomes

Since the launch of the initial blog website, the Future Agenda programme has provided a series of both planned and unplanned outcomes.

First and foremost, this book in your hands provides a synthesis of what the Future Agenda programme has revealed. Examining the key issues highlighted by the multiple workshops and online discussions, it explores what is certain about the next decade, what are probable changes, what are seen as the moderators of the future and what are the main implications for governments, companies and individuals. There is a more detailed explanation below of how the book is structured and how you might wish to use it.

Secondly, the accompanying futureagenda.org website allows anyone to access the insights gained from the programme in an interactive and dynamic manner, with linkages not only between the varied topics and issues but also to the source materials, be they the initial perspectives, the raw comments received from participants or reports and documents shared as part of the programme. This website provides a snapshot of the insights and interdependencies identified to date.

Thirdly, many of the organisations which participated in the programme have already used the insights that they gained and shared about the future to inform and direct some of their priorities. Some companies have identified new opportunity areas and already started developing new products and services to meet associated needs. Other organisations have gained a deeper understanding of key issues that were previously not on their radar and now have not only a better recognition of how they might be affected in the future but also an improved understanding of how they may need to respond differently. Numerous academics participating in the programme have found new areas for research and application of their knowledge. In addition, several government bodies have used the insights both to validate existing assumptions and to challenge others. We hope that the book and the website will help to stimulate more actions such as these.

The intention of the Future Agenda programme was never just to share, challenge and collate as many different views as possible of the key challenges for the next decade and provide synthesised generic outputs for individuals and organisations to use. That is indeed the first step, but the primary focus is to do so while simultaneously providing a platform for new and higher levels of innovation.

Many of the breakthroughs that we need in the future will, just as those in the past, most likely emerge at the intersections between different areas. While innovations in a few arenas, such as pharmaceutical development, do occur largely within one discipline, many others occur from the convergence of challenges and opportunities in several separate sectors. For example, significant decisions about the future of food need to factor in the impacts and implications of water and waste; those relating to the issues of identity are increasingly driven by such topics as choice, data and connectivity; and the way in which we choose to go about designing our cities is significantly predicated on changes that are likely to occur in transport, migration and work.

In creating, choreographing, running and reporting on the Future Agenda programme, we have seen many opportunities for positive change being suggested, discussed, assessed and refined to a point at which they can now start to stimulate new ideas – ideas about how to tackle some of the big challenges we face in such areas as climate change, sustainable health and food supply; ideas about how to use policy to best influence choice and steer the right path over the next decade; and ideas for new products, services and business models that will ensure the legacy of the past does not become a burden on the future.

We would like to thank all those who have contributed to the process; this book could only have been written with their support and thoughtfulness. We hope that you find it useful, thought-provoking, stimulating and, ultimately, a source of new insights leading to innovation in your own field.

Tim Jones and Caroline Dewing, November 2010

Navigating this book

The Future Agenda programme kicked off sixteen parallel discussions. As views on these were shared and built upon, it became clear that as well as the vertical conversations within each topic, there were a host of issues bubbling to the surface that cut across several areas. Some of these are critical drivers of the future; some are issues that will moderate how the future unfolds. As such, in the synthesis of the insights from the programme, we have sought to highlight these issues and group them accordingly so that you, the reader, can see how they interrelate, and can therefore also choose which chapters of the book you will find most interesting.

In Part 1, we detail what we see as the four macro-scale certainties for the next decade – the things that, unless there is an unexpected, massive and fundamental global shift, will most definitely occur and so are the certitudes upon which everything else is built. These certainties are:

- a continued imbalance in population growth
- more constraints on key resources
- an accelerating shift of economic power to Asia
- universal data access.

Each of these is covered separately so that you can gain a good understanding of why these macro-drivers of change are occurring, what the core characteristics of these shifts are and, therefore, how they will influence the world between today and 2020.

Part 2 explores some of the key insights we have gained into how the world and our lives will probably change over the next decade. These are the key changes highlighted by the programme that will occur in many different areas, some influenced by just one of the four certainties, others by two or more. These changes are detailed by providing both the signals from today that give evidence to support the direction of change and the future implications over the next ten years. They are grouped into six clusters – health, wealth, happiness, mobility, security and locality – which seem to encompass all the issues highlighted. Each change that is depicted in this part is variously linked to a number of others and so we have used margin indicators to help you see these links clearly and so move from one topic to another. This navigation replicates in a somewhat limited printed form some of the more dynamic interactions that can be found between these topics on the accompanying website.

In Part 3, we look at four themes that have come up in many of the discussions as the key moderators of the future. These are not specific issues where there will be a clear change between 2010 and 2020 but are the themes that will most likely influence the extent to which the changes detailed in Part 2 take place. These four themes – trust, privacy, choice and global/local action – are themselves interrelated and so, as well as sharing perspectives on them in isolation, this part also shows how these interrelations work;

how they provide a moderating influence that may either accelerate or decelerate change; and how their interrelationships allow us to see a number of alternative scenarios in the future.

Part 4 then goes into more detail on the impacts and implications of outcomes from the Future Agenda programme. Linking together many of the earlier certainties, probable changes and moderators of the future, it brings together some conclusions and questions for the next decade. These have been grouped into three areas – those that will most likely concern governments and so provide questions for future policy and regulation; those that will potentially relate to organisations and so provide stimuli for innovation and change in approach at that level; and lastly those that raise questions for us as individuals in how we see our role in the future and how and where we may wish to exert influence. It is the 'so what?' from the programme and hopefully provokes as many questions as it provides answers.

Finally, there is a section giving resources and references which brings together some of the multiple sources of information that have been shared and used in the Future Agenda programme. You may well find these useful to you in exploring some of the issues raised in more detail or on a continuing basis.

PART 1
The four certainties

Context

In any look forward in time, we are dealing with differences that may or may not be predictable. If we look to next year, we can usually identify a number of things that will be largely the same, such as the food available for us to eat, the nature of our work or where we choose to live. Equally there are several aspects of life that we can pretty well guarantee will change slightly, for example by being faster, slower, smaller or bigger than today: faster computers, slower traffic, smaller cars and bigger networks. All of these are relatively predictable – in fact, almost certain.

One of the core assumptions of many futures programmes is that there are certainties and uncertainties, so, assuming you can identify what they are, it should be perfectly possible to build alternative views of the future based on combinations of these. As we look further out, to, say, two to three years, we can see a range of trends that might have an increasing impact in the world. These are things that are emerging or accelerating today and may become more influential as they become mainstream; alternatively, of course, they may give way to the next fad or ideology. Although these are more 'possible' than 'guaranteed' futures, they are extrapolations of the world today and so we can be reasonably confident that they will come about.

The challenge in looking further out, say to the future in five to ten years' time, is that many of the changes that could take place may be significant departures from today's reality and so not on our collective radar.

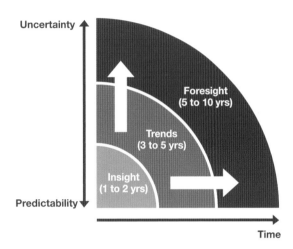

As such, our confidence in what those changes might be, let alone their impact, could be quite low. Think back to 2000 and ask how many saw what effect the recently launched Google would have on the internet, never mind the advent of social networks. Or consider how 'green' we have now become and observe how sustainability is now a hygiene factor for us all rather than a niche issue for some.

All in all, there are a host of changes that we need to think about when considering the next ten years. Some are incremental evolutions – some are radical revolutions. The big challenge in any foresight programme is in differentiating these and gaining a clear understanding of which changes are most likely.

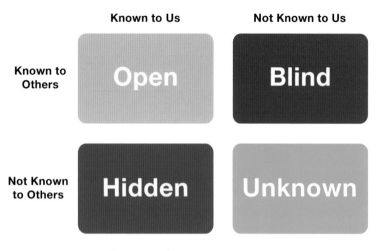

Known to Us   **Not Known to Us**

Known to Others   Open   Blind

Not Known to Others   Hidden   Unknown

Knowns vs unknowns

In order to distinguish what many term the 'probable futures' from the 'possible futures', futures programmes such as the IFTF's Map of the Decade, IBM's Global Innovation Outlook use a range of different techniques to highlight developments in which there is more collective confidence, rather than those considered less predictable, and group them accordingly. For example, Nokia's Wildcards programme looks specifically at the low probability events that could have a significant impact while other scenario programmes, such as those undertaken by the likes of GBN, seek to explore possible outcomes of the interaction of certainties and uncertainties and the implications for the world, a market or a business.

Another school of thought looks at the future on a known versus unknown dimension. So we have 'known knowns' – things like population growth – that we can predict quite clearly, and then we have 'known unknowns' – such as the future price of oil. The interesting bit comes when we consider the 'unknown knowns' – those things that are definitely occurring but the impact of which we do not fully understand, such as, perhaps, a shift in values or another environmental impact of our actions alongside CFCs and carbon. These are the nuggets that many futures programmes seek to uncover by bringing together different views and making new connections. As if this wasn't complicated enough, we finally come to the 'unknown unknowns' – the events that will take us all by surprise and which we therefore find difficult to prepare for. All of this was famously hijacked by Donald Rumsfeld in his NATO speech in 2002. The principle, however, is still clear.

The intention of the Future Agenda project is to clarify which issues fit into these types of categories. By doing so, we want to enable people, companies and governments to make more informed choices and place more intelligent bets. However, although it is easy to put certainties into the 'known known' group, the problem is that we have to challenge ourselves as to which issues really are certain.

We believe that it is a pivotal issue to get the certainties for the future clear up front. Once we have clarity on the 'known knowns', we can build a better understanding of the options and possibilities that exist on top of these. Of course, the process is problematic. For example, we tend to have greater confidence in those things happening within our industry or field of expertise and could quite possibly discount events or developments from other areas. We have tried to avoid this by using the varied initial perspectives on the different topics and the subsequent discussions around these to help us highlight, test, challenge and validate the themes that participants from around the world agree are the driving forces of how the world will develop over the coming decade.

This first part of the book therefore details what, from the programme, we see as the four macro-certainties for the next decade. Unless there is a massive and fundamental global shift that we have not anticipated, these are the things that will most definitely occur. They are, therefore, those certainties upon which everything else is built. Signals of these global trends can be seen today and are already being factored into plans and strategic approaches by some governments, institutions and businesses.

The four certainties are:

- a continued imbalance in population growth
- more constraints on key resources
- an accelerating shift of economic power to Asia
- universal data access.

Imbalanced population growth

By 2020, we will add another 750M people to the planet, most in places least able to accommodate them.

Over the next ten years, improvements in health, education and living standards will continue to drive population growth. Longer life expectancy will offset the trend towards having fewer children, which means that by 2020 there will be more of us and more of us will be older. Regional differences in growth rates will result in a larger proportion of people living in Asia. In addition, continued migration from rural areas means that a greater number of us will live in cities than ever before.

This suggests that, as long as there are no disasters on a huge scale – natural or man-made – over the next decade, demographic changes are much more certain than many other long-term predictions. The macro-trends are clear: the human population has grown massively over the past century or so. All things being equal, this growth trend looks set to continue.

It's easy to suggest that there are just too many of us around these days and that this has put unsustainable pressure on the resources available, but this is not strictly true. The questions that matter are not only around general growth but also around balance. Are people in the right places? Do we have the right skills? Can we reduce child mortality in emerging economies? Do we have enough people of working age to support economic growth? As the population ages, are there enough people to support the old? How can we close the gap between the 'haves' and 'have-nots'? These are all-important questions that

we need to address in order to understand the primary implications for the world in 2020.

To start with, let's take a closer look at the overall population numbers. We crossed the 1 billion mark in the mid-nineteenth century to reach 1.6 billion at the start of the twentieth century. We hit 2.3 billion at the end of the Second World War and from then on the global population has been increasing at around 75 million per annum. By 2008, we totalled 6.7 billion and now, in 2010, we are approaching 7 billion, with China accounting for over 1.3 billion and India for over 1.1 billion. This means that by 2020 there will be around 7.7 billion people living on Earth. Most likely we will be split between around 1.4 billion in each of China and India, 515 million in Europe and 335 million in the US. In the absence of major pandemics, global natural disasters or multi-regional wars, organisations such as the UN and OECD estimate that the world population will reach around 9 billion people in 2050 and peak at around 9.2 billion in 2075. Taken at this level, an extra 750 million of us in the next decade and an extra 2 billion in the next forty years inevitably means a more crowded world with ever more of us competing for the same resources.

On top of this, child mortality rates are declining and more of us are living longer. Today, our average life expectancy across the globe is 68 at birth. Of course this varies from region to region, with North Americans

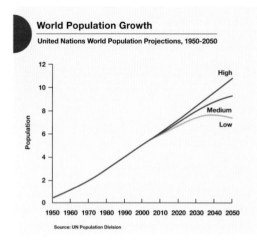

World Population Growth

United Nations World Population Projections, 1950-2050

Source: UN Population Division

Our children can expect to live on average to celebrate 97 years, and from 2030 onwards it will not be surprising if life expectancy reaches 106.

boasting 79 years as opposed to an average of 54 in Africa. But, wherever you are, expect to be here at least ten years longer than your parents. Looking forward, our children can expect to live on average to celebrate 97 years, and from 2030 onwards it will not be surprising if life expectancy reaches 106. What is clear is that if, as predicted, the proportion of the world population aged 65 years or older increases by a third and the average number of people who live for more than a century increases ninefold, the concept of 'old age' will have to be redefined. In many developed economies, 55 is already the new middle age and we can clearly see a future where what used to be the average age of retirement becomes the mid-point of the average adult life.

This has huge social and economic implications and is certainly bad news for those who, having worked for the traditional forty years, were looking forward to a long and happy retirement. Pension providers will have to re-evaluate their business model. In relatively recent times, people who retired at 65 did so, on average, only a few years short of their life expectancy. If the current threshold stays in place, our children can reasonably expect to live in 'retirement' for an additional 32 years. It's a pity that their pension funds are unlikely to be able to pay for this: most pensions have been designed to accommodate an upper quartile life expectancy where retirement age is 'death minus ten'. It looks like there is no alternative – we will all have to work longer than our parents.

On the other side of the coin, an overall increase in the working population could also result in increasing numbers of people finding themselves unable to find a job as the decade progresses, the global recession bites, and economies adapt to changing technologies, resource constraints and different methods of working. This has the potential to lead to a sense of frustration and exclusion amongst those who are unable to find work, which in turn will have significant political and social ramifications, particularly in the more vulnerable economies – probably in Europe and the West.

Overall, while the macro-trend around global population increase is clear, four factors shape the balance of the growth both in terms of scale and location. They each have influence and are shifting future projections. These four factors are:

- changing fertility rates
- decreasing child mortality
- people living longer
- international and urban migration.

Fertility

We are currently experiencing an extraordinary fertility decline. The fertility rate represents the number of children an average woman is likely to have during her childbearing years (15–49). Taking typical averages into account, the natural replacement rate by which a population stays level is 2.1 children per woman. So, a rate of below 2.1 is the point at which population growth begins to slow or even fall. Globally we will reach that point by around 2020 for the first time. Small wonder, therefore, that fertility has become a primary focus for local political parties and national governments as well as transnational and global agencies.

It's worth remembering that a decline in fertility does not mean a decline in population, which can continue to rise while fertility goes down. For example, high fertility in an earlier generation can lead to an increased number of women of childbearing age all having fewer children but together increasing the overall number of children. This is why the UN and OECD see a peak population accruing around 30 years after we reach the natural replacement rate in 2020.

There are several reasons for the decline in overall fertility. There is, for example, clear evidence to suggest that as we get richer we want smaller families. This trend was first noticed in nineteenth-century industrialised Britain and is fairly well established. As poor countries now race to catch up and more of us are becoming richer, the global population looks set for a relatively speedy decline – so much so, in fact, that the transition in fertility rate from five children to two, which took place over 130 years in Britain (1800–1930), happened in just twenty years (1965–85) in South Korea. In

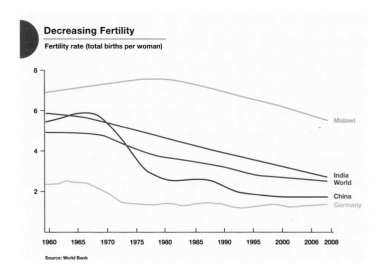

Bangladesh the fertility rate dropped from five to three in twenty years (1980–2000) and in Mauritius it took ten (1963–73). Some countries are experiencing an even more dramatic change. Take Iran, for example, where the national fertility rate dropped from 7.0 in 1984 to 1.9 in 2006 and in Tehran it has now dropped to a mere 1.5.

Such declines in fertility at one level have a lot to do with the movement of people from the countryside to the towns and cities: tilling the land is generally labour intensive and an extra pair of hands to help is welcome but it's a different matter altogether in the restricted space of the city where the cost of feeding and housing a larger family is often prohibitive. It's a simple matter of economics and living standards. Generally speaking, fertility starts to drop when the annual income per person is $1,000–2,000 and falls until it reaches the replacement level at $4,000–10,000. Poorer agricultural regions often have higher fertility rates so it's not surprising that although India's average fertility rate in 2010 was 2.68, its poorest state, Bihar, had a fertility rate of 4.0 while it's richest, including Andhra Pradesh, Goa and Tamil Nadu, have rates of only 1.8.

Fertility is also falling because more women are better educated and are therefore more likely to go out to work and demand contraception and less likely to want large families. The impact of female education on fertility is perhaps most evident in Iran where in 1976 only 10% of rural women aged between 20 and 24 were literate. That share is now 91%. As more women become literate, so their economic roles and societal views change, and the desire for fewer children increases. In addition, the widespread availability and use of contraception has also played a fundamental role in changing fertility trends. Family planning has helped many people reduce the number of children they have – and research even suggests that fertility in some countries would be even lower if family planning services were more widely available. The impact of female education and use of contraception in controlling population growth highlights why both issues are so high on the agendas of the likes of the UN and several major NGOs as well as many national governments.

Over the next ten years we can expect to see further declines in fertility to a point where nearly

Fertility is also falling because more women are better educated and are therefore more likely to go out to work and demand contraception and less likely to want large families.

all major economies are below the replacement level of 2.1 children per woman. German fertility dipped below replacement in 1970 and is still low. In the likes of France, Korea and Russia, a host of incentive programmes are already under way to encourage families to grow. This is driving some change – take France, for example, where the fertility rate is now 1.98 children per woman after having been as low as 1.7 in the mid-1990s. The US seems to have been most successful in encouraging its population to grow – it is the only rich country that, having fallen below the replacement rate, has risen back above it.

In general, it is in many developing countries where the more stable fertility rates will continue to be found over the next decade, and so where the rates of population growth will be highest. Some countries, particularly those with little or no infrastructure because of war or low living standards, will continue to have high fertility rates – think of Malawi, Uganda, Angola, Chad, Mali and Sierra Leone, which are currently running at over 6.0. Associated population growth rates for these countries range from 2.5% to 3.3%. This means that around 250 million people will be added to the African population over the next decade – over twice the rates in Asia and South America. Compare this with projections for Europe, which are largely flat, and North America, where the population growth is expected to be around 8% over the decade. To put it another way, one-third of the net global population growth between today and 2020 will take place in Africa.

The main problem with all of this is that, because fertility rates decline as standards of living rise, it would seem clear that the majority of the world's population growth will occur in the nations least able to sustain it. Furthermore, as fertility falls it changes the structure of the population by increasing the size of the workforce relative to the number of children and old people. More women can work and, because there are fewer dependants, they have more money to spend. That said, consider how quickly fertility rates in some high-population developing economies such as India and Indonesia are falling and how low they are going. This could lead to change that will shift the world's long-term population growth in a more sustainable direction.

Infant mortality

The flip side of the influence of fertility on population growth is that of infant mortality – which is essentially measured by the number of infant deaths per 1,000 births. With advances in public health and wider availability of medical support, some of the primary causes of infant mortality have been significantly controlled over recent years. During the past half century, average infant mortality has been cut from 116 to 47 and, based on the UN constant fertility scenario, is expected to fall to around 40 by 2020 and 30 by 2050. However, the story varies significantly from region to region.

In Western Europe, infant mortality is already down to four deaths per 1,000, but in Latin America and China it is currently at 22, and in many parts of Central Africa it is not expected to drop much below 100 over the next decade. Essentially this means that a child born in a developing country is over thirteen times more likely to die within the first five years of life than a child born in an industrialised country. Although reducing child mortality by two-thirds from 1990 to 2015 is one of the UN's Millennium Development Goals, it looks highly unlikely that it will be achieved.

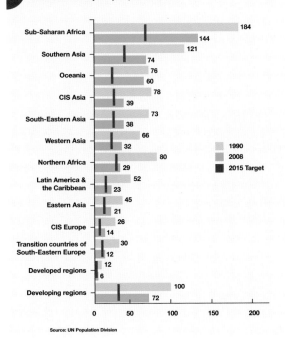

Child Mortality

Under-five mortality rate per 1,000 live births

Region	1990	2008
Sub-Saharan Africa	184	144
Southern Asia	121	74
Oceania	76	60
CIS Asia	78	39
South-Eastern Asia	73	38
Western Asia	66	32
Northern Africa	80	29
Latin America & the Caribbean	52	23
Eastern Asia	45	21
CIS Europe	26	14
Transition countries of South-Eastern Europe	30	12
Developed regions	12	6
Developing regions	100	72

Legend: 1990, 2008, 2015 Target

Source: UN Population Division

On a positive note, there is rising investment from global agencies and philanthropic ventures, like the Gates Foundation, which are working hard to reduce the incidence of the leading causes of childhood deaths, such as measles, malaria and diarrhoea, which are the scourge of the young and vulnerable. However, success is patchy: mortality rates are higher for children from rural and poor families and whose mothers lack a basic education.

By 2020, the overall impact of reducing infant mortality on the global population may not, in isolation, be significant but, combined with the possibility of decreasing fertility rates in the regions

Although reducing child mortality by two-thirds from 1990 to 2015 is one of the UN's Millennium Development Goals, it looks highly unlikely that it will be achieved.

of continued high child mortality, such as found in Central Africa, some have argued that we could see a reduction in the rate of local population growth combined with a decrease in child mortality that will help improve the quality of life of millions.

Taken together, declining fertility and infant mortality rates have great potential to slow, if not immediately halt, population growth in some important regions. While getting the world as a whole to below the natural replenishment rate looks probable in the next decade or so, the big challenge is really in the areas where this is taking place slowly if at all. For all the obvious reasons relating to sustainability, food availability and economic growth, Africa is always high on the agenda of many organisations when the topic of imbalanced population growth is discussed, but other countries with high fertility rates, such as Pakistan, should not be ignored.

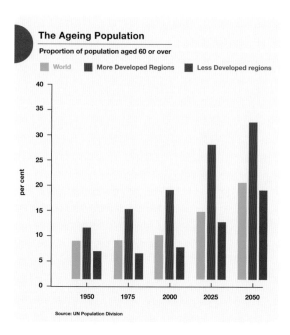

The Ageing Population
Proportion of population aged 60 or over

World | More Developed Regions | Less Developed regions

Source: UN Population Division

People living longer

Of course, reductions in fertility and increases in the life expectancy of children are not going to solve the problem of there being too many people on the planet. It really is a question of balance. Extremes at the other end of the spectrum are already significant cause for concern.

In most major economies of the world, the population is getting older. The percentage of the population over 65 has been rising steadily in all OECD countries and today 7.7% of the world's population is over 65. By 2020, this figure will be 9.4%. At the moment, the developed world is at the forefront of this demographic revolution; by 2050, UN statistics suggest that pensioners in the 'rich

By 2020, the dependency ratio is expected to be above 50% in Finland, Italy and Japan.

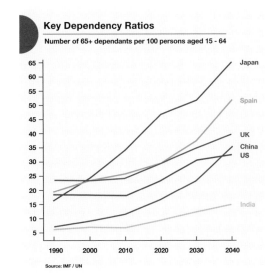

Key Dependency Ratios

Number of 65+ dependants per 100 persons aged 15 - 64

Source: IMF / UN

world' will comprise one-third of the population and one-tenth will be over 80. But emerging economies are not far behind (take Mexico, for example: in 1980 the average Mexican was 17 years old; today, he is 28). Many governments now have to contemplate the prospect of slowing growth and low productivity, rising public spending – particularly on healthcare – and labour shortages.

From an economic perspective, this mass ageing is already producing significant pressure and, going forward, many see it as a time bomb for healthcare, pensions, taxation and wider social dynamics. The key measure for this is the dependency ratio – the portion of population which is inactive in relation to the total labour force. This is equal to the number of citizens aged below 15 or above 64 divided by the number of individuals aged 15 to 64, and so is expressed as a percentage. The higher the figure, the greater the economic burden on the state and hence the labour force. By 2020, the dependency ratio is expected to be above 50% in Finland, Italy and Japan. So, for every elderly inactive person there will be less than two people in the labour force – they are the people paying the taxes to support the elderly. By 2050, most of the world will have reached this point and, in the likes of Spain, Italy, Japan and Korea, where the dependency ratios will have passed the 90% mark, there will be nearly one pensioner for every worker. Whereas some economies, such as the Nordics, are used to high taxation in order to provide

high levels of social support, in most countries where low taxation has been a key political foundation in the past there will need to be significant changes in opinion in order to cope with higher dependency. Today's smaller families will find it harder to care for elderly relatives and public healthcare and pensions will have to adapt. This is bad news when many global economies are still having to cope with financial crises and existing debt.

Living longer is, of course, a cause for much celebration rather than despair, particularly as we are also living better. The active elderly are out and about and doing many of the things that governments would otherwise have to take care of: for instance, voluntary work and family duties such as looking after grandchildren. Such unpaid work is difficult to measure but it certainly makes a positive difference to government finances. In addition, people are staying healthier for longer so the 'compression of morbidity', the period of ill health that precedes death, has got shorter – mainly because we are living more healthily and have access to better healthcare services. However, there is no getting away from the fact that, at some time or other, the elderly do need more looking after than young people, mainly because they tend to suffer from long-term, chronic conditions that are, unfortunately, expensive to treat (eg, diabetes, high blood pressure and heart conditions).

Most pensions currently operate on a pay-as-you-go principle, whereby today's workers pay for today's pensioners. They are based on the understanding that tomorrow's workers will do the same for them when their time comes. However, given the increasing number of pensioners dependent on a decreasing number of workers, the pension pot in many economies is beginning to look rather empty and the possibility of filling it challenging. Unpopular decisions will have to be made regarding the system – including raising the age of retirement and increasing the amount we contribute.

Many agree that getting people to work for a few more years would solve a lot of the problems associated with ageing populations. Given the impacts of the recent global financial crisis, many governments are already planning increases in the retirement age; an average of 70 by 2020 is considered highly likely by many in the EU. By carrying on working either full or part time, people will not only save government expenditure by not drawing a pension but they will also feed the public purse by continuing to pay taxes and social security contributions; so, from a government perspective, those extra years are doubly valuable. Those who today are in their early sixties and getting ready to become pensioners may, of course, not see things the same way.

Most of this international migration, however, is occurring within regions, albeit from one country to another.

Add an increasingly ageing (and arguably economically non-productive) population on top of the decreasing number of young people in many countries and it is easy to see why concern about the dependency ratio is such a major concern for many government agendas. Even without overall growth in numbers, the fundamental age imbalance of the population within countries such as Japan, Germany and Italy is already provoking political actions. Looking ahead to 2020, as this imbalance increases, the desire for companies to remain economically competitive is driving further changes in attitudes and priorities for population growth.

International migration

The impact of migrant workers on the labour force is beginning to be apparent to all. Despite the current global recession, many countries, especially those in Europe, are heading for a period of labour shortages. As far back as 2007, a study by the Institute for the German Economy in Cologne identified a shortage of about 70,000 engineers, which was 50% up on the previous year. The obvious place to look to fill such gaps is among well-qualified older people, and indeed the Institute found that companies had stepped up their recruitment of engineers over 50.

However, in the absence of sufficient local workers, immigrants have been filling the gaps in numerous countries. Immigration in the developed world is the highest it has ever been, and is making a useful difference. In many areas of still-fertile America, it currently accounts for about 40% of total population growth.

On the face of it, immigration seems like a good idea that benefits everyone. Many developing countries have lots of young people in need of jobs; many rich countries need workers to boost tax revenues and maintain economic growth. But, over the next few decades, labour forces in developed countries are set to shrink so much that inflows of immigrants would have to increase enormously to compensate – to at least twice their current size in Western Europe's most youthful countries, and three times in the older ones. This has cultural and political implications, with public opinion polls clearly showing that people in most rich countries already think that immigration is too high.

The migration issue does cause a lot of agitation but the truth is not as alarming as some would suggest.

Today, there are over 213 million international migrants, which is equivalent to 3.1% of the world population. Of these, 15 million are classified by the UN as refugees, so just under 200 million can be seen as economic migrants. Each year, 2.7 million people are moving from the developing to the developed world: 1.3 million into European countries and 1.2 million into North American countries. Most of this international migration, however, is occurring within regions, albeit from one country to another. Within Europe, the free flow of economic migrants from East to West and back again has been a visible social and political issue for the past decade. In 2010, in Asia, net annual migration out of China was around 346,000, from India 200,000 and from the Philippines around 160,000.

Although a real and tangible challenge for many border authorities in the West and an emotional and political issue for many receiving countries – especially the US – taken as a whole, when compared with natural rising populations, international migration is not a major driver of population growth.

By 2015, 32 people an hour will be moving into Shanghai, 39 into Kinshasa and Jakarta, 42 into Mumbai and Karachi, 50 into Dhaka and 58 into Lagos.

Largest Cities in 2020

Rank	City/Urban area	Country	Population in 2020 (m)
1	Tokyo	Japan	37.28
2	Mumbai	India	25.97
3	Delhi	India	25.83
4	Dhaka	Bangladesh	22.04
5	Mexico City	Mexico	21.81
6	São Paulo	Brazil	21.57
7	Lagos	Nigeria	21.51
8	Jakarta	Indonesia	20.77
9	New York	USA	20.43
10	Karachi	Pakistan	18.94
11	Calcutta	India	18.54
12	Buenos Aires	Argentina	15.48
13	Cairo	Egypt	14.02
14	Metro Manila	Philippines	13.4
15	Los Angeles	USA	13.25
16	Rio de Janeiro	Brazil	13.23
17	Istanbul	Turkey	12.76
18	Shanghai	China	12.63
19	Moscow	Russia	11.73
20	Osaka, Kobe	Japan	11.53

Source: www.citymayors.com

Urban migration

What is globally more significant than cross-border migration is the continued shift from rural to urban environments: 2006 was notably the year when, on average, more of us lived in cities than in rural areas. Over the past decade, the shift of people into China's cities has been cited as the largest peacetime movement of population in history. By 2050, 75% of us will be living in cities.

The speed of urban change can be clearly measured by the number of people added to cities every hour. By 2015, 32 people an hour will be moving into Shanghai, 39 into Kinshasa and Jakarta, 42 into Mumbai and Karachi, 50 into Dhaka and 58 into Lagos. Compare that with 12 into New York, 6 into London and zero into Berlin and it is clear that again the places of major change are to be found in Africa and Asia. By 2020, there will be 27 cities with populations over 10 million – the so-called mega-cities. But there will also be 73 cities with more than 5 million people.

The primary driver of this increasingly urban world is evidently economic migration and this is a global phenomenon. Whether internal migration within India, China and Nigeria or intra-regional migration in Europe, people generally move in search of a better life. As long as they believe that this can be found in cities, they will seek to relocate. In many areas, such as Cairo, Mumbai and New York, this will continue to involve the relocation of the whole family but in others it will be just the workers. So, as has happened in the past decade in places like Nairobi and Mexico City, a good proportion of migrants will be only those seeking work and the family will, initially at least, be left behind.

The imbalance

We can clearly see a world in 2020 where not only are there another 750 million people on the planet but also, more significantly, they have mostly been added into cities and developing economies. Globally, population growth is a definite certainty for the next ten years and probably for the next forty. Although the rate of growth is gradually decreasing as lower fertility rates have an impact, the extra 250 million Africans added over the decade will most likely be an economic burden in the short term. Such a geographic imbalance of population growth is clearly a strain on the impacted regions but it also affects us all.

Globally, population growth is a certainty for the next ten years and probably for the next forty.

Given declining fertility rates globally and the increasing life expectancy of the growing older proportion of the population, the major imbalance that we will all experience is that of the demographic shift towards an ageing population and increasing dependency ratios. Without significant increases in the number of children being born – which would only add to the growing population problem anyhow – most countries will find this economic imbalance between the retired and the workers a massive problem.

In addition, while net economic migration from Africa, Asia and Central America into Europe and North America will in some way help to adjust the country-to-country population growth differences, most international migration will be added to the cities, and so merely compound the problem created by internal urban migration.

Key resource constraints

We will see economic, physical and political shortages of key materials that will result in major changes in our perspectives.

In 2020, the world will be demanding and consuming more of nature's finite resources. Delays in investment in infrastructure and the inability of legacy infrastructure to cope with changing demand will result in supply and demand gaps, market opportunities and price volatility. Countries will no longer be concerned just about energy security but also about resource security – land, food, water, metals and so on. While resources will not yet have physically run out, the perception of 'peak' resources will drive political and commercial behaviour.

The sad news is that resource supply over the short term is fairly inelastic compared with demand. By 2020, this will result in supply struggling to keep up with demand, increasing supply security concerns and higher prices. This will be particularly relevant as the trend towards urbanisation increases because cities require resources to be 'imported', leading to greater demand on the existing infrastructure.

Economic growth is coupled to resource consumption – as people become more wealthy they use more energy (eg, for air conditioning, heating, computing, mobility), eat and waste more food. They also use more water (think of all those thirsty golf courses). So far, many efficiency gains have been offset by 'the rebound effect', where the improvements have led to greater consumption. For example, improvements in fuel efficiency have been offset because we now drive further or faster than before.

The trouble is that it has taken the industrialised world over a century to develop the infrastructure to supply natural resources to the point of use (pipelines, sewage farms, ports, rail and road links, electricity grids) and making significant changes to this infrastructure will take decades. This is particularly true because resources tend to be geographically concentrated – often in areas that are 'difficult' in terms of physical accessibility or ease of doing business.

The situation will be made worse by the fact that the resources that were easier to get at have already been greatly depleted and those that are left are more technically challenging and expensive to acquire. In turn, business investment in the supply side requires confidence in the financial returns, particularly because projects are highly capital intensive and require specific skills to develop which are often in short supply. Furthermore the risk of failure is significant, particularly given that price volatility regularly leads to on/off investment cycles.

As with many things, there is a high level of interdependence between resources and a rising price of one resource has knock-on effects. For example, the energy industry is resource intensive, using large quantities of steel for construction of oil rigs, refineries and pipelines, and it also uses large quantities of water. Higher steel prices therefore drive up the costs of producing energy; as aluminium production from bauxite requires large amounts of energy, the higher steel prices in turn increase the cost of aluminium. And even when those challenges are overcome, there are also very real concerns about the long-term availability.

Growing populations and economies are placing increasing pressure on many natural resources as we collectively consume more and need more food, water, materials and land. This is placing major demands on the system with some areas now well recognised as pivotal – think of oil, water and arable land. An increasing number of experts believe that within the next twenty years some of what are now considered basic supplies will either have run out or be politically or economically beyond the reach of many. Credible people are making depressing predictions. For instance, John Beddington, Britain's chief scientific adviser, forecasts that by 2030 the world's population could rise by up to a third, demand for food and energy will rise by half and demand for fresh water will increase by 30%. To make matters worse, the spectre of climate change looms, with all its associated challenges, and furthermore some poorly thought-out government policies are making the situation even more difficult to manage.

Even those who were previously sceptics acknowledge that the crunch will come and that we cannot continue on the current consumption growth trajectory. When you consider that BHP Billiton estimates that the world could consume more copper, aluminium and steel in the next twenty-five years than it has done throughout history, this viewpoint almost feels like a statement of the obvious. The question is, of course, what should be done to mitigate the damage?

Who can blame emerging nations, which for years have suffered from relative poverty, when they embrace economic development? How can the countries that have already profited from exploiting global resources now try to curtail the use of the same resources by the next generation of growth economies? The answer surely is that they can't. The growing economic power of China and India, the world's most populous countries, has brought millions of people increased wealth and an improved quality of life which previous generations could only dream of. But this new-found prosperity has knock-on effects on the demand for resources, and especially for the countries that are traditionally the big consumers.

The US currently consumes around 22% of the world's oil and 20% of the world's gas.

Energy

Energy has been top of many political agendas for the past century and, in many eyes, has been the resource over which we have been fighting many of the recent wars. In terms of oil, the US currently consumes one-third more than the whole of the European Union, around twice the volume of China and seven times as much as each of India and Russia. Equally, for natural gas, US consumption currently outpaces that of the whole of the EU, is 50% greater than that of Russia and is eight times that of China. No question, then, as to which country is the big oil and gas consumer: the US currently consumes around 22% of the world's oil and 20% of the world's gas. Alongside the now widely recognised obvious issue of unsustainable consumption in itself, there are two key problems here. First, overall global oil and gas demand is growing faster than new reserves are being found and, second, most of the oil is in the Middle East and most of the gas is in the Middle East, Europe and Russia. Today, US energy demand is well outpacing its domestic supply and so it is hugely dependent on imports. Going forward, unless behaviours shift fundamentally or policies on arctic and offshore drilling are changed, the US will continue to need to try to secure more of an increasingly constrained resource. Add in increasing demand from China, never mind other growing economies, and the geopolitics of oil and gas are all too evident. Oil, which quite literally drives the world forward, is in crisis, with the chief economist of the International Energy Agency (IEA) predicting that 'the output of conventional oil will peak in 2020 if oil demands grow on a business-as-usual basis'. Globally, oil and gas supplies are both physically and politically constrained resources. Or, to put it another way, in the language of the energy sector, the 'days of easy oil are over' and from now on it gets more difficult. There

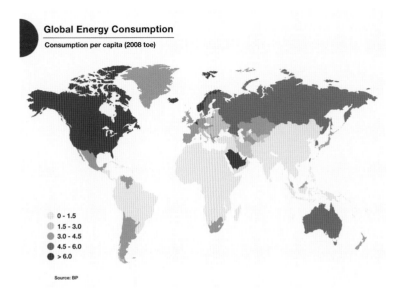

Global Energy Consumption

Consumption per capita (2008 toe)

- 0 - 1.5
- 1.5 - 3.0
- 3.0 - 4.5
- 4.5 - 6.0
- > 6.0

Source: BP

are more known resources out there but they are in deeper waters, in more environmentally sensitive areas, in more complex geological structures and in less secure regions of the world. But that has not stopped our increasing demand.

In terms of other energy sources, the next big one on the list is coal. Here the US faces less of a supply problem, as it has around 30% of the world's reserves compared with Russia's 19%, China's 14% and Australia's 9%. In the coal arena, faced with limited oil and gas supplies, it is China which is already the No 1 consumer and its consumption is growing quickly. In 2008, China produced and consumed over 42% of the world's coal (compared with 17% in the US). The one thing the US has plenty of at current rates of consumption is coal – the problem is that it is a very dirty fuel and a major source of carbon emissions. You can see the important role of coal in China when

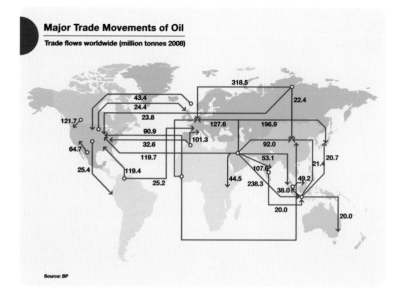

Major Trade Movements of Oil

Trade flows worldwide (million tonnes 2008)

318.5
43.4
24.4
23.8
121.7
90.9
127.6
196.9
101.3
64.7
32.6
92.0
119.7
53.1
25.4
107.6
21.4
20.7
119.4
44.5
49.2
25.2
238.3
38.0
22.4
20.0
20.0

Source: BP

than 5.5%. While there are now a large number of projects under way to construct new dams and new reactors around the world, the timescales required to construct and commission many of these facilities are too long to have a significant impact over the next decade. It is true that, looking fifty years out, the energy scenarios mapped out by the likes of the IEA and Shell reflect a greater share for renewable supplies, but right now the view is that energy supply is still primarily fossil fuel based and hence under increasing, not decreasing, constraints. As BP and others state: 'Although renewable energy continues to play only a small role in the world's energy mix, the share is rising rapidly in some countries and there are the beginnings of a material impact.' As highlighted shortly, bio-fuels are evidently also on the increase, but, at the moment, not without some serious stresses on the food chain.

you look at electricity consumption, as this is an area where China is already using more than anyone else. At the moment most of China's power is coming from coal. Going forward this has to change but this is a problem given the steadily increasing demand. According to the Economist Intelligence Unit and BP, while the US accounts for 20% of total primary energy consumption, Asia is already consuming 35% of the world's overall energy (up from 26% in 1995) and has accounted for two-thirds of the increase in world energy demand since 2000.

There are clearly alternatives – renewable energy from hydro, geothermal, wind, wave and solar generation, and also nuclear power. However, over the next ten years, the challenges of scaling these up to make a significant contribution are considerable. Hydroelectricity accounts for less than 6.4% of the world's current energy supply and nuclear for less

Looking ahead to 2020, energy demand and supply from fossil fuels are clearly going to be stressing the system. There are a number of well-regarded scenarios for the future of energy, some of which factor in action on climate change, some not. Some make assumptions about huge investments and government subsidies in renewable energy schemes and others make assumptions about the speed at which, for example,

Over the next twenty years, global energy demand will increase by around 40% – so an average of 1.5% a year – with the vast majority of the growth coming from non-OECD countries such as China, India etc.

the world will shift to electric mobility. To ground our views in a more probable world, the best place to see the baseline view of the future is the International Energy Agency's Reference Scenario.

The IEA Reference Scenario proposes that, over the next twenty years, global energy demand will increase by around 40% – so an average of 1.5% a year – with the vast majority of the growth coming from non-OECD countries such as China, India etc. Oil will remain the largest single fuel, providing 30% of the total energy mix, with more and more transport accounting for 97% of the increase in its use. Gas supply will also increase by around 45% by 2030 to provide just over a fifth of the world's energy needs. World electricity demand will grow at an average of 2.5% a year, adding a supply equivalent to around five times the current capacity of the US. In 2009, 13–14% of the world's electricity came from nuclear power and its use is expected to grow in most regions except Europe. However, its overall share of electricity generation is expected to fall. That said, technical innovations around nuclear fusion might mean that different sources of nuclear energy become commercially available in the future. In absolute terms, however, the biggest increases in demand will be met by coal-based power generation. The growing use of renewable energies – wind, wave, solar, hydro and geothermal – will start to make an impact but, in comparison to the other energy sources, their individual shares of the mix will still be in single figures at the end of this decade.

To provide all of this extra capacity will require huge capital investment – around $26 trillion – and over half of this will occur in developing countries. The financing of this by the energy sector and governments is, therefore, not straightforward and

the cost of energy will continue to rise. In terms of spending on energy imports, China will overtake the US around 2025 while India will take over from Japan as the world's third largest importer by 2020. If we think energy is an issue now, just imagine what it will be like in 2020!

Associated with this type of view, there is a continued rise in carbon emissions. By 2020, an additional 5,000 million tonnes will be being emitted annually, and double that by 2030. So, without a massive and fundamental global shift in energy consumption behaviour, any chance of slowing CO_2 emissions is years away. While the US and Europe have finally started to talk about levelling off, if not reducing, carbon emissions, the challenges elsewhere are considerable. For instance, in 1990 the combined emissions for China and India accounted for 13% of the world's total, and, because they are the world's fastest-growing economies, their emissions will continue to rise markedly. In 2008, non-OECD primary energy consumption exceeded OECD consumption for the first time and further growth of 34% can be expected by 2030 – of which China will account for 29%.

Although Copenhagen failed to get any significant agreement on climate change, it is clear that, over the next decade, new agreements on climate protection will variously come into place, whether regionally or globally. According to the IEA 450 Scenario, to limit the probability of a global average temperature rise of 2°C even to a 50/50 bet requires all OECD+ countries to take on emission reduction commitments from 2013, with everyone else joining in by the end of the decade. This impetus to reduce carbon emissions will place another restraint on the use of oil, gas and coal and so add to the constrained supply of these fundamental energy resources.

Between now and 2030 we will consume more copper, more aluminium and more steel than we have in history.

Metals

Alongside energy, the growth in consumption of many of the world's main metals is also on the rise. As mentioned above, according to BHP Billiton projections, between now and 2030 we will consume more copper, more aluminium and more steel than we have in history. But who will be responsible for what consumption? Today China consumes around 25% of the world's refined copper, 16% of the world's nickel, 25% of the world's aluminium and 45% of the world's iron ore. So, in comparison to other economies, China is already consuming eight times as much refined copper and steel as the US and almost four times as much steel as the EU.

With all the construction under way and planned, as well as increased production of vehicles and domestic appliances, China's demand for steel is expected to double by the 2020s, while in India the government's target for steel production in 2020 is four times the levels of 2010. Driven by demand from the construction industry, global cement supply is also on the up, rising at just over 4% a year despite the recession. India, the world's second largest cement market, is expecting 'some of the most rapid advances of any country in the world'. Other fast-growing markets for cement in Asia include the Philippines, Taiwan and Vietnam, all with growth rates exceeding 6% per year.

So far we have not started to reach peak production of these core metals but, given the escalating growth in demand, current reserves will not last for ever. Although industry experts estimate that there is another 1,000 years' worth of aluminium available around the world, for nickel we are talking about 90 years and for copper the projection is down to only 60 years. When you consider the large amounts of copper required in each wind turbine as well as in connections between wind farms, this starts to place growth constraints on some renewable energy options.

The difference between metals and hydrocarbons, however, is that metals can be recycled and reused. But, historically, wealthy economies are not very good at recycling. Take aluminium as an example. Every three months, Americans discard enough aluminium to completely rebuild every single commercial aircraft in the USA. Aluminium can be recycled over and over without loss of performance. In theory, we have an inexhaustible supply of it in circulation right now. In fact, if we recycled all our aluminium, we'd never have to make more.

Compared with primary production, recycling aluminium requires only 5% of the energy and produces only 5% of the CO_2 emissions as well as reducing the waste going to landfill. Aluminium is also the most cost-effective material to recycle. Similarly, every tonne of steel packaging recycled makes the following environmental savings: 1.5 tonnes of iron ore; 0.5 tonnes of coal; 40% of the water required in production; 75% of the energy needed to make steel from virgin materials; 1.28 tonnes of solid waste; reduction of air emissions by 86%; and reduction of water pollution by 76%.

Other metals such as copper, gold, silver and brass are less frequently sent to landfill as their value is more generally recognised and consequently the recycling infrastructure is more developed. That said, handling large quantities of electronic equipment in order to recover precious metals has led to the exporting of equipment to places where little regard is paid to the health of workers and the environmental consequences of poor treatment of this waste stream.

Rare metals

While the increasing focus on climate change is, in itself, proving problematic for many concerned with resource supply and demand, the focus on green technologies has meant that we may have overlooked other equally important and increasingly scarce commodities. Take, for example, worldwide demand for rare earth minerals, covering fifteen elements on the periodic table. Unless major new production sources are developed and there is a significant shift in the global balance, the US Geological Survey expects demand to exceed supply by some 40,000 tonnes per year within the next decade. This matters not only because they are vital to the production of advanced electronics equipment – cell phones, batteries, plasma screens – but also because they are part of the 'green technology revolution', being essentials in the construction of hybrid cars and wind turbines. Thus, for companies focusing on green technology, securing a supply of rare earth metals – or developing replacement materials or technologies – is crucial. In the same way as many people have been focused on the date of 'peak oil', others are now starting to talk about 'peak minerals' as the supply/demand balance is tipped more towards constraint.

How Long Will It Last

Years left at current consumption levels

Material	Uses	Years
Aluminium	Transportation, consumer products	1027
Arsenic	Semiconductors, solar cells	20
Antimony	Pharmaceuticals	30
Cadmium	Batteries	70
Copper	Wires, plumbing, coins	61
Germanium	Semiconductors, solar cells	5
Gold	Jewellery, dentistry	45
Hafnium	Computer chips, nuclear control rods	20
Indium	Solar cells, LCDs	13
Lead	Pipes, batteries	42
Nickel	Batteries, turbine blades	90
Platinum	Jewellery, catalysts, fuel-cells	360
Selenium	Semiconductors, solar cells	120
Silver	Jewellery, catalysts	29
Thallium	High temperature supercondutors	65
Tin	Cans, solder	40
Uranium	Nuclear power and weapons	59
Zinc	Galvanizing steel	46

Source: New Scientist

As another example, consider platinum. As well as being used for jewellery, platinum is also a primary material for catalytic converters and fuel cells for cars. The majority (88%) of the world's platinum is produced by just two mines in South Africa and most of the rest comes from a single mine in Russia. Platinum is recovered at a rate of about 200 tonnes per year. Say we wanted to use all of it to increase the number of cars powered by fuel cells, then this is only enough to produce 2 million such vehicles by 2030, which is only around 5% of the world's current car fleet. So, given the growth in demand for transport, as well as competing requirements for platinum, any major plans for the mass introduction of vehicles running on fuel cells are significantly constrained not just by lack of investment and political will, but more fundamentally by a limited supply of a pivotal material.

Water

Unlike most of the resources we consume, there is no alternative for water. As GDP per capita rises, so does water demand and by 2025 two-thirds of the world's population are expected to be living in water-stressed regions. This problem is not new, as over 1 billion people currently experience water scarcity, having less than the minimum 50 litres a day recommended by the UN. In Europe, we use around 300 litres a day and the average US citizen consumes twice that.

Over the next ten years, industry will have to change its water use; agriculture will have to adapt; and governments will have to work out ways of ensuring the general public are more aware of the problem. To be fair, major steps have already been taken. Led by the likes of Australia and Singapore, national governments have been paying increasing attention to their water supply and use and, in doing so, several are now implementing major water strategies. Singapore, with a clear reason for reducing its dependency on neighbouring Malaysia for water, is focused on four tasks: 1) increasing the water available from the local catchment area, 2) reclaiming and treating waste water so that it can be reused by industry, 3) managing the importation of water and 4) building new desalination plants. In some countries where water stress is already evident, regulation concerning water usage is coming into force to limit fresh water consumption, shift some primary users from blue to grey water and increase overall water recycling. Emerging design standards are seeking to move government and corporate facilities towards water-neutral status and so preserve precious resources.

With 20% of the population but only 7% of global water supplies, China is particularly vulnerable. The World Bank reports that half of China's 660 cities suffer from water shortages, affecting 160 million people. Worse, it seems that about 90% of cities' groundwater and 75% of the rivers and lakes are also polluted. Small wonder that China has a strong interest in Tibet, the source of ten of Asia's largest rivers.

Water issues are also becoming increasingly political. Dan Smith, the Secretary-General of the British-based peace-building organisation International Alert, said: 'Water is a basic condition for life. Its availability and quality is fundamental for all societies, especially in relation to agriculture and health. There are places – West Africa today, the Ganges-Brahmaputra river system in Nepal, Bangladesh and India, and Peru within ten years – where major changes in the rivers generate a significant risk of violent conflict. Good water management is part of peace building.'

Water scarcity is not only a social challenge but a commercial one. Materials companies such as Dow, DuPont, Alcan and Corus are therefore all looking at ways in which they can innovate more in relation to the water they use as part of their production processes. Equally, the automotive industry, the IT sector and the food and drinks industry are also concerned about both future 'security of supply' issues as well as emerging consumer sentiment. Everything that people have been worried about regarding energy can evidently be applied to water – price, security of supply and scarcity. In these companies, concern about managing water use is seen as a priority for both internal resource risk and external reputation risk. They are busy getting accurate views of their individual water footprints so that they have the data to track and guide improvements going forward.

The price of water does not reflect its true economic value in most countries, which distorts our understanding.

Looking ahead, better education and understanding will be critical. While consumers are easily able to see the water we use for drinking, cooking and washing, we are often less aware of the water used throughout the supply chain to produce the goods and services that we consume. Expect to see more awareness-driven initiatives such as water footprinting and labelling in the future. When you consider that Ford, on average, uses 400,000 litres of water to make each of its cars and the manufacture of a kilogram of microchips (which require constant cleaning to remove chemicals) consumes about 16,000 litres, you can better understand the problem.

Despite all of the bad news, water is still however a renewable resource: we are not running out of it. A significant part of the problem is the huge and often deeply inefficient use of water – the UK loses about 3.3 billion litres of clean water a day through leakage, for example. Thankfully, much of this will be returned in various forms to the system – although not necessarily in the right location or in a quality that can be effectively reused. In addition, throughout many parts of the world, rainfall and river flows are strongly seasonal, with too much water arriving during monsoon periods followed by maybe seven or eight months of water scarcity. Climate change will exacerbate this and we 'will increasingly get the wrong water in the wrong places and the wrong times of year'. To address the scarcity problem, supply can often be increased through storage during wet periods or the use of technology – drilling boreholes

to access groundwater, for example. Reservoirs and big dams have their opponents, but they can also aid development and store monsoon runoff.

One last point about water: it's a fact that the price of water does not reflect its true economic value in most countries, which distorts our understanding. Government subsidies are therefore creating the wrong behaviours. One only has to look at cities such as Las Vegas or Dubai to realise this cannot continue long term.

Land and food

To a certain extent, government interventions are also having a negative effect on food supplies. While growing – and, more specifically, supplying – food to feed ever more people is in itself a major challenge that has already led to riots and government changes in places such as Madagascar, the bigger immediate challenge concerns bio-fuels and associated regulations that have been passed in recent years. The worst example of this is perhaps America's support programme for home-grown corn ethanol, which is coupled with tariffs on cheaper sugar-cane ethanol from Brazil. The programme has raised global food prices and consequently increased malnutrition among the world's poorest. It has also tarnished the reputation of policies to cut carbon emissions – and cut little carbon. The EU's decision to set a target for bio-fuels to make up 10% of all transport fuels by 2020 is proving equally disastrous for the poor. Subsistence farmers in countries such as Bangladesh can barely support a household and have little if any extra production to sell, which means they do not benefit from higher prices for corn or wheat. In addition, poor slum-dwellers in Delhi and Nairobi, for instance, produce no food at all and need to spend as much as 90% of their meagre household incomes just to eat.

In March 2009 there was a coup in Madagascar where it was announced that South Korea's Daewoo Logistics would lease half the island's arable land from the government to grow food. The deal was that the company would get the land rent-free; existing farmers would not be compensated; all the food would be exported. When news of this seeped out, the reaction gave impetus to a surge of opposition that swept the government from power. The new president's first act was to quash the deal. It was a salutary lesson, as other parts of Africa and Asia have signed similar deals. (The Economist)

The good news is we are we are already working on solutions, including improvements in farming efficiency and new fuels. Ashok Gulati of the International Food Policy Research Institute points out that an additional rupee spent on agricultural research yields 9.5 rupees of output. Better storage and transport facilities would also allow farmers to profit from growing fruit, vegetables and flowers. These offer better prospects than staple cereals, like wheat and rice, which preoccupy policymakers. According to the World Bank, transporting grapes to the Netherlands from India costs more than twice as much as transporting them from Chile, even though Chile is twice as far away.

As economies grow, the demand for energy, food, protein, water and metals all pretty well scale linearly: increasing GDP per capita is largely directly linked to per capita resource consumption.

The constraints

So, whether energy, metals, water or food, the next decade is clearly a challenging time for management of some of the key resources that keep the world going. While there are real physical shortages of some resources discussed above, the reasons for apparent shortages of the majority of resources – shortages that will have an impact on commodity prices around the world – are more geographical, economic and political. The main resource constraints in the next ten years are largely the result of a number of influential countries wanting to secure their own supplies, or continue to use above their equitable share; a number of influential companies seeking to either profit from higher prices or else ensure that they control the supply of resources in demand; and, most significantly, a huge number of us wanting more.

As economies grow, the demand for energy, food, protein, water and metals all pretty well scale linearly: increasing GDP per capita is largely directly linked to per capita resource consumption. If you have no money, you can access few resources. However, once you, whether an individual or a country, start to create more wealth, then you can spend it and this is usually on food, homes, transport and possessions. As you continue to grow, you continue to want more and this relationship keeps on going. Of course, the big challenge going forward is to decouple resource use from economic growth by essentially using less and yet continuing to allow economies to grow. This is where innovation will have an essential role. Already some countries have levelled off demand – as with average energy consumption per capita in Japan and Europe – but in most and for most resources this has yet to occur. As in other areas, such as mobile money, perhaps the first places to deliver real change will be in emerging economies unencumbered by existing infrastructures and industry models. In an expanding world with more people and increasing economic growth, our demands are already pushing hard against supply limits. As we move forward over the next decade, some of these resource constraints are going to generate a host of problems. We don't know exactly when and where, but we do know it is a question of when, not if.

Asian wealth shift

The centre of gravity of global wealth shifts east with decreasing influence for the US and Europe.

It is difficult to make generalisations for a continent of 3 billion people with a wide social, political and cultural diversity. However, given the much anticipated economic dominance of Asia over the next ten years, it is certainly worth trying to do so.

It is clear that the world's centre of gravity has gradually been sliding eastwards for a while now. Over the past ten years, Asia has accounted for half the world's GDP growth and, from an Asian perspective, things are looking pretty good for the future. At the end of 2008, Asia's GDP was just under US$14 trillion – roughly the same as the US – and all indications are that its growth will continue to outpace Europe and the US as we head into the next decade.

Some emerging countries barely noticed the recession while developed countries continue to struggle. In the last quarter of 2009, Thailand grew at an annual rate of 15.3% and Taiwan at 18%. Many economists expect growth in emerging markets to be four percentage points higher than growth in the rich world for at least the next five years. Indeed, thanks to rapid advances, many Asian companies have established their place in the global economy. Take for example India's ArcelorMittal, the world's largest steel company, or Lenovo, the China-based computer technology company which did not exist in 1990, bought IBM's personal computer business five years ago and is now the world's fourth largest PC maker, after Hewlett-Packard, Acer and Dell.

Nirmalya Kumar of the London Business School says that the combination of rapid growth and extensive internal restructuring has left many Asian companies with plenty of cash in their pockets. Profit margins of 10% are common – double the average in the West. And, because ownership is concentrated, companies find it easier to take risks. Even as Western companies were reeling from the recent recession, emerging-market giants were shopping. India's Tata Consultancy Services bought Citigroup Global Services, the outsourcing division of the American bank, for $512 million in October 2008. HCL, the Taiwanese technology group, snapped up Britain's Axon Group for $672 million two months later. Reliance Industries, another Indian company, is pursuing LyondellBasell Industries, a chemical company, in a $14.5 billion bid, and Bharti Airtel, headquartered in New Delhi, has gobbled up Zain, a leading African telecoms company, for $9 billion.

Looking more closely, we might have underestimated Asia's growth already. GDP figures converted at market exchange rates can understate real expansion because they don't take into consideration that the price of many domestic products, food, clothes, electronic goods and so on are always cheaper in low-income countries (Thailand, China, Indonesia,

GDP Growth to 2020 ($bn)

2020 Rank	Country	GDP 2010	GDP 2015	GDP 2020
1	United States	14,535	16,194	17,978
2	China	4,667	8,133	12,630
3	Japan	4,604	4,861	5,224
4	Germany	3,083	3,326	3,519
5	United Kingdom	2,546	2,835	3,101
6	India	1,256	1,900	2,848
7	France	2,366	2,577	2,815
8	Russia	1,371	1,900	2,554
9	Italy	1,914	2,072	2,224
10	Brazil	1,346	1,720	2,194

Source: Goldman Sachs

important to consider consumer spending in dollar terms. Over three-fifths of the world's population live in Asia and their purchasing power accounts for a little over one-fifth of global private consumption. Although, overall, Asia is still a poor continent, with more than 71% of people living on less than a dollar a day, Asian consumers are clearly growing richer, with average earnings in many countries doubling in the past five years. Asians are now able to use their newly acquired disposable incomes to buy everything from mobile phones (43% of all sales are now to Asian consumers) to cars (35% of all car sales last year were in Asia).

Asia's growth has been built primarily on Western consumption – or, more accurately, over-consumption. Export-led development has lifted significant markets out of poverty; in fact, the per capita income of people in the 'Tiger' economies of Hong Kong, Singapore, South Korea and Taiwan now rival, or in some cases exceed, that of many European countries. This is by no means a new phenomenon. A century ago, Japan was the first to understand the West's almost insatiable desire for imports and began with a focus on light goods, such as raw silk and pottery, before moving on to heavier industrial materials like steel and chemicals. As early as 1914, almost a quarter of the world's cotton and yarn exports were from Japan. In the 1960s, Singapore, Hong Kong, Taiwan and South Korea imitated Japan and flourished.

India etc). This means that the average households in Asia do not need to spend as much money buying goods as their Western counterparts. Also, many Asian currencies are still recovering from the dramatic tumble they took during the financial crisis of the late 1990s, and Japan has also had to deal with a period of deflation. Given this, some argue that it is much better to measure growth through purchasing power parity (PPP), which takes lower prices into account. Through this lens, it is even clearer that Asia has done pretty well over the past couple of decades. Its share of the world economy has risen steadily, from 18% in 1980 to 27% in 1995 and 34% in 2009, and, all things being equal, Asian PPP will probably exceed the combined sum of America's and Europe's within four years. This isn't surprising when you consider that three of the world's four biggest economies by PPP (China, Japan and India) are Asian.

We must tread carefully, however, because another school of thought suggests that PPP measures exaggerate the numbers and it is much more

Asia's growth has been built primarily on Western consumption – or, more accurately, over-consumption.

China also boomed after opening up its economy in 1978. Its 'Special Economic Zones' were designed to attract foreign capital to build factories to make 'stuff' for the Western market. Millions of products were quite literally 'made in China' and then shipped off to shops in London, Paris and New York. Malaysia, Thailand, Indonesia and, later, Vietnam all forged similar export-led paths to growth, so much so that the past ten years have seen Asia's exports as a share of its GDP grow from 37% to 47%. Of course, the story is not the same everywhere: Singapore's exports hit 186% of GDP in 2007 while Indonesia's were less than 30%. Some countries, mainly for political reasons, have not jumped on the bandwagon – Myanmar and North Korea, for example, remain poor.

The export model has helped Asian countries improve their living standards quickly. Evidence suggests that China has benefited most from this arrangement, with a quadrupling of GDP and an increase in exports by a factor of five over the past decade, not to mention the ability to attract Western technology and expertise and the creation of millions of manufacturing jobs for the poor. It has been a dramatic shift in industry and the sheer speed of change has made it particularly challenging to maintain cheap and competitive manufacturing labour markets and yet ensure acceptable standards of living for the workers. But, so long as incomes are increasing, both government and the people have been content to ignore things like social services and good governance – privileges that Western societies take for granted. The main problem, perhaps, is that the 'easy money' obtained through exports has tempted some governments to put off other areas of economic development, the encouragement of domestic demand being a prominent example.

Until very recently this production of goods in Asia for Western consumers proved very satisfactory for all involved and Asian economies have grown on the back of the seemingly insatiable Western appetite for cheap clothes, electronics and toys. In their discussion of this, economic historians Niall Ferguson and Moritz Schularick have coined the term 'Chimerica' because both the US and China have played pivotal roles in the unfolding drama.

China, in particular, has used its exports to build up its currency reserves to an unprecedented high. In 2000, it was of the order of US$1,654 billion, or slightly more than 10% of GDP. By 2009, it was US$2.3 trillion, equivalent to more than 50% of China's annual output – or, to put it another way, enough to buy two-thirds of all the NASDAQ-quoted companies. China is also the world's second largest net creditor after Japan (the net credit position takes account of equities as well as debt). America, on the other hand, simply consumed more and saved less, but, because the Chinese currency was pegged to the dollar, it still maintained low interest rates and a stable rate of investment. In retrospect, it was clearly unsustainable as over-consumption meant that between 2000 and 2008 the US outspent its national income. According to Helmut Reisen, head of research of the OECD Development Centre, total US spending over the period was 45% higher than total income – and a third of this consumption was imports from China.

Like all bubbles, this level of growth was unsustainable in the long term and the financial and economic crisis of 2007 to 2009 has meant that even the American thirst for buying now and paying later has ground to a halt under the pressure of toxic loans and bad debt. Not good for the US but equally not good for Asia, dependent as it is on foreign buyers.

But what happens next? Asian economies, although not in themselves built on debt, have been buoyed up along with all the other assets including American houses and shares during the credit bubble of the past decade. The markets are clearly interconnected. The Asian Development Bank estimates that, because of the amount that is exported to the West, a decline of one percentage point in America's growth rate knocks 0.3 of a percentage point off Asia's.

So, because the once profligate Western consumer is now saving – or, at least, not spending as much – Asia needs a new market. This new market might well be Asia's own population. Trade within Asia is already growing at roughly twice the pace of trade with the outside world. From almost nothing twenty years ago, China is now India's biggest trading partner, with bilateral trade that may top $60 billion this year. Central Asia's trade with China jumped from $160 million in 1990 to $7 billion in 2006. And China is now the biggest merchandise exporter to the Middle East. In fact, over the past few years, China has been exemplary in using bilateral trade agreements to build up a strong network of partners that helps drive sustained export growth.

However, for now, Asia as a whole also needs to manage its finances. It is in a good position because its foreign assets have provided a cushion against the vicissitudes of the recession. As Asian growth continues to outstrip that of the US, it gets harder for Asia's exporters both to keep exporting in volume and to keep importing the greenback. In truth, the average Asian exporters don't necessarily want their currency to strengthen because a strong currency effectively raises their prices abroad and reduces their competitive advantage. It is therefore understandable that places like China would like to

continue to keep the yuan undervalued to ensure it retains Western buyers for its myriad product ranges. It is a situation that Ferguson and Schularick argue 'would introduce new and dangerous distortion to the global economy'.

On top of this, although increasing numbers of Asian consumers have developed a taste for shopping, private consumption currently accounts for only about half of Asia's GDP (compared with 72% in the US), so there is considerable room for growth. Three billion Asians currently spend a little less than US$7 trillion on consumer goods; in comparison, 300 million Americans spend up to US$10 trillion. Today China has 55 million middle-class households: by 2025, this is expected to more than quadruple to nearly 280 million. As prosperity filters through and the middle classes become big spenders, there is the expectation that the region's emerging economies could soon grow enough to offset falling consumption in the US and the EU. So, as American and European belts tighten, expect the Asian consumers to drive the new markets of the next decade.

China is, of course, the movie star of Asia, with exponential growth potential. China now has a market-orientated economy with a flourishing private sector and it has an increasing presence on the international stage – goodbye collective agriculture; hello liberalised prices, fiscal decentralisation, increased autonomy for state enterprises, diversified banking systems, stock markets, and perhaps, most importantly, foreign trade and investment. As a result it has quadrupled its GDP since 2000, raised exports by a factor of five and has now overtaken Germany to become the world's largest exporter. Chinese exports, which jumped ahead after WTO accession in 2001, are generating higher and higher

China is already well on the way to becoming the world's biggest market for pretty much anything you can think of.

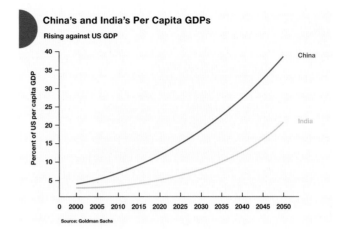

China's and India's Per Capita GDPs

Rising against US GDP

Source: Goldman Sachs

trade surpluses. Not bad for a country which not so long ago had a centrally planned economy and was closed to international trade.

It is difficult for many people in the West to comprehend China's size and scale. China is now the world's biggest market for many household products, including TVs, refrigerators and air conditioners. It tops the world car sales charts despite car ownership currently resting at fewer than fourteen vehicles per thousand citizens (compared with more than 400 per thousand in the US). It has 400 million internet users compared with America's 240 million and India's 80 million. And the Chinese market is only going to get bigger. In fact, China is already well on the way to becoming the world's biggest market for pretty much anything you can think of.

Of course, this growth is not without its problems. The Chinese government faces numerous development challenges, including reducing its high domestic savings rate and correspondingly low domestic demand; creating jobs for approximately 200 million rural labourers and their families as they relocate from the countryside to the towns (10.8% of people still live on less than $1 a day); and containing the environmental damage resulting from the economy's rapid transformation. It also sits on a demographic time bomb as a consequence of the 'one child' policy, which means that China is now one of the most rapidly ageing countries in the world. The government

in Beijing is doing its best to find solutions to these onerous problems and is also actively seeking to add energy production from sources other than coal and oil. However, like everything in China, the solutions it needs are enormous in scale.

Given China's problems, it is worth discussing the other drivers of Asian wealth. Take India, for example, which is second only to China as a fast-growing large economy. Unlike the giant export-driven Chinese economy, India has emerged relatively 'unscathed' by the global economic downturn according to the Asian Development Bank. During the past two decades, it has moved away from its former 'command and control' policies to become a market-based economy. Like China it has a large domestic market with substantial numbers of poor people. However, unlike many of its Asian counterparts, India has a limited reliance on exports, which account for less than 20% of gross domestic product. In fact, the resilience of the economy rests on a huge domestic market, and, even better, India's domestic demand

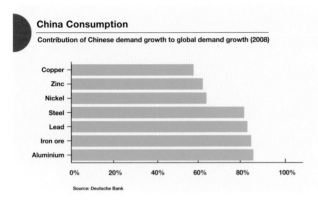

China Consumption

Contribution of Chinese demand growth to global demand growth (2008)

Source: Deutsche Bank

was largely uninterrupted by the financial crisis. Some export sectors did suffer, though, including textiles, but are now recovering.

India's fast-growing economy, with its strong internal focus, also has global ambition. India is increasingly a leading source of process and business model innovations. For example, the launch of the Tata Nano, the world's cheapest car, a couple of years ago has done a lot to position the Indian automotive industry as the centre for low-cost innovation, particularly in small vehicles. The industrial sector is also on the rise, currently expanding at a double-digit rate, and the services sector is now at 55% of GDP. Only agriculture, accounting for 20% of GDP, is under-performing, curtailed as it is by poor harvests and low rainfall.

Education and knowledge have played a key part in India's growth. India produces 3 million graduates a year and about twice as many engineering and computing graduates as America, counting those with bachelor's or master's degrees. In addition, partially because of inadequate physical infrastructure, India is also witnessing some of the fastest rates of adoption for distance learning. Since 2001, 24x7 Learning,

one of the country's leading e-learning technology platforms, has welcomed over 1 million students to the various courses that it hosts for both academic institutions and corporate universities. The thirst for knowledge is strongly supported by the state: Indian legislation ensures that a government or public sector employee who earns an online degree will benefit from an increase in both pay scale and pension.

A young (70% of the 1.2 billion population is under 35), educated workforce has attracted the hi-techs, such as HP, IBM, Microsoft and Accenture. Global drug giants, such as Novartis, GSK, Eli Lilly, Pfizer and AstraZeneca, have all begun turning to India as a base for R&D and Indian-born companies are increasingly carrying out original research themselves – at much lower cost than elsewhere. Today, India has some 110 drug manufacturing facilities approved by the US Food and Drugs Administration. Although the drug discovery business is unlikely to reach the size of the country's IT and software industry, the market for contract pharmaceutical work is about US$38 billion so the opportunities for well-educated, hard-working Indian professionals are considerable.

However, although India's growth rate has been among the highest in the world, it remains a low-income country, with inadequate infrastructure being a significant barrier to development, particularly in rural areas, home to 70% of India's population and the 52% of the workforce that is primarily engaged in agriculture and related activities. Any development strategy will need to contend with the harsh realities of low productivity in the countryside, a massive movement of people to the cities (India's urban population is expected to double over the next two decades to 575 million), and extensive poverty in both rural and urban areas. India plans roughly to double investment in infrastructure to $500 billion over the next five years, or about 8% of GDP each year, with private investors contributing 40% of the total, not only to expand capacity but also to improve the quality of service. India's stated aim is to grow inclusively, which means that it may take a little longer than other nations. Manmohan Singh, the prime minister, may have put his finger on it: 'It is probably true that we are a slow-moving elephant but it is equally true that with each step forward we leave behind a deep imprint. There is a price that we pay in trying to carry all sections of our people along ... It is perhaps a price worth paying.'

No discussion about Asia can be complete without considering the impact that Japan continues to have on economic growth. Despite being at the forefront of innovation and trade in the post-WWII era, Japan was one of the hardest hit countries during the global financial crisis. It is doing its best to address this by finding new domestic markets and markets closer to home – namely, in China – but Japan has deep-seated problems of deflation, huge public debt, ugly demographics and, worst of all, indecisive leadership. Unless things change radically, Japan's difficulties may well hold back economic recovery for years to come.

The finance ministers of the Association of Southeast Asian Nations (ASEAN, comprising a monarchy, a military dictatorship, communist states and democracies) are only slightly less ebullient than their counterparts in Asia's major players, predicting that the region's economy is expected to expand by between 4.9% and 5.6% in the next year. Incrementally, their resource-rich region of 584 million people, with a combined gross domestic product of $2.7 trillion, is stitching together an economic community, even if their political and security harmony is more of a pipe dream at the moment. ASEAN leaders have already agreed to coordinate policies, including rate cuts, credit support and government spending after their export-orientated economies fell into a sharp but short recession during the global financial crisis. Maintaining a positive economic relationship with Myanmar, however, is an obvious challenge that will test ASEAN's political cohesiveness. The nation's military rulers face criticism from some members over its new election laws because of its treatment of political detainees, notably democracy icon Aung San Suu Kyi.

The shift

Given all of the above, it is evident that, as a whole, Asian economic growth will continue to outpace that of the West. Led by the sheer scale of growth in India and China, but also influenced heavily by the likes of Japan, South Korea, Indonesia and Vietnam, the centre of wealth generation is clearly shifting eastwards. The point at which China's economy eclipses that of the US in absolute terms is, according to varied forecasts, just a few years out beyond 2020, but there is little doubt that, given the importance of the GDP PPP view, China itself will already be the centre of gravity for the future world economy at the end of the decade. Add in the rest of the ASEAN countries and it is clear why our third certainty looking forward is that there will be a steady and increasing shift of wealth to Asia from Europe and the US. The shift of economic power to Asia is pretty much a safe bet for 2020.

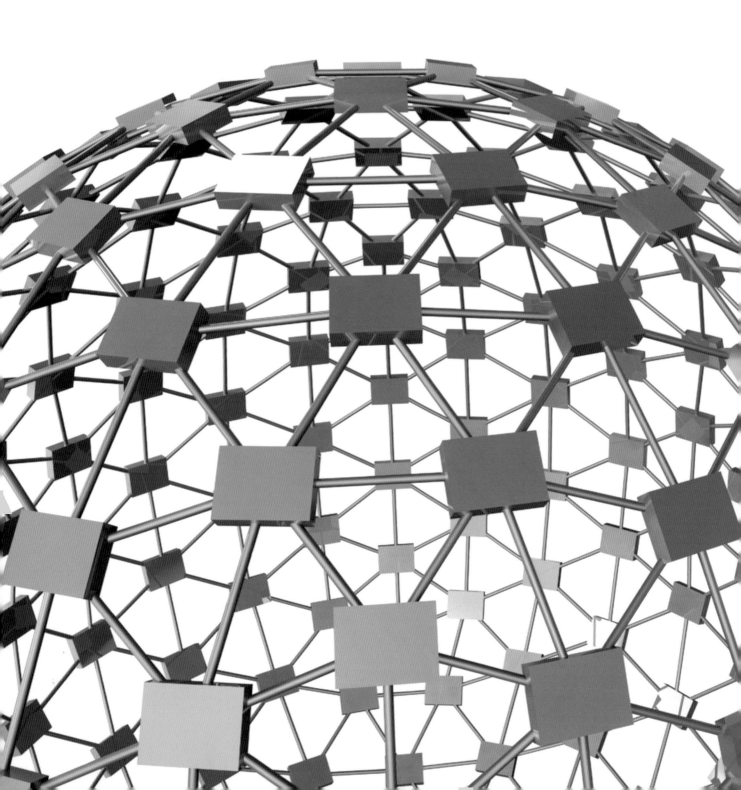

Universal data access

We will be connected everywhere – everything that can benefit from a network connection will have one.

The internet is one of the transformational technologies to emerge from the twentieth century. Another is the mobile phone. These two platforms are now coming together and, as they do so, are bringing with them more opportunities for transformation. Certainly their convergence means that global connectivity – for many, the great goal of recent years – is almost upon us. It's easy to see the attraction of this given that the ability to communicate and interact with billions of people has the potential to, quite literally, redesign society.

Today, it is perfectly possible to envisage a world where we will all be 'connected' – we will be able to communicate with anybody and everybody, anywhere they and we might be. Through these universal interconnections, we will train and learn, educate and entertain, buy and sell, trade and barter. As well as being connected to each other, we will have remote access to our machines (computers, electrical goods, boilers, water pumps and so on). Indeed, the whole 'machine-to-machine' concept is about to hit the big time – smart systems have the potential to reduce the overall impact we have on the environment by helping to regulate the temperature in our homes, monitor utilities, manage traffic flow and myriad other applications that will both reduce costs and increase sustainability. We will probably go on to do all sorts of other things via the internet that have not yet even been considered.

Ten years ago, there were around 700 million mobile devices, most of which didn't connect to the World Wide Web, 370 million people had access to the internet, and the likes of Google (incorporated 1998) and Facebook (2004) were barely gathering momentum or unknown. There are now around 4.6 billion mobile devices worldwide, many of which do connect to the internet (mobile internet subscriptions have already overtaken fixed-line broadband) and internet penetration has grown to 76% in the US, 53% in Europe and many emerging economies are catching up quickly. Consider China, for example, where internet penetration has grown from 2% in 2000 to 27% in 2009. Today's China not only has 370 million fixed-line subscribers and more than 530 million mobile subscribers but also has over 360 million internet users and has become the world's biggest internet market, easily overtaking both the US and the whole of Western Europe. Internet access in South America is also on the rise, with Brazil now having more internet users than any European country. Without a doubt, connectivity is a global phenomenon.

All in all, around 1.8 billion people now have access to the internet. It has become a source of information and, increasingly importantly, entertainment. Although, in the West, access is primarily via fixed-line broadband connections at home or at work, the burgeoning take-up of mobile broadband

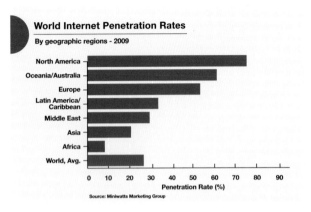

World Internet Penetration Rates
By geographic regions - 2009

Source: Miniwatts Marketing Group

connectivity is transforming the landscape and making access more convenient. This means that time spent online is growing substantially – to some extent at the expense of other, more traditional media. This is emphasised in a German study that suggested the internet's share of media consumption time would grow from 4% in 2000 to 24% by 2015.

As the internet is now being used for an increasing range of everyday activities, from shopping (56% of people in the US are reported to have bought products online in 2009) to banking, to sharing photos and watching TV, a host of interesting statistics abound. For example, Google currently runs over 1 million servers in data centres around the world, and processes over 1 billion search requests and twenty petabytes of user-generated data every day. The rise and rise of social networking continues to amaze: since its launch, Facebook has built up more than 500 million active users and, incredibly, 5% of all time online is currently spent on that website alone. It's no longer just the written word being shared: self-generated video content is having a field day and we are all keen to share our creations so we upload at

least 24 hours of video onto YouTube every minute. The great name of the game is to profit from this – alongside time, the amount of money spent online is set to increase.

Mobile devices are becoming a key means to access the internet, driven by the availability and increasing affordability of smart phones as well as high-speed data modems and USB dongles that provide internet access for laptops. This trend is expected to continue, with growth for smart phones projected to increase from 54 million today to 289 million in 2013, which will increase consumers' choice as to how they access the internet. Perhaps more significantly, though, it is increasingly likely that the first internet experience for the majority of people who live in an emerging economy will be through a mobile rather than a PC. By 2020, the vast majority of us will have internet access to much of the world's data, and most of this will be via mobile.

Jeffrey Sachs, Director of the Earth Institute at Columbia University, has described the mobile phone as 'the single most transformative tool for development' and it certainly seems to be the case. Mobiles do not have the same barriers to access as PCs – they are inexpensive and relatively simple to use, so standard voice and text messaging has

Jeffrey Sachs, Director of the Earth Institute at Columbia University, has described the mobile phone as 'the single most transformative tool for development.

been able to transform the way people in the developing world communicate, look for work, stay in touch with friends and family, send and receive information and even save money. The impact of this on economic growth is significantly larger than that seen in more developed economies, which already had a well-established communications infrastructure. Essentially, mobiles are taking on the same crucial role played by fixed telephony in richer economies during the 1970s and 1980s. In particular, Africa, despite its poverty, has become a centre for both growth and innovation in mobile use – for example, M-PESA, the world's leading mobile money transfer payment service, was launched in Kenya. So, 'connectivity' in emerging economies really means 'mobile connectivity'.

One of the main reasons for this is that the pre-pay charging model has ensured that even the poorest can now choose to have access to a mobile. The pre-pay model began by facilitating the spread of mobile phones among Western teenagers in the late 1990s but, more importantly, it has also dramatically expanded the market for mobile phones in poor countries. The Grameen model of micro-entrepreneurship built on this to enable 'telephone ladies' to be set up with mobiles in rural areas, essentially establishing themselves as living public telephone facilities for fellow villagers. Alongside all of this, the fact that the price of handsets has been steadily falling – from around $250 in 1997 to less than $10 today – has cemented the mobile phone as the main vehicle for connectivity.

You don't have to look far to see the impact of this simple, convenient technology. India, for example, has one of the fastest-growing telecommunication services in the world; on average 20.3 million new

Globally, some predictions suggest that we will reach 6.5 billion mobile phone subscribers by the end of 2014 – equivalent to a 91% penetration rate.

mobile connections are made every month. The current estimate is that there are 584.3 million Indian mobile phone users, compared with 37 million fixed-line subscribers, and by the time this book goes to press you can probably add another 50 million. Globally, some predictions suggest that we will reach 6.5 billion mobile phone subscribers by the end of 2014 – equivalent to a 91% penetration rate. The reason for this is that mobiles are helping to drive growth in the economy. In 2009, the Indian Council for Research on International Economic Relations (ICRIER) found clear evidence to suggest that Indian states with a 10% higher mobile phone penetration enjoy an annual average growth rate 1.2% greater than states with a lower teledensity.

The numbers are impressive but perhaps the best illustrations to give are examples of real scenarios. Take, for instance, a migrant worker recently arrived from the countryside: if potential employers can't contact him because he has nowhere permanent to live, then his chances of getting work are reduced. Also, when the alternative to a phone call is a time-consuming journey along poor and possibly dangerous roads, the value of connectivity is greater. So, if you live in a remote rural community and you need to go to the nearest town to buy or sell some goods, a simple phone call, or text message, can tell you immediately if the journey will be worth while, thus saving you time and money on unnecessary trips.

Connectivity can also help build businesses – small or large. Ranjeet Gupta, an Indian henna artist, is a good case in point. His speciality is decorating the hands and feet of brides in preparation for their wedding day. He came to Delhi from the countryside in 2001 and began plying his trade on a pavement, preparing brides from the poorest families. In 2002 he bought a mobile phone and was then able to prepare brides from slightly richer families, who he could visit in their own homes. He was also then able to order dry henna over the phone rather than having to go to a shop to buy it. As time and privacy became less of a problem, customers asked for more intricate designs and his decorative repertoire grew. He next went on to buy a camera phone and used that as a portfolio to show his designs to customers. Building on his success, Ranjeet was able to buy another camera phone which he gave to his son who lives with the main family in a village outside Delhi. His son has now started training to become a henna artist using the different designs sent to him by his father. Mobile connectivity has allowed Ranjeet to make a livelihood in a situation where the modestly educated and relatively poor often struggle.

As already noted, connectivity does not have to be just between people. In the future, the number of machines that will be connected remotely is expected to increase considerably. Machine-to-machine (M2M) technology is set to be used in the battle against one of the most pressing challenges facing society – namely, climate change. Expectations of the benefits of this are high. A recent joint report by Accenture and Vodafone suggested M2M connectivity could cut Europe's annual energy bill by at least €43 billion and effect a reduction in annual greenhouse gas emissions by at least 113 million tonnes CO_2e by 2020. This represents 18% of the UK's annual CO_2e output in 2008 and approximately 2.4% of expected EU emissions in 2020. Clearly, however, these predictions come with many provisos – most importantly, to be successful they can only be realised if industry and governments are prepared to collaborate.

Connectivity, be that mobile or fixed-line and internet connectivity, can only take us so far. Sir Tim Berners-Lee, founder of the internet, envisaged a world of global collaboration, where people could share and build ideas without the confines of time and place. Twenty-five years on this is almost a reality. The internet was born on a PC but its natural home is on the more personalised 'always available, always connected' mobile device. It is here that the internet comes alive, offering not only access to information but also interaction with information. Mobiles have given people, from all corners of the world, who would not otherwise have access, the chance to join in. Indeed, the concept of sending and receiving information via mobile has acted as a stepping-stone for many people as they make the transition from two-way conversations to receiving text-based information via their handsets. The next iteration is, of course, social networking which burst onto the scene about five years ago and which will again fundamentally change the way that people

Over the next ten years, expect that fast, efficient connectivity will facilitate the growing trend towards virtual companies as knowledge workers increasingly become free agents.

relate to one another, as well as with businesses and governments.

Social networking has given us all the ability to host global interactive debates on anything with anyone with the simple click of a mouse or touch of a screen. It has made the sharing of ideas easy. It also means that many of us now live in a 24/7/365 world where it is possible to talk, email or even video call wherever we are, whenever we want with whomever we want. Not so long ago, this would have been possible for only a few highly technical, well-funded institutions. We can create a global discussion – such as that of the Future Agenda – for anyone to join in. Although this is exciting and has huge benefits in breaking down barriers, Web2.0 is also a noisy world and, despite the ability to make information public, the flurry of opinion, websites, blogs and personal pages does not necessarily mean that amongst the clamour it is any easier to sort fact from fiction. Also, how do you work out who you should trust in a world where millions of people use multiple identities?

Increasingly, information no longer has value but understanding information and analysing what it means still does. Those people who are able to take this understanding and connect with others across borders (be they national, professional or social) will be able to build on their knowledge and create their own networks. This will present interesting challenges as businesses come to terms with a world in which collaboration, open innovation and crowd sourcing may make the traditional corporate structure seem very outdated. Over the next ten years, expect that fast, efficient connectivity will facilitate the growing trend towards virtual companies as knowledge workers increasingly become free agents. What is

clear is that the barriers between work and play are continuing to crumble and busy executives will now have to manage the blurring of what used to be quite distinctive areas. It will no longer be a question of work–life balance but more a question of work–life integration.

All of this sounds relentlessly upbeat but there is a darker side to this universal data access. Over the course of the workshops we have been running, three clear themes have emerged and have evoked considerable debate. Roughly speaking they can be characterised as content, contact and commercialism.

The increasing wealth of information available means that more and more individuals will be left to judge what to believe and what to trust. Consider those who want to reach out to others in community chat rooms and in so doing get help and support at times of need: websites such as patientslikeme.com, which provides a way for people with life-changing diseases to share experiences and learn from others with similar conditions, are great examples of how social networking can work to the benefit of others. But sites like this are juxtaposed with sites that are designed to misinform or undermine. It will be left to the user to decide what is accurate and to respond accordingly and decisions around this will become more difficult as the amount of information available increases.

In particular, parents will have to deal with the challenges of ensuring their children do not have access to inappropriate information, be that of a sexual, violent or otherwise offensive nature. This will be increasingly difficult because many adults will continue to struggle with technology that seems almost second nature to their children. There have been many discussions around the grooming of children in chat rooms but, as one workshop participant pointed out, 'one of the biggest challenges may be from the local community'. In the past, school bullying generally stopped at the front door of a child's home but increasingly sophisticated mobile devices mean that not only can a child receive abusive messages, but also their location, who they are with and what they are doing will be shared with others at the mere press of a button. All of this could happen without their parents' knowledge or control. Not only that, but there is also the need to address the dramatic increase in child pornography driven by the ability of the internet to connect those with common but morally unacceptable tastes.

The abuse of content extends across all sectors and is currently most visible as a threat to the creative industries as data is shared indiscriminately and without cost. As Chris Meyer said in his initial perspective, 'Enterprise 2.0 has reduced the marginal cost of IP to essentially zero.' Journalism, the movie business and the music industry have been wrestling with ways in which to retain their value, derived as it is from the sharing of information. Journalism is particularly vulnerable as YouTube, Twitter and any wealth of blogs makes reporters of us all and undermines the traditional business model. Already, many publications feel obliged to provide online content free of charge. Despite the attempts of News International to halt it, this trend seems set to continue. In the short term, the media may well continue to make a profit both

Enterprise 2.0 has reduced the marginal cost of IP to essentially zero.

through sales and advertising spend as, at the time of writing, it is still more convenient to read a traditional paper – on the train for example – rather than look at the news through a computer screen. But as new devices, such as the iPad and the Kindle, continue to improve their functionality and become more widely available, this may well change and business models will have to change too.

The commercial challenge is not faced just by journalists. Although internet shopping may well be more convenient for some over the next ten years, it will also have a huge impact on our high streets as the demand for a physical space in which to buy books, clothes and food declines. Furthermore, the number of people necessary to manage a warehouse is significantly less than the number required to staff a shop so expect significant changes in working patterns in the retail industry. This will reduce job prospects for not only the young but also the poorly qualified. It may also have an impact on local communities, leaving the sick and the old, who frequently use shopping routines as a way of keeping in touch with society, with fewer options for interaction with others.

Finally, problems are looming with regard to how to ensure the next generation of networks manage to support the increased demand from its users. Millions of people are now accessing data, buying goods, browsing websites, sending emails, downloading and swapping music, catching up on television shows, watching movies, or playing video games online. This is putting pressure on the network capacity.

Over the next ten years, key decisions will have to be made around how networks are managed so that as many people as possible are able to benefit from the internet. The current view is that messages must queue up to be delivered and, the more demand that is placed on the network, the longer and slower the queue gets for everyone. This means that a large video file will reduce the speed at which another short email arrives at its destination. Effectively all applications are treated alike and network operators do not interfere with the data they send or receive – with the important exceptions of prioritising calls to the emergency services and blocking illegal content such as child pornography. However, this means that those people who do not wish to use high bandwidth services are forced to queue alongside those who do. It is becoming increasingly important to identify a way in which networks can be monetised and those who need to use more capacity can do so. The most contentious decision will be over who should have priority when demand is high and the system is put under pressure.

Finally, during the next ten years, increasing connectivity means that, whether we like it or not, we will all have a virtual presence. As a result, individuals will have to decide the amount and value of the data we produce and who it is we should share it with. We will have to balance the benefits of sharing our personal information – around our health, for example – with concern for our privacy. There is a gradual public realisation that faster search results and the convenience of tailored information come at a price and that price is sharing personal information with organisations. Already today many people are taking information off their Facebook and MySpace profiles and restricting what data is open to the public. Going forward, we can only expect this to increase as the private data/public data balance changes. It's not all doom and gloom, however, as the younger generation, which has matured alongside the internet, is likely to find the negotiation between public and private online lives much easier.

Universal access

So, expect the majority of the world's population to be connecting to the internet via a mobile device by 2020, with the major share of new users coming from China and India. Universal data access will be here: imagine a world where there may be as many as 50 billion devices all connected to each other, offering new types of services and opportunity for people, business and government. Of course, as well as opportunity there will be challenges – interception, the right to privacy, the difficulties in distinguishing fact from fiction – but in a world that will be constrained in almost every other area – food, health, resources and so on – perhaps it is here that we have most reason to be optimistic.

PART 2
Drivers of change:
key insights

Whereas Part 1 examined four certainties for the next decade that everybody agrees about, here we look at the probable changes that could occur between now and 2020. These are events and shifts across many different areas considered likely to happen by the thousands of people engaged as part of the Future Agenda programme workshops and online discussions. However, they are not certainties. Some factors make these changes appear highly probable but, because of their technology dependencies and links to unpredictable social trends, political will and regulation, there is a chance that they will not play out as expected. For each of the forty-eight probable futures outlined here we have therefore sought to explain the context and the likely changes by 2020, but have also indicated some of the variations that may occur and likely consequences. In addition, as many of these are interconnected or share common issues, we have highlighted in the margins which other topics each one connects to so that you can navigate your way through.

We have grouped the forty-eight probable futures into six of what we have called clusters, each of which contains eight insights that address similar themes. These clusters are health, wealth, happiness, mobility, security and locality and, as we address each in turn, we hope that the connections and dependencies are clear.

The future of health

The world of health and nutrition is one in which there are many significant technological and social changes on the horizon. For instance, stem cell research and more detailed use of the information we have on the human genome are providing a plethora of new development opportunities. Equally, with a generally larger, older, fatter population on the 2020 horizon, there are a number of major policy decisions around food supply, health funding and even end-of-life management that will demand attention. Some of these will be more relevant to certain countries than others. At the same time, we must not forget that there are some fundamental global issues that connect us all, such as the likelihood of new global pandemics. New business models will also move rapidly around the world to make healthcare more efficient.

The many discussions that we held focusing on the future of health highlighted a host of issues and possible changes for the next decade, as well as some things that will stay the same. We have chosen eight that not only sparked a lot of debate but also were felt to be some of the most significant probable changes in this area. They range from the inevitable to the controversial and provide an interesting view of how this important area may evolve over the next decade.

The topics covered in the following pages are:

Automated people-care

Clinical enhancement

Diabesity

Global pandemics

Halting Alzheimer's

Mass medical tourism

Pharma foods

Systemic euthanasia

Automated people-care

Robotic assisted care and remote monitoring provide economically viable support for the sick and elderly so people can stay home for longer.

One of the key challenges for healthcare providers is to provide ongoing medical support of the elderly and the chronically sick at home. Given that people are living longer and the costs of hospital-based care are so great, or, as in the case of many emerging economies, simply not available, many countries are increasingly focused on providing solutions that help people within their own space. The traditional approach to this has been through using carers who either live with patients or visit them on a regular timetable to monitor their health, advise on diet and exercise, and alleviate isolation and loneliness. It has been argued consistently that supporting people in this way avoids, or at least delays, the need to admit them into primary or secondary healthcare units, which saves both the social and financial costs of entering hospitals or care homes. Many cultures and societies traditionally encourage long-term family cohesion and recognise home-care to be far better for the individual than the institutional alternatives. However, with escalating costs, increasing dependency ratios and the mushrooming of the populations over 65 in many countries, this is fast becoming economically unsustainable. As one workshop participant explained: 'We can no longer afford to provide our elders with the level of personal support they have traditionally had but we also need to keep them out of hospitals for longer.'

Similar levels of support are also provided to those in younger age brackets who suffer from long-term chronic diseases such as diabetes, asthma, heart conditions and HIV and AIDS. The latter is particularly pertinent to South Africa where an estimated 5.7 million people are currently living with the condition. These diseases typically require daily monitoring and diagnosis coupled with informed support. In response, a host of programmes are currently being designed which will not only allow healthcare workers to have access to more detailed information and so give better support in the field but will also help patients to manage their condition independently.

Over the next decade, many predict that automated people-care, where assistance is provided either remotely or by technology-enabled products within the home, will be a major focus of attention for many different sectors. Beyond pure healthcare providers, automated people-care has become an increasingly attractive arena for telecoms companies, software developers and IT hardware manufacturers. In the UK, one of the last pieces of legislation passed by the outgoing Labour administration in 2010 was the Personal Care Bill which ensured free personal care at home for around 400,000 people with the greatest needs. Given the economic considerations, this level of support can only be achieved with significant technological input. In South Africa, the hope is that 'e-health' will help to increase public access to the limited number of healthcare workers and, in particular, give people access to health information so that they are better prepared to manage their conditions.

Today, growing numbers of public and private organisations have moved on from basic systems of nurse visits and are already providing telehealth-based support to monitor vital signs through data links, give advice over the phone and even allow remote imaging. Text-based support of multiple patients has proved highly effective from both therapeutic and economic perspectives in many countries – from the Philippines and Brazil to Germany and South Africa, services have been launched to help diabetes, TB, HIV and Alzheimer's patients as well as to improve the more day-to-day check-ups. Given the impact that can be achieved, McKinsey estimates the telehealth or mhealth industry to be worth over $50 billion by the end of the decade. Alongside the mobile phone networks, firms like GE, Philips and Siemens are all placing big bets in this area. Telemedicine connectivity will therefore soon be providing widespread 24/7 medical data sharing between patients and healthcare professionals. Over the next couple of years, additional services planned for rollout include the use of video links, fully wearable monitoring equipment as well as in-home sensors to track movement, body temperature and other vital signs. In addition, remote dispensing and monitoring of drugs is on the cards for many conditions.

Text-based support of multiple patients has proved highly effective from both therapeutic and economic perspectives in many countries – from the Philippines and Brazil to Germany and South Africa.

One interesting development in this area is the combination and integration of telecare, remote monitoring, virtual support and robotics: iRobot, a company known equally for the Roomba robotic vacuum cleaner and the bomb-disposal remote guided vehicles used in many battlefield environments, is also active in people-care. In 2009, iRobot established a healthcare business unit and launched its prototype robotic telepresence nurse:

"iRobot believes that next-generation practical robots have the potential to help caregivers perform critical work and extend the time that people can live independently. Robots may be capable of assisting in senior care in a variety of real-life situations, including household chores and the on-time administration of medication. This could ultimately lower the cost of care."

With advances such as these, many see that the assisted living arena will be one of significant innovation and investment. In the US, current healthcare costs are around 17% of GDP, or over $2 trillion dollars a year. As such, and with the increasingly ageing population, any solutions that act to both reduce and prevent the onset of significant healthcare support requirements are being embraced by government, HMOs and healthcare insurance companies alike.

A recent study by Plum Consulting quantified some of the key arguments and concluded that the ageing population in the UK will increase demand for social care by nearly 50% over the next twenty years while the supply of informal carers will hardly have changed. Given the higher dependency ratios, the statistics are even more challenging in countries like Japan, Korea and Italy. With continuing improvement in price/performance of electronic devices and the growing ubiquity of always-on fixed and wireless broadband communications, over the next decade we can expect to see strong demand for assisted-living services. These will include telehealth services, which use a combination of sensors, hubs and remote servers to provide better and more cost-efficient management of chronic conditions; telecare services, which provide continuous lifestyle monitoring of older and disabled people in the home; augmented reality services for those with cognitive disabilities, and services to locate dementia sufferers who wander and become lost; and digital participation services, which will connect, engage, stimulate and entertain people with disabilities and the elderly in their homes.

Many of the enabling technologies are already available but rapid take-up of such services is by no means guaranteed: the way in which organisations delivering health and social care respond to options for change will be crucial. Whether funded through insurance-based schemes or directly by government, there are several hurdles ahead. These include the need for large-scale, controlled trials (some of which

are now being scheduled); training and building up expertise; and, most critically, the rollout of integrated electronic patient care records that help to make everything function.

By 2020, industry experts see that, in many economies, 'we will have an advanced integrated system of automated people-care in place.' As a consequence, patients will be enabled to retain their independent lives for longer and so better enjoy life outside the mainstream care system. Many commentators therefore envisage a slow-down in the recent growth of nursing homes as a greater share of the elderly remain living at home. While for some this could mean greater physical isolation, the ambition for many in the healthcare sector is to use technology to prevent people feeling isolated. In a world where, on average, family support for the older generation will continue to decline and the cost of providing personal carers will continue to rise, patients with long-term chronic diseases and the elderly are increasingly likely to see some step changes in support over the next few years.

Related
insights

Page 65

Page 77

Page 117

Clinical enhancement

Enhanced functionality will shift from an external add-on to an integrated capability to provide the option for superhuman performance.

A potentially controversial topic raised when looking at the future relates to the advances being made in replacement organs and limbs. Different people have varied perspectives on where this is going and what the mass impacts will be. Some point to the high-tech developments that have taken place in prosthetics over the past few years, which have allowed people to regain near full limb movement. Some take this further in a military context and mix in the topic of exoskeletons as a possible option for enhanced battlefield performance. Then there are also developments like those at UCLA where digital cameras have been hardwired into the back of the retina of visually impaired patients to provide first black and white and now colour image recognition. In the world of cosmetic surgery, some experts are talking about sight and hearing enhancement being offered in key clinics within the next decade. If we can replace vital organs and limbs, why can't performance be tweaked to a higher standard with embedded technologies? Higher frequency ranges of hearing and infra-red vision are often mentioned in this context. While this may sound like science fiction to some, a number of recent developments are bringing enhanced performance closer to the market than you might think.

For some context in looking at how quickly the world of clinical enhancement is changing, it is worth considering the massive growth that has taken place in cosmetic surgery over recent years. In the US alone, the number of cosmetic treatments has more than doubled in the past decade to reach over 11 million a year. In terms of surgical operations, around half a million breast augmentations and liposuction operations and over 200,000 tummy tucks are undertaken each year. In non-surgical treatments, Botox accounts for nearly 3 million a year and well over 1 million laser hair removal and hyaluronic acid procedures are carried out. In total in 2008, Americans spent almost $12 billion on cosmetic procedures and, interestingly, men accounted for nearly one in ten of these. Globally, particularly as China's increasing appetite for enhancement grows, it is estimated that the cosmetic surgery industry could be worth over $200 billion a year by 2020. It's hardly surprising, therefore, that many countries have been setting themselves up as centres of excellence – from Switzerland to Brazil to South Africa – and the expectation is that frequent cosmetic changes to the body will become commonplace as more people search for physical perfection.

The desire for the 'ultimate look' is being replicated by a similar ambition for 'ultimate ability' as people seek to improve their physical and mental performance. In sport, the use of drugs to enhance performance is a long-standing problem that, despite all the bad publicity and shame that comes from being caught out, is still a big issue in almost all disciplines from cycling and weightlifting to running and football. Outside the professional sports arena and into

The cosmetic surgery industry could be worth over $200 billion a year by 2020.

the world of body-building, the use of steroids to enhance muscle structure has long been widespread. In parallel with this there is also momentum building around drugs that can provide improved mental performance. New lifestyle drugs and the wider use of cogniceuticals are giving us the ability to manage the 'highs and lows'. Not only can individuals control their emotions and senses with pharmaceutical products but they can also get by with less sleep.

At the start of the Future Agenda programme in 2009, an article in *Scientific American* on 'turbo-charging the brain' provided a good overview of some of the drugs that have been designed for one purpose and have proven to demonstrate cognitive enhancement as a side effect. Methylphenidate, amphetamines, modafinil and donepezil were all cited as medicines that have been approved for neurological disorders but also 'have the potential to improve mental functioning in unimpaired people'. The article also suggested that some drugs that are being developed to address and limit Alzheimer's and Parkinson's, and counteract dementia and ADHD (attention-deficit hyperactivity disorder), might be used by healthy people to enhance their cognitive performance. Although students, the military and older people who don't suffer from dementia are the primary markets, the potential for mass enhancement of capability when it is needed is just around the corner. How far this will go is a key question but several companies such as Helicon Therapeutics and Cephalon are already nudging the enhanced performance agenda forward.

Interestingly, significant advances are taking place in the military arena that may soon scale up to the commercial world. Starting with the improvements achieved in areas such as prosthetics as a consequence of injuries sustained in Iraq and Afghanistan, the US military in particular has been trying not only to repair the damage but also to go several steps further towards achieving 'superhuman' performance. DARPA (the US Defence Advanced Research Projects Agency) has been making significant investment in the area of exoskeletons and has already invested in the development of an exoskeleton suit for ground troops. This wearable robotic system could give soldiers the ability to run faster, carry heavier weapons and leap over large obstacles. Within the next few years, exoskeletal systems are expected to give soldiers augmented strength and speed as well as increased endurance; and they will also have built-in computers to help troops navigate through foreign terrains.

On top of this, enhanced sight and hearing is also advancing quickly. Building on some of the pioneering work undertaken in the past decade at institutions such as UCLA (which has been hard-wiring digital cameras to retinas to restore sight in blind people), the same technologies are now being applied physically and virtually on the battlefield. Under such programmes as 'Future Soldier 2030', the US Army is investing heavily in making the idea of the soldier as a system a reality. Alongside such advances as

Significant advances are taking place in the military arena that may soon scale up to the commercial world.

neural prosthetics and embedding magnets in finger tips to enhance sensing, one fast-developing area is that of providing augmented reality vision and data. Integrating many of the established data projection techniques used in fighter planes, information related to where the eye is looking is increasingly being provided to pilots and soldiers. Whether this will be navigational, environmental, 'friend or foe' identification or just layered contextual information on buildings and landmarks, through glasses and active contact lenses or more embedded linkages, what you see could be enhanced both in terms of data and also in terms of the visible spectrum as infra-red sight becomes an added function.

It is clear that an increasing number of people see that the next decade will be one where more and more of us seek to take the option of improving our normal human performance. The symbol H+ is used by some futurists to denote an enhanced version of humanity and for an increasing proportion of the population this is fast becoming a reality. By 2020, permanent rather than just a temporary change of

By 2020, permanent rather than just temporary change of capability from drugs, doping, implants or surgery will be available.

capability from drugs, doping, implants or surgery will be available. Experts predict that, led by the advances taking place in the military, wearable robotics will become increasingly embedded in humans and providing this to the mainstream will become part of everyday cosmetic surgery.

The ethical debate surrounding mass enhancement capability is still wide open and, as yet, it is unclear how the regulatory bodies might respond. However, those with the will and the resources will certainly have access to clinical enhancement, created for restorative surgery and then applied to the commercial mainstream. The world of the 'Bionic man' is (finally) not so far away.

Related insights

Page 69

Page 201

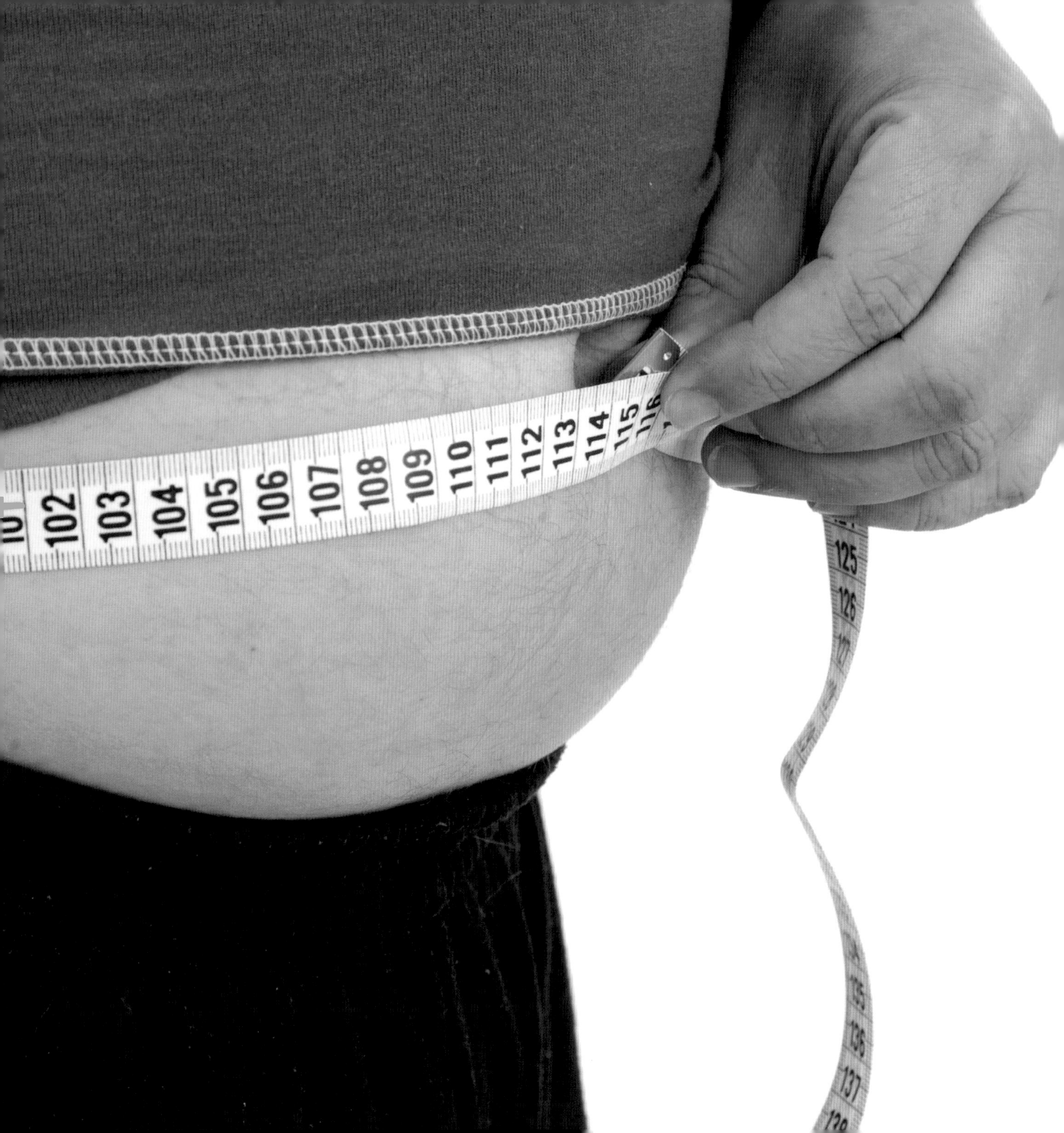
102
103
104
105
106
107
108
109
110
111
112
113
114
115
125
126
135
136
137

Diabesity

With diabetes consuming 5% of GDP, a combination of fat taxation, patient data mining and personal budgets play a role in stabilising the obesity epidemic.

Diabetes is the world's most costly epidemic. Over the next ten years there will be an increasing number of technical solutions to help manage the condition but few expect this to counter its growth, particularly the escalation of type 2 diabetes, which is mostly caused by a high-calorie diet and sedentary lifestyle. If governments and public healthcare systems are to manage the direct and indirect costs, significant action to change behaviour is critical.

The World Diabetes Foundation estimates that 285 million people – corresponding to 6.4% of the world's adult population – already suffer from diabetes. That number is expected to grow to 438 million by 2030, corresponding to 7.8% of the adult population. In Europe alone, approximately 33 million adults are suffering from the disease. It is no longer a rich-nation problem, as over 70% of people with diabetes now live in low- and middle-income countries: in Saharan Africa, it is projected that the number of sufferers will double, reaching 24 million by 2030. Type 2 diabetes, which affects over 90% of the diabetic population, is the big growth challenge. It already afflicts 92.4 million adults in China and over 10% of the population of countries such as the US, Malaysia and Indonesia are expected to be diabetic by 2020.

The current cost of managing the disease in Europe is around €15 billion per year, with associated medical complications accounting for up to 8% of the total health budget. In the next ten years, roughly 5% of global GDP and over 25% of many public healthcare budgets across the world will be spent on dealing with its consequences. Furthermore the problem is affecting the working population. The average age of impact for type 2 diabetes has already fallen from 54 to 46 but, going forward, this is expected to drop further. By 2020, the behaviour change needed to reduce the impact of diabetes in society will be among people who are today between 30 and 35.

As well as the direct costs of treating diabetes, there are other hidden costs. For the patient, significantly higher insurance premiums are common in developed societies, and in countries such as India, 15% to 25% of an average household income can be required to cover treatment. Add on the impacts of increased susceptibility to other conditions as well as more days off work, early retirement and below average productivity and the hidden costs of diabetes escalate further. Globally, by 2025, it is expected that the direct costs of diabetes to society will be €300bn, nearly double today's figure. Add on the indirect costs and estimates for the 2020 burden are in the order of €500bn.

In the next ten years, new non-invasive technologies, improved low-cost business models and more hard-hitting public health campaigns will have all been

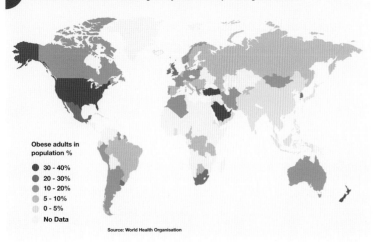

The Global Obesity Problem

An obese adult is classified as having a Body Mass Index equal to or greater than 30

Obese adults in
population %

● 30 - 40%
● 20 - 30%
● 10 - 20%
● 5 - 10%
● 0 - 5%
No Data

Source: World Health Organisation

influence citizen choice and better manage the risks associated with diabetes.

From discussions in our workshops in the UK, the US and Spain, there are several areas where action is seen as highly probable and potentially effective. In particular, there was strong support for the introduction of fat taxes, the improved use of patient data and an increase in individuals taking responsibility for their own healthcare costs.

Given that higher taxes on cigarettes proved to be one of the best ways to reduce smoking rates, a parallel approach is now on the agenda for obesity. For example, the Mayor of New York City, Michael Bloomberg, is planning to tackle the American fondness for fizzy drinks with a so-called 'soda tax'. With potential regulation at an EU level coming by the middle of the decade, many are now predicting the widespread use of financial levies on either key products (fizzy drinks, sugary snacks and so on) or their manufacturers as an option that many governments will pursue. Some countries, such as New Zealand, are also experimenting with incentives to encourage people to eat more fresh fruit and vegetables but most policymakers we spoke to say the option of making unhealthy, high-calorie foods more expensive will have a greater impact and is easier to implement and manage.

From another view, there is also potential to make better use of patient data. Tech-savvy diabetic sufferers already benefit from a growing number of mobile phone applications that can help to record and track individual measures, diet and performance and there are increasing numbers of systems that allow the sharing of data between patients and their doctors. Building on this, several organisations support the

deployed around the world in various ways to try to mitigate the impact, manage the consequences and control the rise of type 2 diabetes. Potential technological breakthroughs, such as drugs that aid weight loss and inoculations for type 1 diabetics, have already yielded positive results in animals but it will be four to five years before clinical trials are complete and humans can start to benefit. Medical developments are now focused around non-invasive devices which provide alternatives to needles and syringes. This means that the introduction of implants, to change the dynamics of testing, and patch-based systems for blood glucose monitoring are all on the horizon. However, the problem is that the scale, cost and timing of the introduction of many of these solutions will have little overall impact in the short to medium term. Any effective changes will be concentrated around government and regional policies to control food consumption,

Globally, by 2025, it is expected that the direct costs of diabetes to society will be €300bn, nearly double today's figure.

notion that peer-to-peer and expert patient groups may have as much influence on individual behaviour as the more traditional patient–healthcare professional relationship. So, expect to see patient data becoming more visible and more shareable across platforms and systems in the years to come.

Improvements in data collection will not only allow improved relative comparisons between one individual and another, but will also facilitate more predictive data analysis. One outcome of this will be more transparency around future patient scenarios and risk so that diabetic sufferers can see how their condition is likely to evolve relative to other sufferers' experience and they will also be able to predict the likely risk of side effects such as limb loss, blindness or additional incapacity.

In general, public understanding of diabetes is low compared to other diseases and there is a pressing need to address this. The media are already broadly engaged (given its link to obesity, some have christened the issue the 'diabesity debate') but many see the need for increased public awareness as the third component for behaviour change alongside taxation and data use, particularly as individuals may well find themselves obliged to take greater personal responsibility for their healthcare costs.

Across many countries the notion of providing financial rewards for reducing the burden on public health is gaining momentum. For example, some regulators are considering recovering above average healthcare costs from patients either through an increase in income tax for the employed, or by reducing benefits for those out of work. While these may seem politically contentious, they do signal the level of action that economically pressured governments are proposing in order to contain the mounting healthcare budgets.

The diabesity challenge is real and tangible. If an epidemic is to be avoided, many say that drastic action is required, fast. Informed healthcare experts see that 'many economies have a diabetes time bomb to deal with, one that requires concerted approaches across many fronts.' Over the next decade, it looks like taxation on high-calorie foods to influence individual choice, improved sharing of personal data to support this choice, and the increased personal responsibility for healthcare costs to reward this choice are pivotal in gaining control.

Related insights

Page 73

Page 239

...tuation and are about the pote...

Swine Flu Sp...

Health officials reached thei...

Global pandemics

We are likely to see two to three major pandemics start in regions with limited public healthcare and rapidly spread globally and so demand fast response.

Since the Spanish Flu pandemic of 1918, which killed over 50 million people and infected 500 million others, national governments have had an eye on the risks from widespread pandemics. With the advent of SARS a decade ago, the avian flu pandemic in Asia in 2007 and the swine flu (H1N1) pandemic that started in Mexico in 2009, the incidence and impacts of such events are causing more and more concern at international levels. The reasons for this are threefold: 1) the speed at which pandemics can spread around the world has significantly accelerated due to increasing mass air travel; 2) the consequential time available to track the source and initial progress is decreasing; and 3) the capability to get the right drugs into the right place at the right time is not necessarily up to the challenge.

To understand the implications of future pandemics, we need to be clear on what the difference is between a pandemic, an epidemic and an outbreak. The Center for Disease Control and Prevention (CDC) in the US defines an outbreak as simply the start of an infection in a localized geographic area. An epidemic occurs when a large geographic area is involved and which has a higher than expected mortality rate. A pandemic is a global outbreak that exceeds the 'normal' levels of mortality and infection levels for typical diseases. The key word here is 'global'. There are two major factors that effect whether or not an outbreak will lead to a pandemic: pathogenesis and virulence. Pathogenesis refers to how a virus will cause disease and how

easily it is spread. The virulence refers to how sick a certain virus will make the host and how easily it can cause death.

The World Health Organisation maps out a pandemic based on six distinct phases. Phase 1 is when non-human infections are spreading and there is no animal-to-human transmission. In Phase 2, an animal influenza virus, which is known to have caused infections in humans, circulates among non-human animals. Phase 3 sees animal-to-human transmission but no person-to-person transmission under normal conditions — when this is seen, the risk of pandemic rises. Phase 4 occurs when there is known human-to-human transmission of the virus. This allows outbreaks then epidemics to occur and even further increases risk of a pandemic. In phase 5, human-to-human spread is documented in at least two countries in one WHO region and may well indicate that a pandemic is imminent. Phase 6, the pandemic phase, is characterized by outbreaks in at least one other country in a different WHO region in addition to the two or more countries defined in phase 5. Designation of this phase indicates that a global pandemic is under way.

A core problem with pandemics is that 'they often arise in regions with low levels of public health and they rapidly spread across the world to more advanced countries'. It is highly unusual for one to start in, say, the US or Europe. In tracing the cause

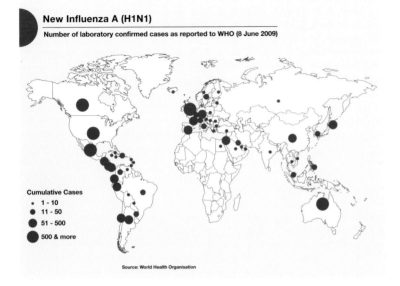

New Influenza A (H1N1)

Number of laboratory confirmed cases as reported to WHO (8 June 2009)

Cumulative Cases
- 1 - 10
- 11 - 50
- 51 - 500
- 500 & more

Source: World Health Organisation

one of the fastest-growing sectors of the global pharmaceuticals industry, many see that current vaccines will not help in the future. A critical issue here is that the rate at which a virus variant can develop is faster than the speed at which new vaccines can be developed: unlike many other diseases where a known condition already has an established therapy in place, pandemics are often caused by new strains of virus and so need a new antiviral vaccine. Typically, creating the new vaccine takes around six months and so there is a significant gap between pandemic outbreak and treatment availability. Much hope is being pinned on DNA-based vaccines, where DNA rather than dead virus particles grown in eggs is used as the base for developing new vaccines. These offer the potential for quicker responses and so enable faster global distribution.

of a pandemic, it is therefore vital to focus on 'patient zero' – the first personal to become ill. So, for example, the 2009 swine flu pandemic started in Mexico and H1N1 patient zero was found in the village of La Gloria, Veracruz, next to a large industrial pig farm. Notably, this highlighted the rising risk from people and animals in many parts of the world increasingly sharing the same limited water sources. Although the 2009 pandemic was in some ways a false alarm, as mortality rates were not excessive, it is seen in many circles as a good model for how global health authorities will need to cooperate in the future when more lethal strains of virus spread.

The swine flu pandemic also highlighted the problems in availability of suitable vaccines – both in terms of the right drugs and their global distribution. Although the re-emergence of influenza as a pandemic threat has stimulated the influenza vaccines market to be

In the next decade, many healthcare organisations agree with Jack Lord's initial view that 'we will see two or three major pandemics that will have a significant global impact'. Given that Spanish flu killed around 3% of the world's population at the time and infected around a third, the consequences of a similar event today are massive. If, for example, a new strain of avian flu were to spread quickly from its source globally, then some estimate that as many as 3 billion people could be infected within twelve months. If the right vaccines are not developed and distributed quickly, one in five of these could die within the year. As was highlighted in one workshop: 'In many ways, a global pandemic has to be seen as a greater threat to us than nuclear terrorism and global warming combined.'

There is, therefore, a significant global focus on ensuring global cooperation between health authorities and on improved monitoring of populations. The WHO has already taken a lead in the former area and, as shown with swine flu, many of the processes are

In many ways, a global pandemic has to be seen as a greater threat to us than nuclear terrorism and global warming combined.

now in place and are being built upon. Potential global hot spots are continuously being identified to highlight emerging virus outbreaks and prevent future pandemics from reaching their full potential. Emerging infectious disease identification is seen as a major area for healthcare investment and is a top priority for public health systems globally.

In terms of monitoring, several organisations believe that this is where we will now see a significant increase in investment. Already several countries have advanced approaches in place. Most notably, Singapore has developed a highly integrated system that ranges from detailed public information through to advanced surveillance. Singapore's 'Quarantine System' was developed during the SARS outbreak and people who had come into contact with infected persons were placed on home quarantine for five or more days. Thermometers were issued to all citizens and daily reporting to a centralised system ensured that early rises in body temperatures were noted as an indication of likely infection so that quarantining could take place.

Emerging economies find the monitoring and tracking of disease particularly challenging. They are hindered by several core obstacles, among them a global shortage of healthcare workers. According to the WHO, among 57 countries, mostly in the developing world, there is a critical shortfall in healthcare workers, representing a total deficit of

2.4 million healthcare workers worldwide. In South Africa, where we held a workshop there are four nurses per 1,000 people, a figure which, although high for an African country, pales in comparison with a developed country such as Norway where there are sixteen nurses per 1,000. This human resources constraint intensifies the already increasing pressure on developing-world health systems as not only must they cope with the need to contain the spread of communicable diseases associated with extreme poverty, they must also contend with the growing incidence of chronic diseases, such as diabetes and heart disease, an effect of new-found (relative) affluence. As a result, in some instances the wherewithal to monitor disease is extremely limited.

Moving forward, many countries expect to roll out more sophisticated systems for full population monitoring. Global bio-surveillance initiatives are in place to, for example, enable enhanced monitoring at border crossings and key transport hubs, such as airports, as these are the primary areas where cross-infection can occur and spread the virus. At a wider level, mass monitoring of vital signs is also under way in some countries where, for example, daily infra-red satellite images are being cross-referenced with location of mobile phones so that the individual body temperature of each member of a population can be monitored and, at the first sign of significant increase, just as in Singapore with SARS, they can be contacted and quarantined.

Global pandemics will happen in the next decade; the problem is that we don't know from exactly where they will emerge and what form they will take. As such, the key challenges are in the fast and effective response to the initial outbreak and ensuring that epidemics do not become pandemics.

Related insights

Page 189

Halting Alzheimer's

Stopping mental degradation from Alzheimer's makes quality ageing more possible by improving cognition and slowing the rate of decline.

In our discussions, one of the big bets for the future in the health arena that many are focused on is being able to halt the rise of Alzheimer's disease. This disease is a physical condition affecting the brain and is the most common cause of dementia. Today, worldwide, 35 million people have Alzheimer's and, as the ageing demographic shift has greater impact, this is projected to rise to 115 million by 2050.

There is currently no cure for Alzheimer's disease. However, drug treatments are available that can alleviate the symptoms and even slow down the disease's progression in some patients. Although the exact causes of the disease are still being investigated, people with Alzheimer's are known to have a shortage of the chemical acetylcholine in their brains. Drugs available to people in the moderate stages of dementia, such as Aricept, Exelon and Reminyl, work by maintaining existing supplies of acetylcholine, the chemical compound which activates muscles. Another drug, the only one that is suitable for use in people in the middle to later stages of dementia, is called Ebixa and works in a different way — it prevents the excess entry of calcium ions into brain cells. Excess calcium in the brain cells damages them and prevents them from receiving messages from other brain cells. These drugs are not a cure for Alzheimer's, as they have no effect on the underlying degenerative process of the disease, but they can stabilise some of the symptoms for a limited period of time.

Finding a way forward for Alzheimer's is a burning issue, especially in the US where there are currently 5.5 million patients and the direct and indirect costs of the disease amount to over $100 billion annually. In addition, the disease is well recognised as placing heavy economic and social burdens on caregivers. By 2050, with more people living longer and so a greater percentage of the population susceptible to the disease, the US is forecast to have 14 million people with Alzheimer's and the burden on the healthcare system could be as high as $500 billion.

While finding a cure for Alzheimer's may take longer than our 2020 horizon, a capability of stopping degradation is highly probable. In fact, over the past few years, there have been some major developments which give hope. Key to many of these is the use of adult stem cells as a base for developing

By 2050, with more people living longer and so a greater percentage of the population susceptible to the disease, the US is forecast to have 14 million people with Alzheimer's and the burden on the healthcare system could be as high as $500 billion.

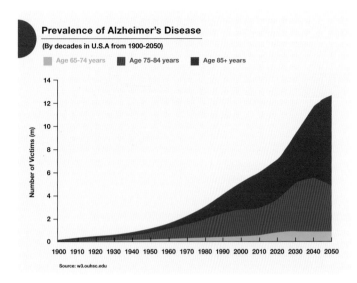

Prevalence of Alzheimer's Disease

(By decades in U.S.A from 1900-2050)

Age 65-74 years   Age 75-84 years   Age 85+ years

Number of Victims (m)

Source: w3.ouhsc.edu

new healthy brain cells. As was highlighted during the Future Agenda programme, 'several treatments in development are designed either to improve cognition or to slow the rate of decline' and some of the most promising avenues of research being undertaken at universities including Berkeley focus on reducing 'amyloid beta' levels.

An increasingly accepted hypothesis about Alzheimer's is that it involves the accumulation of a particular protein known as amyloid beta, which is a peptide of around forty amino acids. In Alzheimer's patients, two enzymes, beta secretase and gamma secretase, effectively cut amyloid beta segments out

Several treatments in development are designed either to improve cognition or to slow the rate of decline.

of larger, normal parent molecules. These segments damage neurons and synapses and, as they build up, either in soluble form or clumped into plaques, cause the early onset of Alzheimer's. Some of the processes under development are focused specifically on preventing amyloid beta from being formed in the first place and also try to stop the molecules from attaching to one another if they do form. Once the symptoms of Alzheimer's, such as memory loss, are evident, a great deal of neurological damage has already been done. Therefore, by monitoring and measuring amyloid beta levels in healthy people before any degradation, the onset of the disease can be detected in advance and remedies applied. Others suggest that 'a broader strategy is needed, one that incorporates the role of newly identified genes and even the chemical processes responsible for killing nerve cells.'

By 2020, these and other new developments in genetics and biotechnology are expected to 'slow the progression of the disease and further alleviate its behavioural and psychological effects'. As a consequence, those diagnosed and treated in the early stages of Alzheimer's will probably enjoy far greater self-sufficiency than is possible today.

In a similar vein, it is increasingly probable that by 2020 we will also be able to halt the decline of patients with Parkinson's disease, the degenerative disorder of the central nervous system that impairs the sufferer's motor skills, speech and other functions. Nearly 1 million people in the US are living with Parkinson's disease in 2010, again with no known cure but medication or surgery providing relief from the symptoms. By 2030, health forecasts predict up to 9 million patients globally, with around half of these in China. Following recent campaigns, including especially the one led by the actor Michael J. Fox, there has been increased investment and focus on this disease. The big hope here is that stem cell-based techniques will play a big part. One approach being pursued in Sweden involves the removal and cloning of adult neural cells and coaxing them to become dopamine-producing neurons for subsequent re-implantation into patients. Another study under way at Oxford University is using induced pluripotent stem cells taken from a patient's skin to grow new brain neurons. These and similar studies could well be the next step in cell replacement therapy for Parkinson's disease.

In the areas of both Alzheimer's and Parkinson's, the new developments on the horizon open the door for even longer and more productive lives. In bringing mental degradation under the same control as physical, this could provide an end to the increasingly common situation of the mind degrading faster than the body – and certainly delay the onset of decline.

It is increasingly probable that by 2020 we will also be able to halt the decline of patients with Parkinson's disease.

Related insights

Page 49

Page 77

Page 117

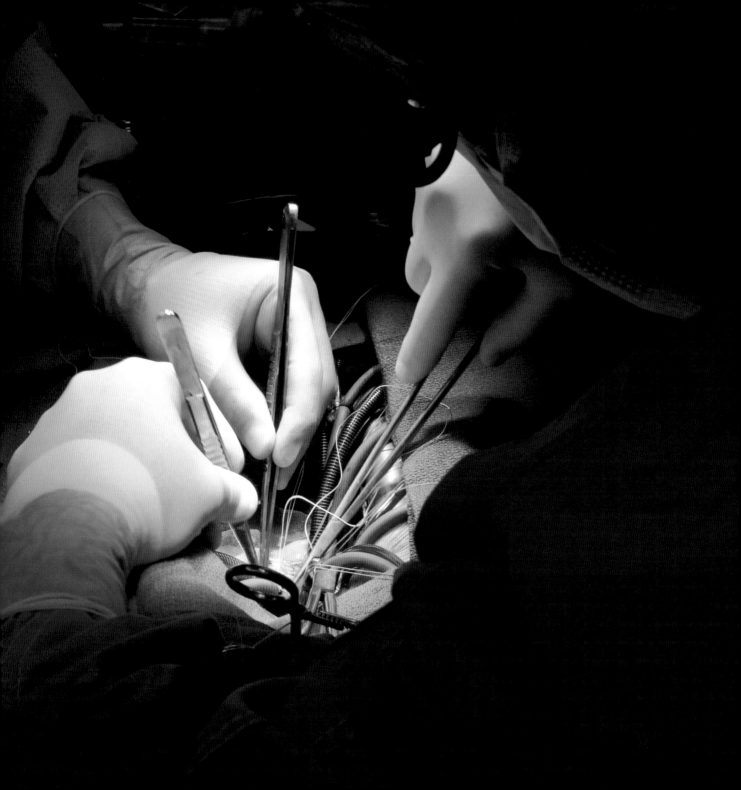

Mass medical tourism

Medical tourism goes mainstream as low-cost cardiac surgery and broader healthcare provision join dentistry and cosmetic surgery to have global impact.

Switzerland has long been a centre for medical holidays – a place where the rich have gone for relaxation and treatment. Over the past few decades, it also became a centre for more surgical vacations, often focused on providing cosmetic enhancement for its customers. In a similar vein, both South Africa and Brazil are also well known as places to go to get good-quality cosmetic surgery. London, LA and Miami are also renowned as centres of cosmetic excellence. Today, new locations such as Dubai, Venezuela, Thailand, Jamaica and the Philippines all variously compete in respective niches as the places for the two-week holiday with an inclusive tummy tuck or breast enhancement. They have all been recruiting leading plastic surgeons and building hotels-cum-hospitals to provide cosmetic services at competitive prices.

While cosmetic surgery has largely paved the way, other areas of medicine have followed suit over the past few years, as high-quality services have been made available in key locations at low cost and so have become attractive destinations for people from different countries. Dentistry has been a primary area here: Hungary fast became a centre for dental tourism in Europe, as has Bangkok in Asia. Costa Rica, El Salvador and Panama have all played a similar role in Central America. In these areas, high-quality dental work at relatively low cost in attractive destinations is provided for those with the money and the desire to travel. In 2007, over 100,000 UK residents went aboard for medical treatment, of which 43% sought dental procedures and 30% went for cosmetic surgery. The average spend for such trips was just under $4,000 per head.

Today there is a shift happening, not just in quality and cost but also in the complexity of operations being made available and, going forward, the niche activity of medical tourism will go increasingly mainstream as low-cost cardiac surgery and broader healthcare provision are added into the mix. New business models and new areas of focus are creating new destinations.

In many cases, it is India that is leading the way. Most significantly at first were the advances made by Aravind Eye Hospitals with cataract operations. Adopting process techniques from the fast food industry, Dr G. Venkataswamy, founder of Aravind Eye Care System, has pioneered change in the speed, scale and cost of operations. Primarily aimed at making life-changing eye surgery available to a wide range of the Indian population, the five Aravind Eye Hospitals in India conduct over 300,000 operations a year, costing on average $50 rather than the usual $500. Today, as the success of the business model scales up, India is also becoming a centre for medical tourism as patients

In many cases, it is India that is leading the way.

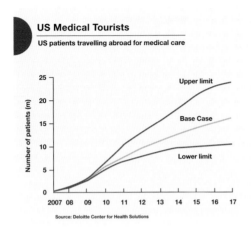

US Medical Tourists

US patients travelling abroad for medical care

Number of patients (m)

25 — Upper limit

20

15 — Base Case

10

5 — Lower limit

0

2007 08 09 10 11 12 13 14 15 16 17

Source: Deloitte Center for Health Solutions

Public health systems in Europe and healthcare insurance companies in the US are all ramping up plans to formally take advantage of the economics associated with this movement.

from the US and Europe fly in for an operation that is done as well as anywhere at a fraction of the price.

Also in India, the Narayana Hrudayalaya Hospital in Bangalore is already performing over 600 heart operations a week – eight times the average at other Indian hospitals, and the highest in the world. What is significant about these examples is not just the volume, nor that the quality of the surgery and success rates are as good as anywhere in the world, but, due to the nature of the business model and process innovation, the costs are significantly lower: Narayana charges just $2,000 for open-heart surgery compared with between $20,000 and $100,000 in the US. With high

quality at this price difference, it is not surprising that there are already around 1 million medical tourists going from the US to India each year and by 2012 this is expected to rise to over 1.6 million. By 2013, the India medical tourism market is expected to be worth more than $2 billion.

The Narayana Hrudayalaya Hospital is the centre of the rapidly developing Narayana Health City in Bangalore. This campus will consist of eight other hospitals and research institutes, ranging from a 1,000-bed cancer hospital to a 500-bed eye hospital to institutes for neuroscience and thrombosis. Over the next decade, the organisation plans to recreate a similar health city and medical university in partnership with the government of the Cayman Islands that will 'revolutionize tertiary healthcare' in the islands, providing medical procedures at half the cost of US facilities. An initial 200-bed facility will open in 2012 and this will eventually develop into a 2,000-bed centre.

Narayana charges just $2,000 for open-heart surgery compared with between $20,000 and $100,000 in the US.

Similar initiatives are under way in other countries as well: Dubai is aiming at being 'GMT+4' centre of cardiac surgery and, as well as attracting the best surgeons, is also building more dedicated hospital hotels, which include post-operative support. Turkey is planning for more revenue from medical tourism than the 'sun and sand' type; the Mexican federal government's Tourism Secretariat has a new initiative to grow medical tourism in the country, with the expectation of 650,000 visitors, who will spend $50 million a year by 2020; and in South Korea, where high-quality medical treatment is around 30% of the price in the US and around 60% of that in Japan, big plans for expansion are also taking shape, targeting 1 million patients by 2020. In addition, public health systems in Europe and healthcare insurance companies in the US are all ramping up plans to formally take advantage of the economics associated with this movement. Overall, the medical tourism market is expected to be worth $100 billion by 2012 and close to $500 billion by 2020. At this scale, what was once a niche option only for the very rich will be a mainstream activity, and one that will increasingly become a credible option for the majority in many developed economies.

Related insights

Page 53

Page 117

Page 151

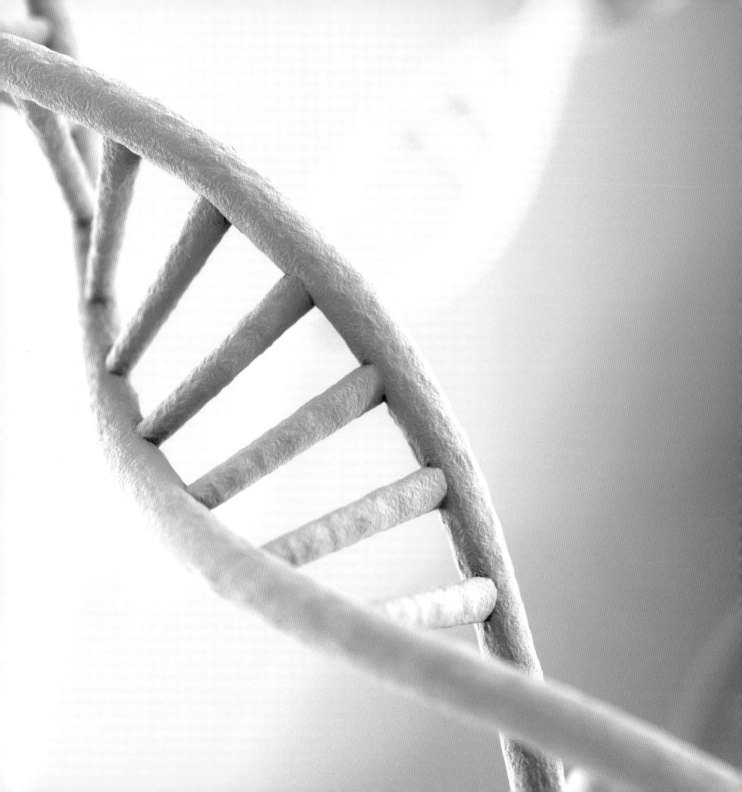

Pharma foods

More customised foods blur the line between pharmaceuticals and food as nutrigenomics allow individualised diets to fit genetic profiles.

As awareness of advances in biotechnology is increasing, a growing area of interest is in the use of foods for medical purposes. There is a long-standing tradition in many cultures of using natural herbs and foods to treat ailments. In recent years, so-called 'superfoods' have started to receive increasing attention, particularly in the media. Interest is now rapidly expanding to foods with clinically enhanced properties. Probiotics, prebiotics, functional foods, clinical foods and nutraceuticals are all talked about and promoted as being good for you either in general or by specifically targeting a bodily function, such as improving digestion, bone density and so on. As technology evolves and more is understood about how to tailor food and drug combinations to better fit individual needs, the opportunities for tailored foods that use improved genetic profiling are burgeoning. By 2020, many in the pharmaceuticals and food industries predict biotechnical advances to combine foods grown in the field and drugs developed in the lab. In the next decade, we can expect to see a shift in some of our basics from traditional 'farmer foods' to more sophisticated 'pharma foods'.

The term nutraceuticals, which comes from a combination of nutrition and pharmaceuticals, is used to describe 'food, or a part of a food, that provides medical or health benefits, including the prevention and/or treatment of a disease'. So, one person's functional food can be another person's nutraceutical. Given that they are cheaper than pharmaceutical products and can sometimes provide some of the benefits, nutraceuticals are a growth sector attracting pharmaceutical and biotech companies, including the likes of Monsanto, DuPont, Abbott, Johnson & Johnson, Novartis and Genzyme Transgenic. Clinical foods, or medical foods, are by contrast specifically formulated to meet certain nutritional requirements of people with specific illnesses. They are regulated and therefore prescribed by physicians. Nutraceuticals are, therefore, not clinical foods.

While these products have been appearing on the market in recent years, the next step now on the horizon is in foods created for medical benefit. The big change is the link between food preparation and nutrigenomics, which is applying the sciences of genomics, transcriptomics, proteomics and metabolomics to human nutrition. Nutrigenomics is a relatively new science and is the application of high-throughput genomic tools in nutrition research: now that human genes have been sequenced and we can understand more about our make-up, nutrigenomics is essentially the science that allows us to tailor food to fit our genetic profiles.

The big change is the link between food preparation and nutrigenomics.

A salmon can be raised in half the normal time, have less fat, more meat and include extra nutrients.

Pharma foods, 'biopharmaceuticals' or 'farmaceuticals', are one outcome of this and are compounds produced from genetically modified crops or animals. They provide higher than usual amounts of various nutrients that can be consumed as foods. What distinguishes them from functional foods, nutraceuticals and their like, are that they are not naturally occurring. They are engineered to provide specific health benefits: for instance, gene 'pharming' allows scientists to alter an animal's DNA by combining it with DNA from another species. The resulting genetically modified animals – transgenic fish, cattle, sheep, goats and chickens – are tailored to provide embedded drugs and proteins for human consumption. Proponents, such as the Biotechnology Industry Organization, see that transgenic animals can not only be provided with traits that will improve disease resistance, but also that they can accelerate growth and increase proteins, provider leaner meats, increased muscle mass and improved nutritional quality. So, for example, a salmon can be raised in half the normal time, have less fat, more meat and include extra nutrients. Although no products are currently on the market, the US National Academy of Science undertook a study that did not identify any food safety concerns. Alongside the ethical issues of blurring the difference between different species, issues around environmental impact and animal welfare are, however, raised by those against this sort of development.

Plant-made pharmaceuticals are produced by using similar technology in plants: transgenic plants are engineered to have resistance to pests and harsh conditions as well as improved shelf life and nutritional value. Modified potatoes have been enhanced with protein and, in 2008, scientists altered a carrot so that it would produce calcium and become a possible cure for osteoporosis. There has also been discussion of the benefit that can be gained for vitamin A deficiency from the consumption of golden rice, which was developed by the International Rice Research Institute to alleviate micronutrient deficiencies in developing countries.

As a group, such pharma foods have been a controversial issue. For example, back in 2007 several food companies lobbied the US Department of Agriculture against the introduction of pharma foods due to 'concerns about their negative impacts on food safety, on markets for food crops and on the integrity of the wider food supply'. PepsiCo saw that 'the significant risk of crop contamination that is present when plant-made pharmaceuticals are produced in food and/or feed crops leads us to the conclusion that the only way to prevent such a contamination is to prohibit their production'. In its 2008 Corporate Social Responsibility report, addressing concern about the testing of plant-made pharmaceuticals, General Mills stated that 'to fully ensure the safety of world production via plants and grains, General Mills currently opposes moving to production of any so-called 'pharma-food' that would use a food crop or food grain to grow or produce plant-made pharmaceuticals'.

However, despite this reticence, and given the increasingly populous and hungry world, many companies are now progressing with the development of pharma foods. In his initial perspective on the future of food, Jim Kirkwood highlighted the opportunities and challenges:

"Pharma-foods, the intersection between food and pharmaceuticals, is an area of growing opportunity for many in the food sector. As consumers demand more technologically sophisticated foods with unique, complex health benefits, food companies will need to respond. We now understand more about individuals' disease propensities from the human genome. Therefore nutrigenomic determination of diet becomes technically possible. Technology is advancing and as natural bioactive components are better understood, the line between pharma and food will blur. The challenge will be how to continue to find new ways to continue to provide

natural, food-delivered preventative health benefits and begin to provide natural, food-delivered disease state improvement benefits without food becoming a drug."

In a New York workshop this view gained clear support. As well as the wider recognition of the global need for more proteins and nutrients, participants saw that 'genetic profiling is advancing very quickly and is now accepted as a good thing', 'business models in the pharmaceuticals sector are encouraging significant investment in the area' and that 'nutrigenomics will fundamentally change consumer healthcare as nutritional screening becomes a standard part of health check-ups and consumers readily provide their genetic profile'. Although a controversial subject, given the benefits to be gained, the fast pace of technology development and a shift in government regulation on the horizon, the advent of widespread availability of pharma foods by 2020 looks increasingly likely. Customised foods that match medical benefit to your genetic profile will be in your shopping basket soon.

Genetic profiling is advancing very quickly and is now accepted as a good thing.

Related insights

Page 57

Page 185

Page 189

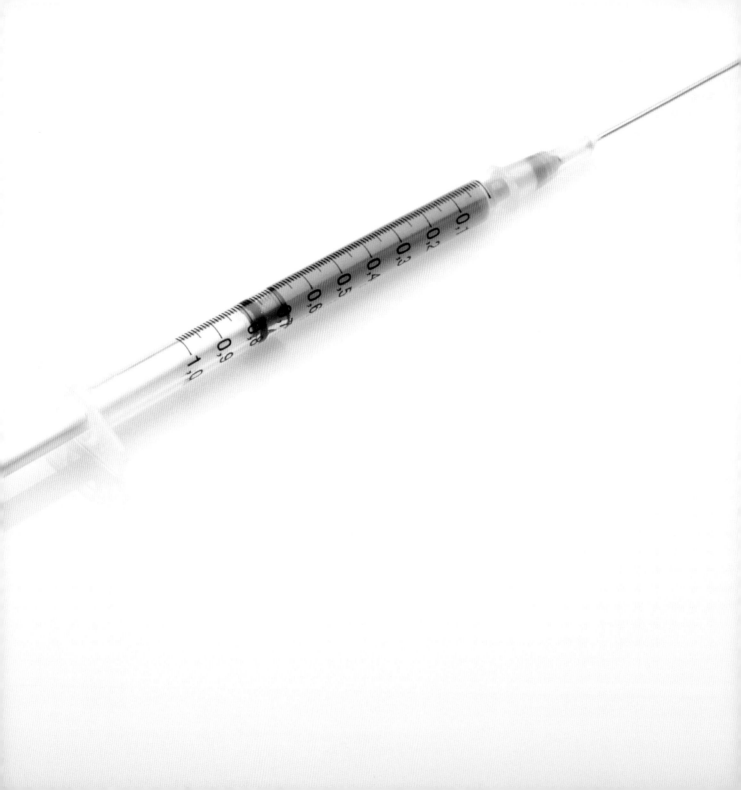

Systemic euthanasia

The escalating economic and social cost of supporting the aged beyond natural lifecycles leads to wider acceptance of assisted suicide.

Given the certainty of imbalanced population growth and the increasingly ageing population, some claim that there are people born today who, if they wish, could live for over 200 years. With the current record at 120 and a host of people already living past 115, there is little doubt that, with technology advancing as quickly as it is, physically adding another 80 years or so is looking possible. Whether or not mental capacity can be sustained for that long may be a greater challenge, but the world will certainly get used to more and more centenarians. In the UK alone there are over 9,000 of them today.

While this may be all well and good at an individual level, many see that, from a societal perspective, the ageing population is presenting us with a major financial burden, especially given that current pensions were not really designed for people living much beyond 75. With increasing dependency ratios in many nations and escalating healthcare costs across the board, some people have been asking the rather difficult questions around whether we can continue to cope with this level of mass long-term ageing.

An increasing number of healthcare professionals see that life-sustaining treatment is frequently not cost-effective. In the US, acute hospital care accounts for over half (55%) of the spending for Medicare beneficiaries in the last two years of life. In many other countries, the high costs of surgery, intensive

A recent study in Brazil confirmed that over 70% of total healthcare costs occur in the twelve months before death.

care and life-extending drugs used towards the end of a patient's life adds up to nearly 80% of total healthcare costs. A recent study in Brazil confirmed that over 70% of total healthcare costs occur in the twelve months before death. And a story on Bloomberg a couple of years ago highlighted the case of one US resident whose healthcare costs totalled $618,616, almost two-thirds of it for the final twenty-four months and, according to his wife, 'much of it for treatments that no one can say for sure helped extend his life'.

Given such predictable trends, a question increasingly being raised in governments and medical policy groups is whether we should continue to put in all these resources and effort, in many cases only to delay the inevitable by a few months. In a US future of health workshop, the question was asked: 'When will the US adopt the Do Not Resuscitate policy used by the National Health Service in the UK?' A DNR order on a patient's file means that a doctor is not required to resuscitate a patient if his or her heart stops and is designed to prevent unnecessary suffering. This is used when a patient is in hospital and

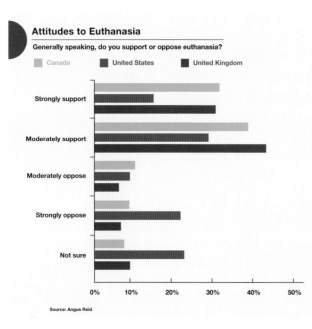

Attitudes to Euthanasia

Generally speaking, do you support or oppose euthanasia?

Canada   United States   United Kingdom

- Strongly support
- Moderately support
- Moderately oppose
- Strongly oppose
- Not sure

0%   10%   20%   30%   40%   50%

Source: Angus Reid

When will the US adopt the Do Not Resuscitate policy used by the National Health Service in the UK?

the benefits of treatment are seen to be outweighed by the burdens of future quality of life. Some regard this as a form of passive euthanasia. At the workshop it was argued that 'if the US were to adopt the same policy, the savings to the healthcare budget would be enormous and unnecessary suffering of patients who had little hope of long-term recovery would be avoided'. However, this is just one step and others are proposing even more significant changes.

Over the past few years, euthanasia and physician-assisted suicide for the terminally ill have become prominent medical and social issues. There are legal and ethical constraints on euthanasia in many countries, but not in all. Physician-assisted suicide and euthanasia are legal in, for example, Colombia, Belgium and the Netherlands (in 1990, 9% of all deaths in the Netherlands were as a result of

physician-assisted suicide or euthanasia). However, in most countries, despite a number of legal challenges, assisted suicide for the terminally ill remains illegal – albeit rarely prosecuted. Acceptance of the concept is not widespread and some workshops, most noticeably in South Africa, rejected the concept for religious reasons. Nevertheless, recent attention in the Western press has specifically been focused on the growing popularity of clinics such as those run by Dignitas and EXIT in Switzerland. Since its foundation in 1998, Dignitas has assisted around 1,000 people to die, 60% of them from Germany and 10% from the UK.

In markets such as the US, where the healthcare system is largely focused on keeping people alive for as long as possible, assisted suicide and DNR are highly controversial topics. Even with increasingly public debate, such as the plea from author Terry Pratchett, who has called for tribunals to give sufferers from incurable diseases the right to medical help to end their lives, wider acceptance of euthanasia is still in the minority. But it is growing.

In ten years, many think that more and more people will start to see that life doesn't need to go on for ever, especially since the option to live for longer in reasonable comfort is really only a luxury for wealthier nations where the healthcare systems, insurance policies and private wealth enable increased levels of support. The argument is that systemic euthanasia should be introduced. Moreover, this should not be limited just to those who have a proven terminal illness but should be an option available to all.

With the economic burdens evident and the trends clear, the rational side of the case is increasingly accepted, but in many influential circles the ethical, emotional and political perspectives are also shifting. Some see that opening the door for euthanasia beyond those with terminal illness is a slippery slope leading to a point where individuals who would not otherwise consider it may be pressurised into asking for assisted suicide by interested parties; others see that the option to proactively check out of life when

The rational side of the case is increasingly accepted, but in many influential circles the ethical, emotional and political perspectives are also shifting.

enough is enough is a sign of a more balanced society. No doubt the debate will continue, and pick up pace as more countries make assisted suicide legal, and, for those that don't, the numbers travelling across borders for the service may well increase.

Related insights

Page 49

Page 65

Page 117

The future of wealth

How wealth is created, valued, shared and used over the next decade is subject to a number of possible changes. Globalisation has connected many of us in ways we never conceived of that allow new ideas to be shared and innovations to accelerate. It has also linked us together in ways that mean shocks in one region can quickly be transferred to another. A flatter world in parts is providing opportunities for those with talent to leapfrog ahead of others, but at the same time there is a growing imbalance between the haves and the have-nots in society. The next decade will see new technologies that will drive new business models that will, in turn, change how wealth is created and shared, but it will also see political and social needs drive other changes in how we manage and use the wealth and resources that we have available. There is also clearly significant influence in this area from the certain shift in the centre of gravity to Asia and the consequences that this will have for wealth creation, trading and even currencies. As with the health cluster, we have chosen eight of the most significant probable changes that came up in the discussions, some of which have global relevance whereas others have a very local impact.

The topics covered in the following pages are:

- Differentiated knowledge
- Dynamic pricing
- Lease everything
- Less energy
- Local currency
- Mobile money
- Richer poorer
- Third global currency

Differentiated knowledge

As information is shared globally and insight is commoditised, the best returns go to those who can produce non-standard, differentiated knowledge.

In his recent books *The World is Flat* and *Hot, Flat and Crowded*, Thomas Friedman, *New York Times* columnist and three-time Pulitzer Prize winner, did an excellent job of sharing how the flattened world of the past decade has been driven by quicker and easier knowledge sharing. Through his multiple examples from India and China, in particular, he highlighted how the alignment of increasing globalisation, high-speed internet connections and new business models all helped the likes of Infosys, Wipro and Tata to become knowledge engines. As outsourcing of call-centres to lower cost economies merged with offshoring of key data-intensive tasks to a similar group of countries, know-how was steadily transferred from the developed to the developing world.

As Harvard's Clayton Christensen, author of numerous books on disruptive innovation, has also highlighted through his stories about the changes in the PC industry, outsourcing drives knowledge sharing and value creation. He focused on the way in which US computer companies such as Compaq and Dell shifted parts manufacture, then assembly and then, finally, design to China and Taiwan. As a result, he shows how the likes of Acer, Lenovo and HTC were able to build up their expertise to a point where they themselves have now become the new incumbent competition and the world's leading brands.

Today, the fast-growth economies are no longer fast-followers but have become global centres of excellence in their own right. Microsoft's lab in Beijing is one of its most advanced in the world; Infosys designs engines for GM and wings for Airbus; and much of the pharmaceutical industry is shifting capability to China and India. Meanwhile, the old economies are finding it more and more difficult to keep pace. New knowledge creation has therefore been the common focus for many and the idea of building knowledge economies has been the policy reactions of many countries which have seen their value-creating manufacturing capabilities disappear.

In the UK, the Work Foundation recently published a report on 'Innovation, Creativity and Entrepreneurship in 2020', which, in headline, argues that:

"To achieve recovery, Britain has no choice but to create a balanced and sustainable knowledge economy by 2020 and therefore must devise new ways of intervention to achieve change. The quest is on for policy levers that can deliver changed behaviour as effectively but more cheaply."

The fast-growth economies are no longer fast-followers but have become global centres of excellence in their own right.

As the half-life of knowledge continues to shrink, 2020 will see greater commoditisation of knowledge.

As such, to build new knowledge, universities around the world have been increasing their status as knowledge hubs. But just as many institutions have been trying to create exclusive content. Leaders such as MIT, for instance, have put all their course materials online free of charge through the OpenCourseWare platform. So, how can others compete?

The future challenge here is that for any knowledge economy to really work, it is a matter of both scale and differentiation. In the initial point of view on the future of work, Chris Meyer argued the case that 'as the half-life of knowledge continues to shrink, 2020 will see greater commoditisation of knowledge'. He sees that, over the next decade, 'the industrialization of information work is certain, and will affect pretty much every business'. Add into the mix a massive imbalance between the US and China in terms of graduates and the US and India in terms of engineers and it is easy to see a one-way shift taking place.

A fundamental issue embedded in this topic is the end of intellectual property (IP). Although this has been on the cards in some sectors for several years, it has now become a more widespread concern. Just as IP in the music and education industries has been challenged by new business models, many see that regulation will fail to keep up with digital collaborative platforms for innovation. With the growth of the creative commons and open source movements, core components of corporate and institutional knowledge will increasingly be shared without restriction and, in the eyes of some, result in the further decline of copyright and weaker patents. As Chris Meyer asked at the start of the programme: 'if IT has reduced the marginal cost of IP to essentially zero, how will incentives for creative work change to recognise these two powerful economic shifts? Will the open innovation movement evolve to a point where know-how and capability rather than pure IP in the traditional sense is the currency? If so, how will organisations monetise collaboration?' An increasing selection of commentators are predicting that commoditised knowledge may even slow down innovation.

However, there is an alternative view – that of creating differentiated commoditised knowledge. Gary Hamel recently commented that 'in a world of commoditised knowledge, the returns go to the companies who can produce non-standard knowledge'. Apple, fiercely protective of its IP, is often cited as a company whose sales and margins are both a reflection of its unique knowledge and know-how. While clear at a company level, the story is less strong at a national level: this view suggests that at a large/global scale, the competition is on to be the differentiated sources of insight. At a national economy scale, where one cannot have everyone producing non-standard knowledge, the challenge is more about speed and efficiency of knowledge development and sharing at a broader scale.

Furthermore, another recent development adds complexity to the argument. Companies like San Francisco-based Maven Research or GLG Group are scaling up and positioning themselves as intermediaries for sharing of expertise – namely, differentiated commoditised knowledge.

"Maven is the Global Knowledge Marketplace. We connect knowledge seekers with knowledgeable individuals for the rapid exchange of expertise, perspective, and opinion. Our Members ('Mavens') include individuals from all professional backgrounds, geographies, and functional roles. Mavens are paid to participate in short telephone consultations and custom surveys conducted by other professionals who seek to learn from their knowledge."

So, here is a development that is further seeking to commoditise knowledge by connecting individuals within companies, academia, governments – in fact, anyone with insight – to people and organisations prepared to pay for that insight. It is early days for Maven but, in principle, this is a good disruption to the knowledge-based consulting and research sectors that erodes differentiation. What are the implications for the future as more programmes such as Maven ramp up and begin to have a major impact, especially in fast-developing knowledge economies? Probably more specialisation of knowledge within boutique consulting companies where it is more about what you do with the insight rather than the accessing of it; probably faster migration up the scale from novice to expert; and possibly further erosion of developing countries' lead in key areas as the channels for personally profitable dissemination of know-how override the economically significant retention and development of non-standard knowledge.

With the evident rebalancing of economic power – and, with it, associated expertise – it is clear that, by 2020, the knowledge creators will be a significantly different set than they were in 2000. Be they individuals, companies or countries, those that rise above the melee will, in their own ways, have worked out not only how to create non-standard knowledge that others value, but they will have also been able to sustain this so that it continues to be differentiated. They may well have moved beyond the IP frameworks designed to protect ideas to operate in a truly open network of information exchange where IP is not the essential tradable asset. The winners in 2020 will be the ones that manage the delicate balance of new knowledge creation and global sharing in a way in which, even if there is less formal protection available for intellectual property, the value of the know-how is in itself not given away.

It is clear that, by 2020, the knowledge creators will be a significantly different set than they were in 2000.

Related insights

Page 193

Page 197

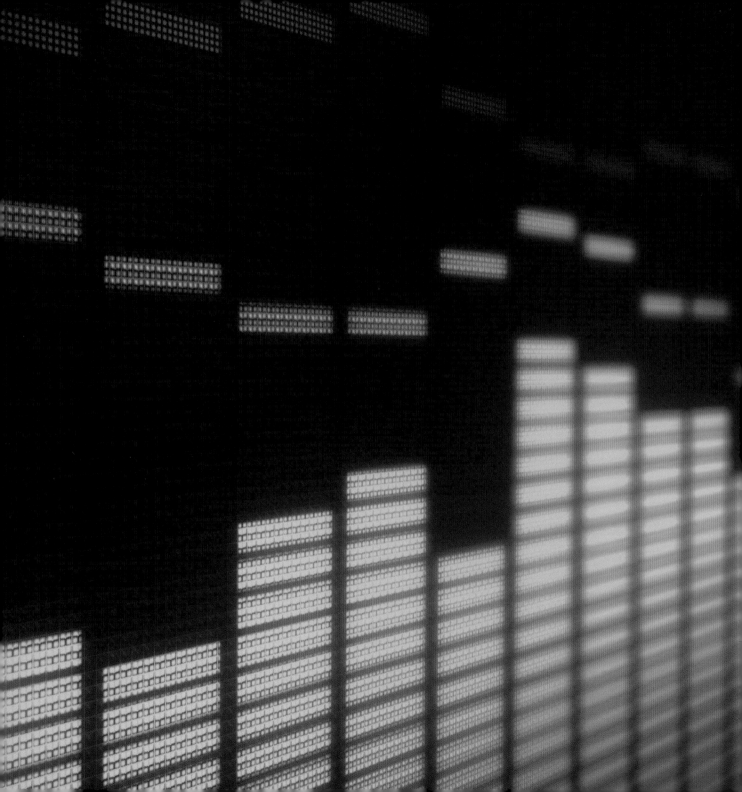

Dynamic pricing

Pervasive smart meters and ubiquitous tracking services create platforms for the dynamic pricing of resources, access and travel to manage demand.

Most of us today are used to the price of goods and services remaining largely stable. The cost of a loaf of bread, a pair of jeans or a bottle of water varies little if at all. Where there is variation because of competing suppliers and retailers changing their prices, this is largely marginal and occurs on a week-to-week or month-to-month basis. While the prices of key commodities, from sugar and coffee to oil and steel, do vary minute by minute on the global stock exchanges, this volatility is not immediately passed on through the supply chain but instead is absorbed by traders, intermediaries and wholesalers. Even when there are spikes in wholesale prices caused by heightened resource constraints resulting from the supply/demand imbalance of rice, wheat or gas, for instance, we as consumers are largely insulated from them. All in all, the vast majority of areas currently experience a pretty stable market where average prices are reactive and lag the supply-side costs by at least a month or so.

Where we do experience price variation on a standard product or service, it is largely predictable and clearly communicated in advance. Off-peak and peak-time ticketing on public transport is a widely adopted mechanism for trying to balance out consumer use of trains, trams and buses in many countries so that those who are able to might decide to save money by travelling outside of rush hour periods or by buying tickets in advance or in bulk. The same principle is applied on many toll roads.

Also in the transport sector, airline seat costs vary not only during the day using a more segmented peak/off-peak model, but also through significant discounts for booking early. In an industry where there is limited capacity the airlines are keen to maximise passenger loading, using variable pricing to attract the majority of customers early and maximise revenue for last-minute or flexible bookings. Over recent years the varied pricing models adopted by the low-cost airlines, from Southwest in the US to RyanAir in Europe and SpiceJet in India, are a well-recognised area of variable pricing understood by customers and refined as a core competence by competing operators.

In a few other areas, we are also experiencing tiered or variable pricing for different experiences. From the timing of a visit to the cinema and the choice of seats at a concert to paying a premium to watch live sport on TV, across the entertainment sector many of us are already used to the concept of paying different fees to experience an identical product depending on the time of day or distance from the stage. In addition, in some countries, we are also used to the concept of peak and off-peak energy use – for domestic as well as industrial users. While these examples are long established in their respective areas, to date they have shown limited variation and none has yet varied in real time. With the widespread introduction and adoption of a number of key technologies, ranging from smart meters to mobile-based location, things are about to change. In response to rising constrained supply of some core resources and in a desire to more finely tune consumer behaviour in an increasingly proactive manner, the advent of dynamic pricing models is on the horizon.

Starting off in the utilities sector, many countries are currently passing regulations to introduce smart meters that will allow real-time monitoring of electricity, gas and water use. At a basic level, remote reading of utility consumption allows the industry to have a better view of demand and so match supply and, at the same time, enables individual domestic and industrial customers to track their consumption and associated cost. However, as highlighted in several of the Future Agenda workshops, the same technology also allows far more sophisticated interaction.

Given that water supply varies on a seasonal basis and consumption on an hourly if not minute-by-minute basis, with increasing physical and economic water stress prevalent in many countries, the capability to use smart meters to introduce dynamic pricing is being increasingly discussed. In Singapore, a country well recognised for its water scarcity, individual households are already given a set quota of basic water supply on a daily basis and a higher price is charged for additional consumption. European regulators are now preparing the way for a similar approach but with more segmented differentiation: 'Every household will get a daily allowance of water sufficient for the essentials but additional use will be charged at different rates that vary depending on the time of day and season.' So, customers will be able to see the immediate cost of having a bath rather than a shower, using their washing machines at peak rather than off-peak times as well as the price of cleaning their cars or watering their lawns.

Customers can, for example, see the cost of catching a train, but also the saving that can be made by waiting half an hour for the next one.

By using dynamic pricing to make supply/demand imbalance both visible and financially significant to customers, utilities companies aim at better managing the overall system. In some markets there may be an initial challenge from consumers who might take time to come to terms with and trust the new technology, but once it has been accepted the same principles apply to electricity and gas with a view to both better managing and better communicating individual and collective use. The concept of reverse charging is also gaining traction whereby individuals who generate their own electricity will be able to sell their excess back into the national grid. This inverts the smart meter model as customers can become net contributors as well as net consumers. Interestingly, one of the RCA projects explored how this might be manifested for electricity supply through simple clear real-time feedback at each socket. Given that the introduction of smart meters is now a legal requirement for 2020 in many countries, this platform for dynamic pricing is clearly being put in place.

Back in the transport sector, transit systems across the world from Japan to India to Europe are also on the verge of introducing more dynamic pricing – mostly enabled by location-based mobile services. As payment goes ticketless, we will increasingly be charged directly when our mobile phone gets on and off a train or bus. Contactless payment systems are already in place in transit systems in places like Hong Kong and London and are rapidly shifting from card to mobile. Given the ability of mobile phones to be positioned within a radius of 50 cm, the widespread use of this platform for transport charging has long been advocated and is now being introduced. Again, as with smart meters, this provides a basic platform upon which more sophisticated pricing systems can be introduced. So, for example, as transport system operators seek to better manage passenger loading and avoid congestion, they can implement real-time increases or decreases of the cost of travel on a train-by-train or journey-by-journey basis. Instead of simply having peak and off-peak cost structures, they can introduce a far more granular segmented model. Customers can, for example, see the cost of catching a train, but also the saving that can be made by waiting half an hour for the next one; they can see the relative real-time costs of alternative transport options to get to the same destination and so decide to take a bus rather than a train; and, it is argued, they can make value-based judgements on the speed/cost of travel to best suit their requirements. Such dynamic systems will provide greater visibility of loading and so allow the use of variable pricing to nudge passengers into making alternative choices and so improve the efficiency of the overall network.

Also, in the arena of road pricing, the introduction of similar technologies is planned to allow passenger and

Real-time predictive traffic forecasting is already possible.

freight vehicles to also experience dynamic changes. Pay-as-you-drive insurance systems have already been trialled by companies such as Aviva to encourage and reward customers for travelling during off-peak hours and on quieter routes. Equally, road haulage firms already benefit from choosing whether or not to use toll-roads and at what time of day, to make their overall journey both time and cost efficient. With the introduction of systems such as those offered by the likes of Airsage, TomTom and Sense Networks, real-time predictive traffic forecasting is already possible. Match that with dynamic pricing and a host of opportunities is unlocked. Take this into areas such as media consumption and a significant change is on the horizon.

While the prices of staple products such as bread, jeans and bottled water, as well as more expensive goods like laptops and TVs, will probably remain largely stable, it is clear that in the areas where variability of cost can lead to efficiency improvements and influence of consumer behaviour, dynamic pricing will take hold over the next decade.

Related insights

Page 91

Page 103

Page 167

Page 175

Page 213

Page 235

Lease everything

Rising sustainability imperatives and increasing cost of ownership shift the balance from ownership to access and we prefer to rent than buy.

The concept of ownership is core to many cultures, but not all. It has also been seen to apply in different ways to different things. Owning your own home rather than renting it has, for example, been higher on the agenda in the US and the UK than in, say, Germany where renting is more widely accepted and housing is seen less as an investment. That said, even in the US, the rich have traditionally had the luxury of home ownership but the poor have had to lease. While the sub-prime bubble in the US temporarily gave an inflated perception of ownership, as Michael Lewis quotes in his recent book *The Big Short*, 'A home without equity is just a rental without debt'. With declining values and increasing mortgage defaults, the ambition of owing our own homes has become less important to many in the developed world, just as it is becoming an increasingly possible option for the growing middle classes in the developing world. Overall, many see that, given the alternatives, with such a high-value, high-cost item as property, a shift is now taking place towards more widespread leasing of flats and houses. This move is, however, not restricted to property and is becoming increasingly prevalent in other areas.

In the transport arena, the alternative of leasing rather than buying a car has been a widespread option for many years. The known monthly cost of having use of a car for, say, three years is more attractive than buying the vehicle – to both the customer and the financial

The aspiration for car ownership can potentially be better met for some by the ability to have temporary access.

services companies facilitating this arrangement. Equally, for short-term use, the option of renting a vehicle is a long-standing need and a successful business model for companies such as Avis, Hertz and their like. What has also been notable in recent years has been the success of short-term, hour-by-hour, rental of vehicles from companies such as Zipcar.com and streetcar.co.uk. Especially in developed urban environments, the ability to have access to a vehicle when you need to make a journey that you can't easily do on public transport, or when you need to transport furniture etc, has been increasingly popular. Going forward, many companies are keen to see how this model can be applied to other urban centres such as Mumbai, Shanghai and Lagos, where the aspiration for car ownership can potentially be better met for some by the ability to have temporary access. The same principles are being increasingly widely adopted for bicycle rental. With headline moves starting off in cities such as Paris, the movement has quickly spread to London, Bucharest, San Francisco, Marrakech and Mexico City, and is now on the to-do lists of many major cities' administrations.

Within the home environment, furniture and domestic appliance rental is on the increase for significant sections of the population who may only be in need of temporary use.

Many can argue that cars are like houses in that they are high-value items that lend themselves to leasing models, where customers see the benefit from a cost of capital perspective. However, what is becoming more evident is how, as we shift from ownership to access, renting is growing as an alternative to buying even for low-cost items. Although, in consumer product areas, ownership has become increasingly important throughout many nations, leasing is gaining traction. The music industry has, somewhat unwillingly, clearly been at the forefront of this, as Napster, iTunes and Spotify have all variously shifted our perception of ownership from having physical product to having temporary or more long-term access to digital versions. Equally, in the mobile communications sector, for many customers ownership of the phone itself has become a by-product of a monthly contract to provide the service.

With these as a reference points, more and more industries are making moves to shift from ownership to access. Jewellery and fashion accessories are frequently leased for the night or a special occasion. Within the home environment, furniture and domestic appliance rental is on the increase for significant sections of the population who may only be in need of temporary use. Students, urban migrants, newly married couples and professionals

on international secondment are increasingly being offered the option to lease, not buy, kit such as washing machines, sofas and beds. While some see this as a return to the days of the hire purchase agreements prevalent in the post-WWII years, the difference is that the intention of ultimate ownership is not there. This is about temporary access for a limited period with the recognition that, as you move on, the product can be returned.

A significant driver in this movement is the sustainability agenda. Reducing waste is clearly a high priority for many industries and local governments so the encouragement of new practices to encourage reuse of products that involve high resource use is an increasing imperative. Voluntary networks such as Freecycle have a role but more fundamental shifts in how products are made available to customers are also in play. Again the automotive industry is playing a leading role here. As lifecycle management has extended into product reuse, the introduction of cars such as the new 95% recyclable Renault Twingo has made increasingly feasible the possibility of key components and materials being leased from, not sold by, the source manufacturer. If the economics work, then it would be possible to lease, not sell, say, an air conditioning unit or even the steel for a car that will be in use for ten years. As long as the components return back to their original source for recycling, a ten-year rental arrangement is increasingly practical.

Taking the same principles into other areas, the concept of leasing, not buying, clothing is also

A significant driver in this movement is the sustainability agenda.

gaining traction for two key reasons. Firstly, given the resources used in manufacture, the ability to recycle is highly attractive. Given the amount of cotton involved, 11,000 litres of water are used in the production of the average pair of jeans, so being able to reuse cotton is therefore just as attractive for the fashion industry as recycling aluminium cans is for the drinks industry. Secondly, in this industry, fashion clearly changes and the products go out of style long before they are worn out. So, expect to see developments where key brands offer customers the option of, say, a three month lease for their clothes. Equally, the same reusage principles apply to computers where, for example, Samsung sees the 'PC becoming a commodity item': given the forthcoming regulations on electronic waste, expect also to be offered PC rental instead of purchase.

By 2020, expect to see that the concept of ownership in sectors such as housing, cars, white goods and clothing has been replaced by that of access. In the end, perhaps it will only be items such as gifts and souvenirs that are kept for a lifetime.

Samsung sees the 'PC becoming a commodity item': given the forthcoming regulations on electronic waste, expect also to be offered PC rental instead of purchase.

Related insights

Page 87

Page 141

Page 219

Page 223

Less energy

Consumers are incentivised to use significantly less energy as escalating growth in carbon emissions forces utilities to change their business models.

As highlighted previously, one of the four main certainties about the next ten years is that we will experience key resource constraints. One of the most significant issues here is clearly energy and, with our continued over-dependency on fossil fuels and the increasing global susceptibility to the impacts of climate change, momentum for change is building. However, we are not yet at a stage where either global agreements will take effect or where technological breakthroughs will provide new solutions; nor are there credible alternative pathways on the table for developing economies.

Few now doubt that the earth is warming, nor that human-related emissions are in many ways responsible. Even so, as ever more varied organisations are now declaring, the rise in carbon emissions shows no sign of slowing. The targets of keeping the amount of carbon dioxide in the atmosphere down to 450 ppm (parts per million) and the average global temperature rise below 2°C are increasingly seen as being unrealistic. In many eyes, 'we have already gone too far' and the challenge is now to mitigate the damage and deal with the consequences over the next twenty years until new options come on line. The more hopeful ambition of taking actions to hit the preferred 350 ppm target is also disappearing fast.

The failure of Copenhagen to agree a binding agreement on greenhouse gases to which all countries can set their targets demonstrates that more time is needed before governments around the world make the necessary tough decisions to halt the growth in carbon emissions. Although the next decade may well see such an agreement come into force, even the optimists recognise that the timescale for its impact will be more like 2050 than 2020. Globally ambitious targets may be set, but global impact is a long way off.

From a technological perspective, the viable 'clean solutions' of nuclear, wind, wave and solar are now all clear to many, but the timescales for action here are also well beyond the ten year horizon. Building and commissioning nuclear power stations takes five to ten years and so, although China and others are now constructing a significant number, it is clear by just looking at which governments are yet to make this decision that any significant global shift to nuclear is a good way off. In addition, although solar, wind and wave are all growing and receiving more investment, the share of the world's energy needs that can be met from these sources by 2020 is at most 25%.

In terms of the main developing economies and their appetite for energy, the 'energy ladder' diagram highlights the challenge. As economies grow, so do their energy consumption levels: hence, as the BRIC

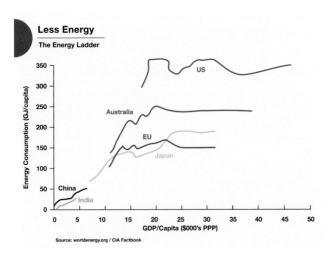

Less Energy

The Energy Ladder

Source: worldenergy.org / CIA Factbook

We cannot stop China and India from growing.

countries and others achieve increasing GDP per capita over the next decade, their average energy consumption is also destined to increase. As Leo Roodhart pointed out in the initial perspective on the future of energy, 'we cannot stop China and India from growing'. Taking all countries' current projections into account, globally, energy demand is likely to double over the first half of this century and, according to the International Energy Agency's reference scenario, 'over the next twenty years, global energy demand will increase around 40%'.

Viewing all this together, it is increasingly clear that, on current projections, it will be at least 2050 before any flattening off of carbon emissions will occur. If an average global temperature rise of even 4°C is to be avoided, then 'an alternative way of thinking is essential'. Action is being called for across many countries and organisations, and in many ways the only option available to us in the next decade is to tackle our thirst for energy. To stand any chance of heading off seemingly inevitable climate change, we all need to halve our annual energy consumption by 2020 – every person and every organisation.

Persuading us to do this is no easy task, but several organisations are starting to make moves in the right direction. In 2010 in Europe, E.ON launched a major campaign focused on 'helping our customers cut their energy use'. In what, from a business growth perspective, appears counter-intuitive for a company that makes money by selling energy, E.ON is encouraging less demand. Other companies are now planning to follow suit: being seen as one of the organisations trying to proactively do something about the problem is arguably good for the brand and good for market share. Going on in a business-as-usual fashion is no longer seen as viable. Singapore has launched a national 10% energy efficiency challenge and Japan, by many steps the world's most energy-frugal developed country, is similarly trying to further cut consumption.

However, to have a meaningful impact on emissions, the biggest challenge is to address the world's largest

To stand any chance of heading off seemingly inevitable climate change, we all need to halve our annual energy consumption by 2020 – every person and every organisation.

The US economy has the potential to reduce annual non-transportation energy consumption by roughly 23% by 2020.

energy consumers, the US and China. While China is able to exert central control and build new nuclear power stations, in the US, the world's largest energy consumer, the issue is all about changing consumer behaviour. According to recent McKinsey research, 'the US economy has the potential to reduce annual non-transportation energy consumption by roughly 23% by 2020, eliminating more than $1.2 trillion in waste – well beyond the $520 billion upfront investment (not including programme costs) that would be required. The reduction in energy use would also result in the abatement of 1.1 gigatons of greenhouse gas emissions annually – the equivalent of taking the entire US fleet of passenger vehicles and light trucks off the roads.' The problem right now is how to persuade a population used to consuming over twice the energy per capita of most other developed nations to drive less, and in smaller cars, turn the thermostats down in the winter and use less air-conditioning in the summer.

Some experts hope that the Deepwater Horizon blow-out may well be the start of a change in attitude, but, if it is not, many see other catalysts ahead. Looking forward to the next few years, many see a tipping point approaching as more natural disasters like hurricane Katrina, increased concerns over energy security and regular brown-outs in major cities become commonplace. Although most do not see that any government will be willing to act to legislate to, say, quadruple the price of energy to force behaviour change, a number of influential commentators do envisage that 'common sense will eventually prevail.' To what extent change will occur by 2020 is clearly an open question, but as many are broadcasting doom and gloom, many others are looking hopeful. As one workshop participant suggested: 'Do not underestimate the influence of the growing middle classes in India and China to set an alternative path and create a better ambition – one that does not seek to emulate the US.' The arguments have been made, action is starting to take place and some companies are proactively seeking to change the status quo. Although in no way certain, we can however be increasingly confident that, by 2020, each of us will, by choice or as a consequence of regulation, be using less energy.

Do not underestimate the influence of the growing middle classes in India and China to set an alternative path and create a better ambition.

Related insights

Local currency

The revitalisation of bartering, decreased trust in banks and increasing community focus broadens the adoption of alternative stores of value for trade.

Allied to the changing role of money globally, several commentators see a rise in the wider adoption of what have been labelled as 'local currencies'. Over the next decade, more people will probably prefer to use more regional, local or even personal currencies. Local currencies have been attracting a lot of attention and there is history in this space ranging from local exchange trading systems, frequently derided as 'babysitting tokens', to Time Banks and so on. However, the next generation of money may be more about so-called 'alternative currency' rather than a return to the approaches of the past.

There have been many variants of local currencies within specific areas for some time but most of these have been limited in terms of scalability. For example, Disney Dollar banknotes are issued and accepted in Disney theme parks and carry pictures of characters including Mickey Mouse, Pluto and Goofy. In South Korea, Samsung employees have also been partially paid in the form of company currency which can be spent in Samsung-owned stores. Equally, but less officially, within prisons cigarettes have been a long-standing form of currency.

In terms of actual local currency that can be used with multiple stakeholders rather than just within one entity, several new examples have recently been appearing. The image opposite is of a local currency used in Cornwall in the 19th century. Two hundred

In 2005, a local currency was introduced in the fishing village of Kinsale in Ireland and since then the idea has been building momentum.

years later, in 2005, a local currency was introduced in the fishing village of Kinsale in Ireland and since then the idea has been building momentum. In the UK alone, there are now several systems in place and, following on from the introduction of the Totnes pound in Devon, the Lewes pound in Sussex and the Stroud pound in Gloucestershire, the Brixton pound was launched just as the Future Agenda programme kicked off. This was the first time the approach had been tried within a city.

"The Brixton pound is money that sticks to Brixton. It's designed to support Brixton businesses and encourage local trade and production. It's a complementary currency, working alongside (not replacing) pounds sterling, for use by independent local shops and traders."

Proponents of such physical local currencies say they boost community economies by keeping money in the area, but critics dismiss them as fashionable gimmicks and tantamount to protectionism.

In places such as Uganda and Ghana, airtime has, for many, become the alternative currency by which people trade goods and labour.

When we looked at this through the village lens, we saw three key elements at play influencing the adoption of alternative currencies:

1) the swapping of time and experience between individuals (piano lessons for golf lessons, for example);

2) the increase in bartering as it provides an alternative to cash that is both more affordable for many and less embarrassing or confrontational than cash; and

3) increasingly, the open exchange of goods through such schemes as Freecycle, where a more connected world has made sharing and reusing products more efficient at a local level. Whether existing as an official local currency or not, examples of the principle of local exchange of value are increasingly visible.

In several African countries, people have swapped the use of cash as means of exchange for a safer store of value – mobile phone minutes. In places such as Uganda and Ghana, airtime has, for many, become the alternative currency by which people trade goods and labour. This local currency is easy to share and exchange, is understood by all, has clear value that can be linked to the national currency, but, importantly, is seen as being outside the government

system. In addition the world of international remittance looks set to change as it is also possible to use airtime to transfer value on a global basis via companies like Transferto and More Magic.

The demonstrable collapse in the trust of traditional banks is one factor nudging Dave Birch, Founder of the Digital Money Forum, towards the future growth of local currencies:

"Many members of the public, whether through financial calculation or outrage, are now prepared to give alternatives a try. In the UK, one such alternative of note is Zopa, the peer-to-peer lending exchange. If regional, local or personal currencies are to disrupt the financial system they need to include an alternative means of saving and lending, not merely spending. A combination of P2P [peer-to-peer] currency and P2P lending could very well deliver the key elements of a new kind of money."

A number of others engaged in the Future Agenda programme specifically mentioned the advantages that informal local means of exchange have in playing outside the tax system. Although the possible avoidance of sales tax or VAT was mentioned as a potential barrier to wider introduction, the shift of more trades out of the national currency systems

The shift of more trades out of the national currency systems at a time of rising public debt and individual tax burdens was seen as a driver of change towards alternatives.

at a time of rising public debt and individual tax burdens was seen as a driver of change towards alternatives. Inventor of the ATM, John Shepherd-Barron, highlighted that 'In Italy the grey economy is thought to be near 20%. In Britain it is nearer 15%.'

Although in no way guaranteed to be pervasive, many involved in the programme felt that local currencies, or alternative means of value exchange, will be prevalent worldwide by 2020. Whether as versions of African mobile airtime, printed local currencies or perhaps more regional extensions of loyalty card points, the ability to use something other than the euro, dollar or other national currency as the means of exchange within your own community is an increasingly likely option for us all.

Related insights

Page 103

Page 111

Page 239

Mobile money

Proven systems built on mobile connectivity and increasingly flexible means of exchange provide a tipping point in the shift towards the cashless society.

The ability to replace cash with digital money transferred via mobile phone has been one of the 'next big things' for well over a decade now. Proponents have for years been predicting widespread use of mobile payments for a range of activities from transportation ticketing to buying a can of cola. They posited that this would all take off in the technology-savvy European markets, probably led by partnerships between banks, IT firms and mobile operators. What few recognised was that regulation and the willingness of consumers to make the shift would be such a barrier; what even fewer saw was that serving the unbanked population in Africa would be the catalyst for change. Today, with more money flowing around Africa by mobile phone, the adoption of micro-payment systems spreading globally and the associated regular coverage of the impacts in the *Financial Times*, *Wall Street Journal* and *The Economist*, many now believe that we really are at a point of change.

The principle has been proved that innovation often occurs where the need for change is greatest. Look to Africa, where there are few banks, poor physical infrastructures and a rural population often dependent on remittances from the city. It is here that technology can really demonstrate value by offering a secure, efficient alternative to cash transactions. Such has been the success of products like M-PESA in Kenya that we are at a point where, looking forward to 2020, many experts, as well as the key players such as banks, governments and retailers,

can see a world, particularly in emerging economies, where the majority of cash transactions have been replaced by digital ones – and where most of these will be made by our phones. Twenty years after the invention of the Mondex electronic cash card system at NatWest Bank in the UK, the reality has come to life on the rugged landscape of the African bush.

Consumer-focused digital money transactions via mobile phone now cover banking services (eg, deposit taking and account management), transfers (eg, distribution of state benefits or person-to-person remittances) and payments (eg, settlements of bills and purchases of goods and services). In 2010, proven examples of these services are up and running, not just in pilot programmes, but in full use by millions of people around the world. In South Africa, Wizzit has positioned itself as a virtual bank and customers can use their phones to make person-to-person payments, transfer money, purchase pre-paid electricity and pre-buy airtime for their mobile. This service is focused on the 16 million South Africans that do not have bank accounts and the same model is in use elsewhere: in Kenya, M-PESA customers (approximately 11 million of them) regularly transfer money from one to another via their mobile, store cash on their phones and access MKESHO, a separate interest-paying account; in Turkey, millions of people send money using Turkcell's mobile service; and in the Philippines, GCash is a highly successful mobile wallet service enabling cashless and cardless micro-

As has been seen in Africa, if systems are successful for the poor unbanked they are quickly adopted as the standard.

transactions, including payments to shops and utilities and transfers to other people. By meeting a clear need to provide simple and secure access to basic financial services to those without bank accounts in the developing world, these and other systems have made money transfer cheap and easy for millions. They are being embraced as part of micro-finance programmes across Asia and Africa and have global support from the World Bank as well as a host of major commercial organisations, including mobile operators and retail banks.

Back in the developed world, where the idea initially failed to take off, we can now see many of the ingredients coming together for the shift to mobile money. Foremost have been pre-pay cards on public transit systems, such as Oyster Card in London, which have now evolved into micro-payment schemes. In Japan over 50 million people carry phones capable of serving as a wallet. With the roll out of NFC (near-field communication) technologies now under way, the ability to migrate these to your mobile is imminent. According to VISA Europe: 'The technology for paying with cell phones by flashing them near reading equipment in stores or on public transport is ready and the initial feedback is good – trials show that consumers overwhelmingly like it. But the biggest problem has been the business model.' With the impetus for change now building and regulators recognising the need to enable

mobile banking to scale, the successes from Africa and Asia are providing the basis for new business models globally. The industry is making strong predictions: analysts at GIA and Berg Insight forecast that 'by 2015, mobile financial services will be used by 1 billion people globally'. Juniper Research predicts that 'as many as one half of the world's mobile subscribers will be making m-payments by 2014, with 500 million people making m-payments on the Indian subcontinent alone'.

In his initial view on the future of money for the Future Agenda programme, Dave Birch suggested that 'Money as an acceptable means of exchange is already undergoing change. Money is useless as a medium unless it is acceptable to both parties in a transaction. In many countries cash is falling as a proportion of transactions.' He asked: 'In a decade, will cash still be there? Why? Might we eliminate money through "turbo barter"? Is cash replacement realistic and under what circumstances? Why now? Which technologies have come together to make this a point in time when the possibility of a change from cash to an alternative means of exchange is not only credible but also increasingly probable?' He then gave his view that:

"The means of exchange is most immediately subject to the pressure of rapid technological change, particularly since we are at one of those inflexion points that come along from time to time. The mobile phone is about to become the most important means of exchange on a global basis and the first technology with the potential to replace notes and coins as the means of exchange for the 'average' person."

Others agree that, with everything that has gone before, the time is right for change: 'Willem Buiter, Professor of European Political Economy at the London School of Economics and former chief economist of the European Bank for Reconstruction and Development, is not the first economist to think about getting rid of cash. But he may be one of the first to think about getting rid of cash in a technological era that actually makes it entirely feasible.'

"If the central problem has been the cost of transactions for poor people, and the central solution is to use mobile phones to make transactions, then the key compromise is straightforward to set out: We must encourage easy-entry competition for low-value, interpersonal transactions and allow not only mobile operators but other newcomers to deliver a service."

More realistic limits for the Know Your Customer (KYC) and Anti Money Laundering (AML) protocols and increasing competition in the provision of mobile payment services will bring hundreds of millions of people into the financial system. This would deliver a significant net welfare increase and make a huge difference to the daily lives of some of the poorest

'People will always need cash for the black economy and in many countries that is significant'.

people. As has been seen in Africa, if systems are successful for the poor unbanked they are quickly adopted as the standard. Designing for the 'bottom of the pyramid' is a widely used challenge, but in mobile money transfer its worth is proven.

So, does this mean the end of cash? The vision of 100% electronic cash has already been bounced around for many years but few people truly see this as a 2020 reality. In a workshop in India, it was highlighted that 'people will always need cash for the black economy and in many countries that is significant'. In the UK, around 15% of cash payments are outside the taxation system; in Italy, it is 20%; in India, around 40%; and in Greece, well over 50%. While some may see that Greece is an extreme case and that as economic growth in India continues more of the money flow will go through the official systems, it is clear that in most countries a good percentage of the money that oils the wheels of society and trade will continue to come from a pocket rather than a phone.

However, now everything – from all three technological, regulatory, business and consumer points of view – is coming together for a major shift to mobile money transactions. Many see that by 2020 there will be fewer credit cards, less cash and well over half of all consumer money transfers will be digital, with the vast majority of these being done on our phones.

Related insights

Page 87

Page 99

Richer poorer

Widening differences in wealth between and within urban and rural communities extends the gap between rich and poor – but they still need each other.

In recent years the gap between richer and poorer households has widened in most areas of the world despite strong economic growth that has created millions of jobs. This has applied not only in the gaps between some rich countries and some poor ones, but also within many nations: the rich–poor gap in the US has increased, just as it has in Brazil. This has been driven by a number of factors, many of which are increasing rather than decreasing as we go forward. Urbanisation is perhaps the most significant issue. The ways in which governments use taxation and spending on social activities to redistribute wealth show little sign of changing; nor do the effects of access to education as a catalyst for greater differentiation of opportunity. Over the next decade, many experts across the world see that the gap between the haves and the have-nots will grow, even though there will be ever more interdependency, in some areas, between wealth generation across the social spectrum.

Experts, such as economist Noriko Hama, see that the big economic issue for the world in the 21st century will be the huge gap between rich and poor: 'About 16% of humanity in the richer countries are better off than at any time in history. However, more than 1.3 billion people are living on a dollar a day or less.' Looking back over the past decade or so, OECD research shows that 'the richest countries have certainly got richer and some of the poorer countries have done relatively badly, but the rapid growth in incomes in China and India has dragged millions upon

millions out of poverty'. The gap between rich and poor is getting bigger in the world's richest countries – and particularly the United States – as top earners' incomes soar while others' stagnate. The income of the richest 10% of people is, on average across OECD countries, nearly nine times that of the poorest 10%. In the US, that gap is even greater – about sixteen times – and, according to the Center on Budget and Policy Priorities, this has more than tripled in the past three decades. 'US cities like New York, Chicago and Washington are less equal than places like Brazzaville in Congo, Managua in Nicaragua and Davao City in the Philippines.'

In a twenty-year study, the OECD said wealthy households are not only widening the gap with the poor, but in countries such as the US, Canada, Italy, Norway and Germany they are also leaving middle-income earners further behind. Earnings of full-time workers have become more, not less, unequal in developed economies over the past decade as high earners have become more so. Research by Professor John Hills at the London School of Economics suggests that increasing inequality in the UK after 2004 has meant that, by 2008, it had reached its highest level in the years since figures began in 1961.

In Mumbai, 'the widening gap between India's rich and poor is an undisputed fact' and, in the process of overall growth, redistribution of wealth has become a secondary issue for many. In Johannesburg it was

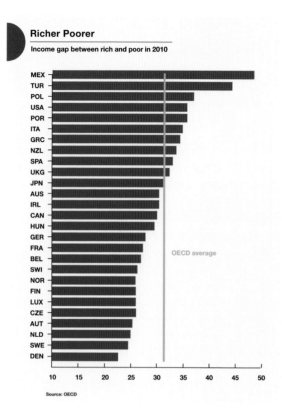

Richer Poorer

Income gap between rich and poor in 2010

MEX
TUR
POL
USA
POR
ITA
GRC
NZL
SPA
UKG
JPN
AUS
IRL
CAN
HUN
GER
FRA
BEL
SWI
NOR
FIN
LUX
CZE
AUT
NLD
SWE
DEN

OECD average

10 15 20 25 30 35 40 45 50

Source: OECD

suggested that the gap between rich and poor was being exacerbated by improved transport systems to the townships – enabling the poor to come into the city more easily and therefore maintaining the old divisions between the black and white populations. But it is in Latin America where the greatest gaps are to be found, and they are increasing. UN research shows that, over the region, the wealthiest 20% holds nearly 60% of the resources but the total income for the poorest 20% is only 3.5% of GDP. In Brazil, the most extreme nation, the richest 10% of the population has over 50% of all income while the bottom 10% has less than 1%.

Increasing urbanisation and escalating migration plus the associated rise of more unplanned slum districts in high-growth cities is leading to rising numbers of urban poor in both the developed and developing world. As Professor Ricky Burdett highlighted in his initial view of the future of cities, 'migration and in-migration has also created an urban underclass which is often allocated to specific areas of the city. Paris is a perfect example. The physical infrastructure, with the beauty and qualities that we all admire, has frozen. This means that all its growth (with increasing immigration from 1945 and onward) has created ghettoisation.' Ismail Serageldin, Director of the Bibliotheca Alexandrina, added that: 'The nature of the economic activity in cities seems to be leading to a greater degree of urban poverty as in-migration and the move to the knowledge society favour the educated and the nimble and drive the gap between the rich and the poor wider. Ghettoisation is a by-product of the income gap as much as it is the result of ossification of the city's physical structure. Are redistributive policies sufficient? Are they politically acceptable at the level that would be required to have an impact on the problem?' But it is not just in cities where the rich–poor gap is increasingly evident: in Brazil, over half the rural population is in poverty; in Mexico, 40.1%; and in Peru, 69.3%. As urbanisation increases, those left behind are getting relatively poorer. Although most of the wealth in rural areas already comes from people in urban areas sending money back, this is not balancing the situation. In India, agriculture in itself produces around 20% of the GDP but more than 60% of the population is involved in this sector.

Looking forward, the rich–poor challenge appears destined to be even greater. As UN findings have highlighted: 'The more unequal that cities become,

The widening gap between India's rich and poor is an undisputed fact.

the higher the risk that economic disparities will result in social and political tension. The likelihood of urban unrest in unequal cities is high.' Today, the countries of the OECD account for around 60% of global wealth. By 2020, China, India, Brazil, Indonesia and Russia will between them account for 30% of global GDP. Within these fast-growing nations, ever greater urbanisation is creating more unplanned ghettos and exacerbating the rich–poor divide. India is trying to rebalance this by, for example, giving slum dwellers money and land on the edges of cities like Mumbai, only to see people sell the land and move back into the city where the promise of wealth is greater.

China is acutely conscious of the potential political instability that could result from greater imbalance and has recently announced several policies that seek to change the underlying dynamic. Concerned that overall GDP growth below 8% could lead to internal conflict, Chinese Premier Wen Jiabao recently announced that China must reverse its widening income gap between rich and poor and that the benefits of a growing economy should be distributed more fairly. In a speech at the start of China's annual parliamentary session he said: 'We will not only make the "pie" of social wealth bigger by developing the economy, but also distribute it well.' As part of this initiative, China is aiming to reform the household registration system that classifies people as either city or rural dwellers. This controversial

system means many migrant workers – farmers who travel to towns and cities to find better-paid work – are unable to get proper services.

In developed economies, the challenges also look too daunting and further polarisation of rich and poor is on the cards. Again according to the OECD, over the past two decades, 'developed countries' governments have been taxing more and spending more to offset the trend towards inequality', but while 'the redistributive effect of government expenditures dampened the rise in poverty in the 1990s, they amplified it in the decade that followed, as benefits became less targeted on the poor.' Governments often try to rebalance wealth distribution, but few have been successful in the past.

As public spending in many developed economies is cut back to help reduce public debt, many see that the rich–poor gap will be much wider in ten years' time. Top-down redistribution and recalibration of wealth generation, as China is partly aiming to achieve, could be one answer, but some question this approach. Others see more focus on improving social mobility as the way to go: By putting in place the means by which individuals and families can climb up the economic ladder, it is argued that more lasting change can be achieved. There are some positive signs – such as the reversal of the digital divide between those connected to the internet and those not, seen as a result of the rollout of mobile connectivity around the world – but overall most experts we spoke to feel that 2020 will be a world where the rich will have got richer and the poor will have become relatively poorer.

Related insights

Page 171

Page 227

Page 231

Page 247

Third global currency

The economic rise of Asia and the need for an alternative to the US dollar as the world's reserve currency produces a parallel broad-basket Asian Currency Unit.

Alongside individual national currencies and regional currencies such as the East Caribbean dollar and the West African franc, today there are essentially two key currencies that can be considered as global reserve currencies: the US dollar and the euro. These are the currencies in which key commodities such as oil, gold, steel and so on are priced; they are the primary currencies against which all others are compared; and they are the currencies that most national governments and central banks hold as part of their national reserves. By implication, they are therefore seen as the currencies of greatest stability and the ones that keep the world's trade systems flowing.

However, things change and global reserve currencies are not immune from this. Going back a century or so, UK sterling was the default global currency, the US dollar was increasing in influence and the euro had not even been conceived. Today, although they are clearly the current leaders, both the dollar and the euro are under increasing pressure. Momentum is building up for a change, or at least the addition of a third, alternative global reserve currency – one that is less dependent on the West and one that more readily supports the future needs of the global financial system. As the G20 has superseded the G7, many have recognised that financial management of the global system must become more equable. Robert Zoellick, President of the World Bank, recently said that the US must 'brace itself' for the dollar to be replaced as the world's reserve currency.

The fundamental drivers of this are the clear shift in the centre of economic gravity towards Asia, the associated growing economic importance of China and the increased risk stemming from growing levels of debt in the US. In addition, the recent problems in the eurozone have raised increasing concern over the long-term credibility and viability of the euro as a common currency across hence many economically varying countries, and so its credibility as a stable global reserve currency.

Given that US public debt has already passed 60% of GDP and could hit 80% in the next decade, many argue that 'the US may require a more flexible fiscal policy than currently exists given its status as the now default primary currency'. With China and others continuing to prosper by lending the US money to buy more of their products and services and so increasing debt and dependency and with the continued rise of the cost of alternative stores of value such as gold, one option for the US government is to devalue the dollar. This would help rebalance the system both domestically and locally, support export growth and also give more economic flexibility. However, at this time, due to its global position as a reserve currency and China's resistance to free-floating the renminbi, this option is not available.

At the same time, many high-growth Asian economies are keen to move on from needing to trade with each other via the dollar. Not only do they want to avoid having to use the dollar as the de facto intermediary for many international trades, they also want to keep their

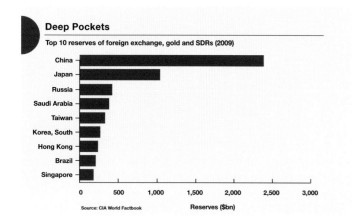

Deep Pockets

Top 10 reserves of foreign exchange, gold and SDRs (2009)

Source: CIA World Factbook · Reserves ($bn)

bias in favour of any one country or group of countries or group of dominant institutions."

During the course of the Future Agenda programme, there was much discussion on this topic. Rajiv Kumar of ICRIER in Delhi authored a challenging initial perspective on the future of currency that was debated in workshops in Europe and Asia. In addition, talk of the decline of the dollar, the US–China exchange rate and the potential for alternatives was increasingly reported in much of the mainstream financial press. All agreed that change is on the horizon but the options and timescales for a third global currency to have an impact were hotly debated. Effectively, most experts see that three alternatives are available.

The China option is one that is seen as increasingly possible, but not the right answer: the rise of China's economic power creates a case for the renminbi revaluation to make it a global reserve currency but there are several fundamental barriers to this. Firstly, the controls exerted by the Chinese government on its currency mean that it is devalued against the rest of the world's currencies, and especially the dollar, to give it export advantage. As Niall Ferguson points out:

"Because Beijing keeps the exchange rate fixed, the dollar cannot devalue against China (and other parts of Asia) despite the large US trade deficits."

Although the Chinese government started to relax the pegging to the dollar in June 2010, the variation being allowed is marginal: analysts at Credit Suisse reckon that the renminbi is undervalued by 50%. These controls prevent the renminbi from having capital account convertibility and so don't allow it to float freely in sync with other currencies; the removal of these controls would be a prerequisite for the renminbi to become

money within their own control with less dependency on the strength of the US economy and the highly US-orientated global financial institutions. 'Why should Asian savings make the round trip to the US?' was a typical comment we encountered. China, India and Japan as well as many others such as Thailand, Vietnam and Malaysia are keen to have an alternative option to the dollar, but this is increasingly seen as not being the euro. The evident weakness in the eurozone, where strong economies like Germany have clearly been carrying weak ones like Greece, creates instability and, besides that, the euro can also be seen to be just as much linked to Western financial imperatives as the dollar.

"Over the next decade, we will move unmistakably towards a multi-polar world which will be characterized by a much broader consultative process that extends to a larger number of jurisdictions. Greater coordination amongst major economies on financial sector regulation will be needed, and this can be facilitated by the newly enlarged Financial Stability Board based in Basle. At its core, the coordination will have to be aimed at achieving greater trust in the transparent and universally applicable working of the financial system. This will especially need to dispel the fear that the global financial system has a

Why should Asian savings make the round trip to the US?

more influential on the world stage. In addition, some argue that, even if the Chinese government allowed their currency to become fully convertible, China may not be prepared politically to assume such a position of global financial leadership and associated responsibility.

A second option is for all countries to adopt what are termed 'special drawing rights' as a parallel reserve currency for international trade. SDRs are the international reserve assets managed by the IMF. They were used to boost global liquidity in 2009, but it is argued that ongoing applications should be made more practical. Several advisers in the US are keen on this approach because it provides an alternative to the dollar but does not give away too much influence as long as the US is still part of the pool. But many suggest that this could constitute a true single world currency and therefore is simply not practical: differential interest rates and selective monetary policies make it impossible and currency harmonisation cannot readily be implemented across countries at different stages of economic development. The considered view is that the IMF is not a super central bank and turning SDRs into a world currency is neither politically possible nor practical. In addition the likes of Martin Feldstein, Professor of Economics at Harvard University, have pointed out that the costs of such a single currency are greater than the benefits of the existence of hedging.

The third option for the third global reserve currency is the creation of what has been termed the Asian Currency Unit or the ACU. This is a basket of Asian currencies that are used not as the primary currency in each country but as a secondary parallel currency

for trade. Given the similarities to what happened in Europe in the late 1990s, many see that the ACU could be a precursor to a common future currency, just as the ECU was for the euro. However, this is not necessarily the case. The ACU is not implicitly linked to Asian monetary union, nor requires it, but is rather a means by which the Asian economies can take greater control of their world:

"If the Asian Development Bank takes the European model forward and creates a parallel currency that is a plural basket of national currencies, the Asian region as a whole will gain some decoupling from the US dollar. This will allow economic agents in the region to invoice financial and trade transactions in a common currency and reduce exchange rate risks as well as channel Asia's savings more efficiently within the region. As a regional benchmark, the ACU will help share the degree of divergence of each participating country's' currencies, which will improve the understanding of generic problems in a particular currency's market and in pursuing macroeconomic policies."

A key question here is whether the ACU would require all nineteen ASEAN countries to participate from the start, or whether it would be more pragmatic to begin with the four big economies – China, India, Japan and South Korea – and then add in more as others gain stability. This would essentially copy the good aspects of the ECU, beginning with the strongest economies without trying to include everyone too soon. It is clear that the concept of the ACU has wide-ranging appeal and benefit, but is also evident that politics could get in the way – especially between China and the other major regional economies. However, given that the alternative is to maintain the dollar as the global currency, with ever-rising pressure on the system, some, but not all, see that by 2020 a more equable model, like the ACU, could well be in play.

Related insights

Page 99

Page 193

Page 243

The future of happiness

As the third of the health, wealth and happiness trio, the topics covered in this cluster address a wide range of possible changes for the next decade. The future of happiness can stretch across a broad spectrum. At one extreme, we can see the impact of societal change that will probably affect all of us as the evident demographic shifts around population growth and ageing are played out. At the other, there are issues that will be very personal in terms of our individual choices around enjoying the life we have, connecting with others and being part of communities that we opt into. In the middle, there are probable changes on the horizon that revolve around some of the choices that governments, companies and social networks may make for us, to which we may as individuals all respond in desired or unexpected ways. In the discussions that led to the selection of the eight topics in this cluster, there were many who see the future as being less happy than today overall; but, on balance, there were slightly more who felt that, with everything that is likely to occur, the world of 2020 could be a happier place.

The topics covered in the following pages are:

Active elderly

Choosing God

Cocktail identities

Enjoying the ordinary

Less variety

Live experiences

Seamless media consumption

Switching off

Active elderly

Wealthier, healthier older people increasingly engage in more active lives having extended careers and becoming more politically involved.

According to the World Health Organization (WHO), by 2020 there will be over a billion elderly people on the planet with 700 million of these in the developing world. In China the proportion of elderly people is on course to double in a period of just thirty years between 2000 and 2030: In France a similar increase took 115 years. In the US, researchers expect the number of people over 65 to move from just under 40 million today to pass 70 million by 2030. Although, as life expectancy continues to lengthen, the number of very old people will rise and so the burden on healthcare systems will increase, for the 55 to 75 age group, improved healthcare and healthier living will result in more active lives than preceding generations. Active ageing is on the rise and, with it, some fundamental changes in society, ranging from employment and parenting to leisure and politics. By 2020, some see that 55 will be the new middle age and many of us will lead independent active lives until our late seventies.

By 2020 there will definitely be a greater proportion of older workers in the workforce than today: experience will be valued as well as economic contribution. Organisations are increasingly aware of the loss of collective memory that occurs when people retire and some, such as P&G, General Mills, Eli Lilly and Boeing, have been using programmes such as yourencore.com to tap into this resource.

Experience will be valued as well as economic contribution.

At the same time, attitudes to continued work are shifting, with up to half of employees increasingly keen to keep working on a full- or part-time basis after retirement age. Third-generation career workers are regarded as knowledgeable, flexible and experienced workers and are rising higher on the wish-list of many organisations. So we can clearly expect continued participation beyond 65 to be on the agenda for more employers by 2020.

What makes this pretty well certain in many countries is the economic pressure to keep people working, delay retirement and so reduce the pension gap. At the extreme in Japan, with an ageing population and one of the lowest birth rates in the world, the number of workers is on course to reduce from 66 million to 56 million over the next twenty years. With gross government debt heading towards 250% of GDP by 2015, Japan clearly needs people to stay in work and remain economically active for longer. Many other developed economies face a similar, though not so extreme, situation. In Germany, for instance, where the country's over-65 population is expected to double by 2035, the retirement age is rising from 64 to 67 starting in 2012 and politicians are talking

Men in their sixties and seventies are also becoming fathers partly because they can and more often because they want to.

about 70 as a long-term target; Taiwan recently increased its retirement age from 60 to 65; due to increasing debt, Greece is planning to shift its official retirement age from 61 to 63 by 2015; and even France is adding a couple of years to its pensionable age by 2018. In 2010, the UK government announced that, as well as bringing women into line with men in terms of working life, retirement age will increase to 66 by 2016, will go up to 68 by 2046 and may also hit 70 not long after that. Whether by desire or need, around the world, over the next decade being old will increasingly mean being economically active.

Beyond working, there are several other areas where there is clear evidence for more active elderly going forward. For instance, older parents: pregnancy over 50 has become increasingly possible thanks to advances in reproductive technology and IVF. Already in the UK there are over 20 births a year to women over 50 and in the US the figure is around 1,000 while in India in 2008 Omkari Panwar gave birth at 70 thanks to IVF. 'Men in their sixties and seventies are also becoming fathers partly because they can and more often because they want to.' Certainly in some markets, Viagra has increased the proportion of the elderly having active sex lives but also there is increasing evidence that more elderly divorced men are keen to start a family and begin again.

Attitudes among the over-sixties are also changing to make them socially more active and so more visible on many a corporate radar. Looking ahead, as the Generation X-ers become elderly, many do not expect their values and behaviours to change. Pensioners windsurf and go to Glastonbury, for example. One of the challenges being faced by many companies is how to market products and services to these people. With 70% of disposable wealth controlled by the over-fifties and more than 1 billion people over 60, companies will soon pay as much attention to understanding the different older groups as they have traditionally done to the under-thirties. The traditional stereotyping of old people as the grey market will be turned on its head as marketers focus more on where the money is. Around 90% of global advertising is currently aimed at the young and many in the industry see that the greater wealth in the older generations will lead to a shift towards seniors being as segmented a market as teenagers.

The active elderly are also becoming more engaged around global and local challenges. In the US there are already over 3 million people aged over 65 taking part in voluntary activities in educational, political and religious organisations. More children are being looked after at key times by their grandparents and, in many parts of the world where migration has separated families, surrogate grandparenting

Companies will soon pay as much attention to understanding the different older groups as they have traditionally done to the under-thirties.

roles are increasingly being taken by active elderly neighbours. In the world of politics, Italian Prime Minister, Silvio Berlusconi, is 74 while Indian Prime Minister, Manmohan Singh, is 78 and there are a host of other government posts around the world being taken by people well past their official retirement age. In some cultures the old have always been respected for their experience and wisdom; in others the ambition and willingness of the active elderly to continue to make a contribution to public life is gaining ground.

Lastly, the seniors of tomorrow will also be more technologically literate than those of today. While around 20% of people in their fifties in developed economies regularly use the internet, as today's middle aged become elderly and connectivity increases, some expect to see even more frequent use. The over-55 group is currently the fastest-growing segment on Facebook and, with more

The over-55 group is currently the fastest growing segment on Facebook.

access to technology and more experience, some see a reducing digital divide between the young and the old in the future.

In many countries, the average pension of the past was designed to last around ten years, as life expectancy was typically around 73. With average life expectancy already approaching 80 in some regions, the 65-year-olds of 2020 may well have twenty years ahead of them. Being more economically active for longer is an increasing certainty for many, but it is highly probable that the elderly will also be more socially and politically active than ever over the next decade.

Related insights

Page 49

Page 65

Page 69

Page 77

Page 227

Choosing God

The increasing fragmentation of society and looser connection between religion and the state in some regions sees more of us turning to God.

There has always been a desire to counterbalance choice and individual responsibility with a sense of moral certainty. As John Micklethwait and Adrian Wooldridge point out in their book, *God is Back*: 'In a world of ever greater competition displacement and opportunity, faith has become a useful attribute for prosperous people. But religion also fulfils a role lower down in society providing support for those who have lost out in global capitalism or feel bewildered by it.' This may well explain why, across the globe, belief in God is on the increase.

Christianity and Islam are the two global religions and in the 20th century Islam has done much better than Christianity in the popularity stakes. The Muslim population has grown from 200 million in 1900 to 1.5 billion today. In comparison, Christianity has declined in the centre (there are more Catholics in the Philippines than there are in Italy) but extended into new geographies, particularly South America. Islam on the other hand is resurgent across the Arab world and some Christian scholars predict that it will overtake Christianity as the world's biggest religion by 2050. Muslim countries are also profoundly Muslim in a way that Christian countries are not – according to Pews Global Attitudes Survey, 99% of Indonesians and 98% of Egyptians say religion plays an important role in their daily lives. That is not to say that the global spread of American-style Evangelical Christianity has failed to have impact.

Indeed, Pentecostal denominations, including charismatics, are the world's fastest-growing religious movements, now comprising one-quarter of the world's Christian population compared with just 6% thirty years ago. According to the World Christian Encyclopedia, about 17 million Africans described themselves as born-again Christians in 1970. Today the figure has soared to more than 400 million, or over one-third of Africa's population. Even in China, a state historically tied to secularism, religion plays an important role, with 31% of the population regarding it as 'very' or 'somewhat' important in their lives and only 11% stating that it is not at all important. Europe alone is wrapped in secularism, with only 21% of Europeans saying religion is very important to them, and this number would be even lower if the migrant population was taken out of the equation – in London 44% of the people going to church are African or Afro-Caribbean.

There are numerous reasons for the rise in spiritual belief. In a world where millions are separated from their homes and find themselves in unfamiliar environments with very different cultural norms, religion offers a sense of security, continuity and purpose. Certainly it provides an anchor for the millions of migrants who are leaving their traditional villages for the new mega-cities. Large numbers of young men, who come to the towns looking for work, have few other traditional structures to keep

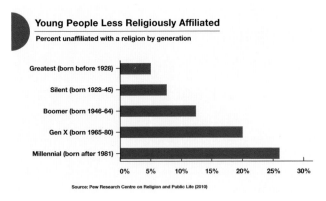

Young People Less Religiously Affiliated

Percent unaffiliated with a religion by generation

Greatest (born before 1928)
Silent (born 1928-45)
Boomer (born 1946-64)
Gen X (born 1965-80)
Millennial (born after 1981)

0% 5% 10% 15% 20% 25% 30%

Source: Pew Research Centre on Religion and Public Life (2010)

benefiting from the spread of Christianity, saying that: 'from the perspective of human society the most successful model is church + market economy. That is to say, the happy combination of a market economy that discourages idleness together with a strong faith (ethics) that discourages dishonesty and injury.' Xiao's assertion is that Christianity is a sign of higher ideas and progress and that spiritual wealth and material wealth go together. Certainly the growth in the Christian fellowship is noticeable. According to the latest surveys done by China Partner and East China Normal University in Shanghai, there are now between 39 and 41 million Protestants in China – a rise from 14 million in 1997. It should also be noted that China is not just open to Christian philosophies; it actually has as many Muslims as Saudi Arabia and nearly twice as many as the entire EU. By 2050, China could have the world's biggest Muslim and biggest Christian populations.

There seems to be an inverse relationship between the generosity of the welfare state and the success of religion. As the state takes on more responsibility for health, education and so on, the need for religious-based activities declines. This may be an additional reason why religion is enjoying growth in many developing countries which are too needy to afford Europe's welfare provision or are philosophically disinclined towards a state welfare model – China and South Korea in particular. Religious philanthropy is not exclusive to any one faith – Christians are to be found feeding the poor but the Taliban also use social welfare as way of engaging with the local population – for example, by funding and stocking hospitals with medical supplies. In general, however, this approach may also shed light on why more wealthy countries with a strong welfare state are generally more secular – take France, for example.

them under control. This is also true for the Muslim population in Europe, which looks set to continue its growth trajectory given the challenges at home and the opportunities in the West. However, the situation is problematic because, although the chances of work in their country of origin may well be limited, many Muslims coming from Europe's southern borders find life difficult: not only are they shocked by the liberalism they find in the European capitals but also they can feel marginalised and isolated as many of them have to pick up the low-skilled or short-term jobs that Europeans don't want any more. Religion provides an alternative to the difficulties they are faced with and offers hope for the future.

From a practical perspective religion can act as an informal club. Signs of religious commitment are generally speaking hard to fake and so provide a reliable signal to others; this produces trust and so makes business easier to transact. This is having an impact in surprising places. In a recent paper, Zhao Xiao, Professor of International Business Economics at Beijing University, argues that China's economy is

Attending religious services weekly rather than not at all has the same effect on happiness as moving from the bottom quartile to the top quartile of overall income distribution.

Although the implications for society of increased interest in religion are huge, there was agreement throughout our discussions that the topic is not often given the significance it deserves. Indeed, quite the reverse. The tide is however turning and the secular institutions are beginning to acknowledge the issue. Until recently, secular-minded governments have tried to keep faith out of state institutions but the rise in religion may mean that many of the electorate want their faith to guide those institutions – and the politicians that run them. This debate is building momentum in primarily Muslim countries like Syria and Egypt, but expect it to affect Europe and the US too – anywhere, in fact, where there is a significant and growing religious population. In addition to migration, the internet and new methods of evangelical practice means that today's world is no longer divided into geographical areas where one faith or another predominates.

Some suggest that the rise of political Islamism, particularly in its extreme form, has prompted a backlash against all religions – and, indeed, it is true that religion is now often blamed for many of the problems we face as a society, stretching from the issues in the Middle East to localised community problems in areas such as Bradford in England or the Parisian suburbs. Certainly religion can be used as a rallying cry for those disenfranchised by their current environments but it's also worth remembering that religion has also inspired many to stand up and defend society against totalitarian states – take, for example, the Saffron Revolution in Myanmar.

Perhaps the increase in religious belief is ultimately driven by the simple wish to be happy. Faith, after all, is a powerful generator of social capital and there is a marked correlation between religion, health and happiness. Pew shows that Americans who attend religious services once or more times a week are happier (43% very happy) than those who do not. This trend has been fairly steady since Pew started the survey in the 1970s and is more robust than the link between happiness and wealth. In fact, 'attending religious services weekly rather than not at all has the same effect on happiness as moving from the bottom quartile to the top quartile of overall income distribution' and, as Micklethwait and Wooldridge point out, it is a lot easier to do. Small wonder more people are trying it.

Related insights

Page 125

Page 171

Page 197

Cocktail identities

The need to differentiate between real and virtual disappears: who you are ceases to be a singular identity as we each have a multiple 'cocktail identity' portfolio.

As the world becomes increasingly 'always on' and 'always connected' a growing number of us manage our time by developing 'multiple identities' which are variously used across our work and social lives. It is quite common today for one individual to have several e-mail addresses – one for work, another for home and another tied into one or more social networks; we could also have a couple of phone numbers and several profiles on Twitter, Facebook and the like. Looking forward, as the number of forms of who we are and groups we may belong to increases, we can expect things to get even more complex. While some see a single universal persona existing across multiple platforms and social interactions, others see a far more fragmented approach being taken. Whatever the case, the growing challenge lies in understanding which or who is the real you.

As Professor Mike Hardy of the British Council highlighted in his initial view on the future of identity:

"The 'dealing-with-multiple-identities' challenge is likely to become more complex and more significant. As our world becomes smaller through migration and mobility, both virtual and real, it may be that people and groups will express themselves more insistently through multiple rather than single identity lenses. So it will be the particular ingredients of the 'cocktail identity' (the combination of personas and their consequences) which will be the more significant. How will we protect and respect apparently contradictory and multiple identities? Will it be through identity personas that we define or will it be from an integrated set of values?"

In one workshop, the comment was made that 'Facebook and similar social networks allow people to customise multiple online identities around themselves – it is becoming the norm'. In another this was brought to life by a 14-year-old girl who had twenty-seven Facebook profiles, and this was seen to be typical in her peer group: one was the profile that her parents and teachers could see and the one that in four years' time would be visible to the universities she hoped to attend; another was specifically for interacting with her school friends and yet another was how she kept her relations back in Pakistan updated. While these three all provided different takes on the same person and were clearly designed to share different aspects of her life to target audiences, her other twenty-four profiles were all made up and ranged from a 14-year-old boy to a 25-year-old woman. Essentially these are social experiments in which, for instance, she is pretending to be a 16-year-old in San Francisco, a 20-year-old in Paris or just someone else she has dreamt up who lives in her street. The girl in question is quite clear which is the real her and which is make-believe, but

This was brought to life by a 14-year-old girl who had twenty-seven Facebook profiles, and this was seen to be typical in her peer group.

how can anyone in the outside world see who she actually is? If a company wanted to market products to her, then which of her multiple identities would they focus on? As she and similar people go to university and enter the workplace, will they have more or fewer identities? Will managing so many fake identities become too exhausting? Will they all merge into one cocktail or will they be kept separate as multiple parallel faces to the world?

If this is not complicated enough, then we also have an underpinning shift occurring in some areas as a consequence of rising migration: as Mike Hardy also suggested, 'as the diaspora space grows, it provides a link between identity, history and now. … Identity in a diaspora space or location develops as an ongoing process that can change with situations and experiences'. As people move from one country to another, they retain their homeland identity but also merge it with their new home – and so become Italian-American or London-Irish. Sometimes this shift happens quickly but not always. One comment from the programme pointed out that 'identity across borders is the true need'. Another highlighted this well in that 'in France we have a broad influx of North African migrants that gradually assume a Moroccan-French, Tunisian-French or similar identity. But this typically takes three or four generations to develop. Yes, we may become Parisian more quickly than that, but, at a fundamental level, I see that

national identity is something we hold on to for as long as possible. Children may be comfortable with being foremost Parisian, but they will still talk more about their grandparent's heritage two or three generations after moving to France.' Going forward, as people from different nations move around and settle a long way from their homeland, the diaspora mix will increase and with it the associated influence on our self-identity.

We also have to consider the impact of increasingly global common interest groups with which people align their priorities. Whether cause-related (eg, Greenpeace), belief based (eg, Christian, Islamic) sports oriented (eg, Boston Red Sox) or lifestyle driven (eg, spiritual, organic food or gay), the growth of the internet has enabled people all over the world to connect and become a community. Many of the connections between the new tribes and clans are increasingly cross-border in nature and influence and so are adding another dimension to the growing identity smorgasbord that we can assemble.

Looking at the decade ahead, people have had alternative views of how this could all play out. At one extreme, some see that we will have the option to inhabit a world where multiple faces to external communities are presented as a coherent mix: in the 'youniverse', everything that can be is centred around the individual. Networks, information, identities and

Identity in a diaspora space or location develops as an ongoing process that can change with situations and experiences.

In the 'youniverse', everything that can be is centred around the individual. Networks, information, identities and relationships are all presented and seen solely through the lens of personal proximity and influence.

relationships are all presented and seen solely through the lens of personal proximity and influence. As was suggested in an LA workshop, 'developments such as Facebook Connect and Opengraft will aggregate your "likes" and make your identity more portable'. At the other end of the spectrum, some see further fragmentation of identity on the horizon to a point where we manage our relationships, interests and

hence our multiple identities in isolation of each other. The coherence is less visible to others, and even to ourselves, but, at heart, still represents an amalgam of who we are.

Cocktail identities are here today and highly likely to increase in the future in both nature and scope. Alongside the identities we create and manage, whether in the real world or online, additional layers based on what others think and say about who we are, what we think and what we do will increasingly be publicly available: professional and amateur critiques on top of and around the real you.

And so we are left with a two-part question. Will we continue to be happy with this cocktail of information about who we are? Or, would it be easier and make us happier to simply consolidate each of our multiple identities back into one and so rediscover the 'real me'?

Related insights

Page 145

Page 197

Page 209

Enjoying the ordinary

Growing satisfaction with the basics of life focuses more on making the most of the day-to-day and increasingly valuing the ordinary.

Even before the economic downturn in Europe and the US that started in 2008, there were several signals that more people in these regions were seeking a less complicated life. As one participant commented: 'After fifty years in a consumer bubble, maybe it is time we again focus on what is really important.' Allied to this, some research shared at one of the early workshops pointed to a shift in attitudes. Europe is going back to basics – but with a twist. From restaurants to holidays, to the simple day-to-day activities like catching a bus, in developed societies there is notable momentum building towards placing a greater value of the ordinary. As austerity measures introduced into the same countries start to bite, some see that, rather than fighting against the economic necessity, many will embrace the opportunity to drop down a gear or two and enjoy the simpler times. This is certainly not currently on the radar in fast-growing emerging economies – where more, not less, is often the priority for many – but some see that this attitude shift may spread as people embrace a more sustainable and more holistic view of life.

At one level, this is fuelled by the continuing interest in the past, albeit a rose-tinted view. Traditional living in terms of values, design and food has been a growing aspiration over the past few years. The widespread popularity of Shaker kitchens, the global success of simple Scandinavian and Japanese product design and the organic food phenomenon can all, in varied ways, be seen as ingredients in enjoyment of the ordinary. Equally, the popularity of organisations such as the Scouts and the enthusiasm for growing your own vegetables also point to a rising interest in the basics. In elements of society today, some commentators see this as a counterpoint to numerous fake, artificial and virtual worlds that we are being presented with. In addition, the continued pressure to perform is seen by many as 'an enemy of happiness' and they hark back to less intense times. But, in doing this, people want to 'connect with a reassuring reality in a non-romanticised way' and often with elements of modern convenience mixed in. So we can, for example, see the return to camping holidays but with extra comforts: from Mongolian yurts in Switzerland to eco-lodges in Portugal and rustic villages in Spain, 'glam camping' is a growing vacation option. Within the online world we can also see fascination in the everyday: already many people use Facebook, Twitter and personal blogs as online diaries and record the most banal comments with an unsentimental focus evoking a 'nothing much happening' view of the world.

Following varied discussions, what appears to be on the horizon for the next decade are two main shifts in attitudes – an increasing backlash against excess

As an increasing majority take satisfaction in 'lagom' or 'just enough', people are beginning to focus on living more sustainable lives.

and a change in the perception of 'ordinary'. While pay restraint, higher taxes and reduced access to easy cash across Europe are now increasingly certain, many believe that the backlash against excess was already building ahead of the austerity programmes that governments are now implementing to reduce debt. As an increasing majority take satisfaction in 'lagom' or 'just enough', people are beginning to focus on living more sustainable lives and use tried and trusted credentials, such as local and familiar, to reinforce the relevance of what is the ordinary day-to-day.

Because we live in an ever faster-moving and ever more virtual world, many more people are now craving a familiar routine. Although there are many benefits to the increasingly connected world, it means that our time does not need to be segmented in the same ways as before – for example, few knowledge workers have a nine-to-five job nowadays. This means, in its simplest form, many want to have a few normal routines in place – having regular meeting times, exercise programmes, social engagements and so on. They do this because it is getting increasingly difficult to fit 'normal' life into the day.

A major consequence of this could be that many will seek to give the ordinary greater value – and in so doing, of course, making it less ordinary! Arguably this is already happening in some sectors (luxury camping, for example), but also consider the way food and drink can be made more ordinary yet can be given a premium value at the same time – it's perfectly possible to pay a small fortune for that English staple of sausage and mash at any number of 'gastro pubs' across the British countryside.

By 2020, several consumer insight experts see that much higher value is expected to be placed on the ordinary and 'premiumisation' is one route through which this can be expressed and communicated. People already pay a premium for the more authentic product or experience. Looking ahead, this could equally apply to the more basic alternatives. 'Ordinary basic interactions are important for many and connections become enhanced both by making them more special and/or more simple.' The disadvantage, of course, is that in the future the 'ordinary' may well only be accessible to those who are wealthy enough to pay for it.

A parallel issue is what is being termed 'slow luxury'. Fuelled partly by image and partly by the sustainability agenda, high-end products and services are focusing more on enjoying experiences for longer. As Mark Philips of Jaguar highlighted in his point of view on the future of transport:

"Luxury goods buyers, I believe, will want to have items that are visually more discreet. At the height of the credit crunch, shoppers on New York's 5th Avenue were

Many will seek to give the ordinary greater value – and in so doing, of course, making it less ordinary!

disguising their designer label purchases in brown bags – and this may not be a short-term fad. In other markets, we are leaving the era of buying disposable IKEA-esque goods and seeking items that offer longevity and quality – a future heirloom perhaps. This is, in some ways, a return to the values of previous generations."

If slow luxury seeks to further promote nostalgia then, as other segments of the market follow on, premiumisation of the ordinary may become even more widespread.

A big question about enjoying the ordinary as a long-term consumer shift is in its global vs. regional scope. Western Europe is seen as the heartland for this, and some suggest that this is because it is in Western Europe where economic growth is starting to plateau, society is increasingly comfortable with itself, and an increasingly secular population is taking a more responsible, sustainable focus on life. The Scandinavian view of the interplay between people and nature is often cited as a role model here but many see this spreading further: 'In Western Europe,

We are leaving the era of buying disposable IKEA-esque goods and seeking items that offer longevity and quality.

a desire for greater simplicity and more "me" and "us" time drives resurgence in the simple everyday.' Some experts, however, also point to similar attitudes emerging in parts of the US while others felt that 'enjoying the ordinary' is largely about adopting some core values that have somehow got lost in the economic scramble of the last few decades.

Maybe, as some have argued, a less consumerist, less consumption-based aspiration will evolve as a global ambition. The American Dream of economic prosperity leading to happiness could, by the end of the decade, be replaced by a more pragmatic goal of making the most of what you have.

Related insights

Page 121

Page 133

Page 137

Page 145

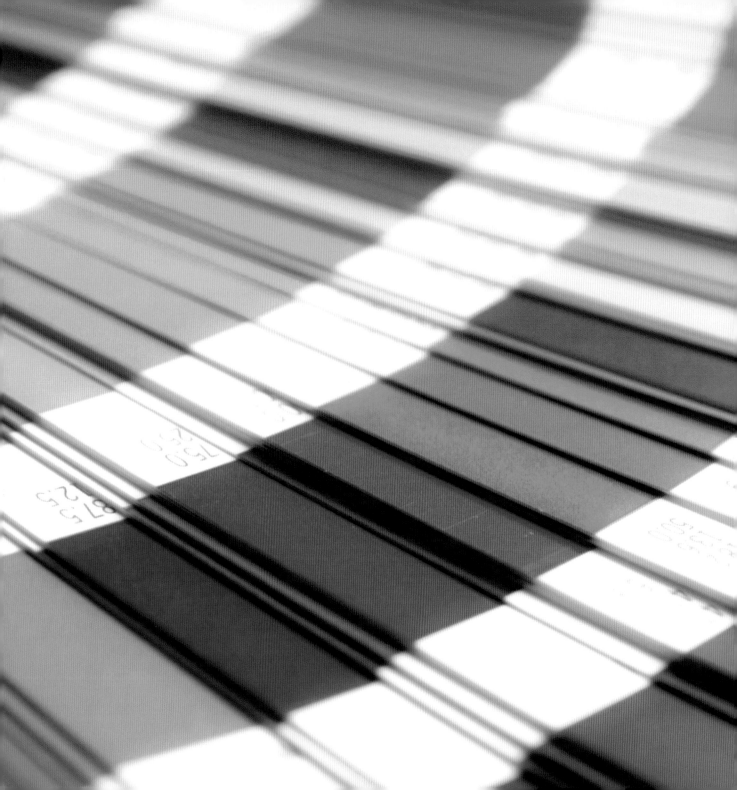

Less variety

The future of choice is about less variety, but not less interest, as retailers provide an increasingly edited portfolio through ever more efficient channels.

One of the most provocative initial viewpoints in the Future Agenda programme was that of the future of choice by Professor Jose Luis Nueno of IESE in Barcelona. In it he indicated that 'as China and India and other fast-developing economies become the primary global marketplaces, the needs and wishes of the 4 billion new consumers will dominate those of the 800 million old ones in the US and Europe. The days when the US set the pace in the consumer mindset are over and this is not going to change.'

In addition, he proposed that 'the realities of global trade are all too clear and we can see the end of variety. In fact we can see a changing balance between variety and cost. Consumers are making a trade-off in a smart way and cost is winning. We therefore face the challenge of how to deal with a reduction in the number of options in the categories of consumption but an expansion in the number of categories.' He also argued the case that 'fewer choices provide higher levels of satisfaction: people like to have lots of variety, but when faced with too many choices, we tend to vacillate and delay decisions. We may want thirty-one options instead of six, but we find it easier to choose one of six than one of thirty-one.'

In many subsequent workshops and discussions with food companies, retailers, media organisations and consumer product manufacturers, there was wide-

Consumers are making a trade-off in a smart way and cost is winning.

ranging debate and reaction to this suggestion. Some recognised that it might be true in certain fields, such as the automotive and fashion industries, but would not apply in areas like food and electronics. Others felt that outside the world of digital products and services, a shift to less, not more, choice is credible. Within this context, the future role of choice editors and choice curators became a strong area of discussion, and one that points to a future of more informed but reduced choice in many fields.

Some experts argued that consumers will always want more choice: 'We see more individualisation and more personalisation taking place in many sectors and this can only lead to more variety' was a typical comment. Especially in the West, it was argued a number of times, people have got used to having ever more variety and they are going to resist having it taken away from them. Also, some highlighted that, especially in China, the desire for labels and the latest products is in many ways already stronger within certain parts of the market than in the US: 'the Shanghai shopping experience is even wider that that in LA.' In many sectors, the market will be

New consumers will want access to new products in the most economical manner and if that means hypermarkets with less SKUs (stock-keeping units) than in the past then so be it.

driven by the consumer and increased consumption around the world will result in more products and hence more variety.

However, many others saw credibility in the argument that greater efficiency within the retail sector will inherently drive towards more effective discount stores providing lower cost products, but with less variety. This is already evident in food retailing with companies such as Aldi and Lidl, and in fashion with the likes of TK Maxx and Primark. The view that physical retailing will split between those focused on speed and those focused on cost was well supported: comments such as 'speed to market is the real challenge – it will be a key issue for many companies in the future and this will be a major battleground for capability' and 'cost is only important in low-innovation categories' highlight the crux of the issue. Fast fashion and its like across the retail sector has a clear place and will, for those able to execute it better that the rest, be a profitable route to follow. Equally, for the discount retailers with scale, and especially with the likely advent of an international 'Asian Aldi' in the next few years, the ability to give customers the basic products at low cost will be paramount. While the hangover from the downturn in the US and Europe could have an impact on this, the growth of the Asian

consumer was seen as more significant in this area: new consumers will want access to new products in the most economical manner and if that means hypermarkets with less SKUs (stock-keeping units) than in the past then so be it. The implicit impacts here are the continued importance of the choice editor and the end of the road for the middle ground. To be successful, both the fast change, high-innovation and the low-cost routes to retail require as small a selection of products as possible – but ones that people want.

As such, the role of the retail buyer as the 'choice editor' on behalf of the consumer is critical. The winners will be the ones who choose the right mix without misses. As one workshop participant put it:

"Going forward, they may want less choice but they will need to transfer their trust to the retail and product brands that best limit their choice. Consumers will want to trust more companies to make choices on their behalf and so choice editors will become more significant. Consumers will most likely trust the brands that make the more informed choice possible."

The role of the department store and its equivalent is therefore limited. Unless they can in themselves be the destination magnets and anchor brands that malls are built around, shops that offer a wider choice but at higher prices will, it was argued, have less impact in the future physical retail world.

In the online environment, where there is no apparent restriction on variety, many see continued expansion of choice. What Amazon has done for books and Rhapsody for music is seen as the business model of the next decade for many other areas. From B2B suppliers to holidays, the pivotal

Consumers will want to trust more companies to make choices on their behalf and so choice editors will become more significant.

issue will be recommendation of purchase from within a wider portfolio. As we tackle the challenge of 'a situation of over-supply where consumers are confused', the continued success of the customers-with-similar-searches-purchased type of approach is seen to be a successful recipe for the future as the successful companies curate rather than edit consumer choice.

Taking the 2020 view, there was another issue that was consistently seen as a catalyst for less variety. This is the increasingly influential sustainability agenda. At an event in the Netherlands we heard that: 'From a sustainability point of view, the less variety option must be the way to go. We can then optimise supply

chains and production for the core and make the non-core the expensive luxury that can subsidise others.' At another workshop it was stated that:

"If we want to encourage consumer choice to have a major role in changing the system, towards for example more sustainable living, then we need to both change the system and encourage the individual to make wiser decisions. The system needs to be changed by moving the boundary conditions to allow better, more informed, better incentivised individual decisions that enable the right thing. We need to start on small things while sharing more knowledge about the big things and their interdependencies."

Many agree that the combination of increasingly competitive business models, more efficient channels and a push on waste reduction, especially in the food industry, will drive the vast majority of us to a future of less variety. However, this does not mean less interest. Designing the next big thing for the next decade will be tougher than ever.

Related insights

Page 129

Page 145

Live experiences

The role of 'live' in an increasingly isolated world becomes more important to create moments for deeper, richer connections and social bonding.

Being part of the moment has always been special. A major international event such as the moon landing or, on a more personal level, a family wedding have been times when people want to collectively come together as part of the live experience. There is arguably nothing new in this and, in many ways, the desire to be part of an event has been steadily growing in line with TV access for many years. However, as more of us live alone and many work alone, we are, on average, spending less time interacting with others. Looking to the future, as virtual connections become more common than real ones, the opportunities to be part of something and share a moment in time with others will become increasingly important. Media companies are placing ever more focus on live events, music festivals and shows are enjoying increased popularity, and informal gatherings in general are on the rise. By 2020, many see that live experiences will be increasingly valuable to us as common touch points in our lives.

Traditionally, live events have either been organised around culture or sport and, in both of these areas, direct participation or involvement as part of the extended global viewing audience has clearly been growing. After the business model of the music industry was turned upside-down by downloading, attention swung back onto live performance. Organisations such as AEG and LiveNation have reinvented the music business model for venues and the top acts and created huge events where the performance, and not the music, is again the core source of revenues. At the same time, there has been a significant growth in live music festivals around the world – from opera to rock. More music events took place in 2009 than ever before and, in the UK, in 2010 there were over seventy rock, folk and jazz festivals in the month of July alone.

In sport, where the physical space in an arena is the limiting factor, being part of the event via the radio, TV or online has always been big but it is also growing steadily. Events such as the Super Bowl attract over 100 million American viewers but this is dwarfed by more international occasions. The 2006 World Cup Final was watched by around 700 million people (one in ten of the world's population) and it is claimed by FIFA that the audience for the 2010 Final reached 800 million. Over half the world's population regularly tune in to the Olympics and the opening ceremony of the 2008 Beijing Olympics is the most watched event to date.

But it is not just sport and culture that people want to be part of. Major news stories attract huge international audiences as stories unfold and people want to be part of the event. On July 20, 1969, over 600 million people watched the Apollo 11 moon landing. The splash-down of Apollo 13 and the funeral of Diana, Princess of Wales, are among the other most notable global news events: the funeral of Princess Diana was watched by 2 billion people around the world. In the US, historically, presidential debates have also drawn large audiences similar to those for other special broadcasts such as the Academy Awards. The most-watched debate so far occurred in the third and final exchange between George Bush, Bill Clinton and Ross Perot in 1992, when more than 97 million viewers tuned in. Around 10 million people watched Britain's first televised election debate in 2010. As 24/7 news channels such as CNN, BBC World, Al Jazeera and their ilk have grown beyond TV and now operate across multiple digital platforms, immediate access to breaking news has become a common expectation, but one which, with the addition of Twitter, blogs and Facebook, is increasingly becoming a shared live experience.

However, in many eyes, the most successful live experience of recent years in purely commercial terms has been the rise of reality TV, from *Big Brother* to *Pop Idol*. Television networks love reality TV because it is a good way to maximise profit. Shows with high ratings earn millions in advertising and they are also largely cheap to make: because reality TV shows are unscripted, networks realise huge savings because they do not have to pay writers. Furthermore, these shows can be easily franchised around the world. According to the *Guinness Book of World Records*, *Strictly Come Dancing* is the world's most successful reality TV format: the BBC has sold the show to 38 countries around the world. The *Pop Idol* format was franchised to 35 while *X Factor* has now reached 26 countries – ranging from the US and Europe to Colombia to Morocco to Russia. In the UK, reality programmes like *I'm a Celebrity ... Get*

Live experiences will be the moments when brands come to life and touch people in new ways.

Me Out of Here! and *X Factor* regularly attract an audience of over 10 million – over one-third of the national audience. In the US, at times, *American Idol* has attracted over 50% market share. Reality shows are big not just because they make money, but also because they create and exploit the immediacy of the event. As such they attract a wide range of audiences: one recent report highlighted that for girls aged between 12 and 17 years old, three out of four of their favourite television shows were reality TV shows.

Alongside formal events, there has also been recent growth of 'grapevine gatherings'. One of the most notable trends of the past few years has been the rising popularity of flash mobs, where a large group of people assemble suddenly in a public place, perform an 'unusual and pointless act' for a brief time, then disperse. The first flash mob was created in Manhattan in May 2003 by Bill Wasik, senior editor of *Harper's Magazine*. Word about a flash mob is now spread via social networking sites, private blogs, public forums, personal websites, as well as by word of mouth, text messaging and email. According to Wikipedia: 'The largest pillow fight flash mob was the Worldwide Pillow Fight Day that took place on March 22, 2008. Over twenty-five cities around the globe participated in the first "international flash mob", which was the world's largest flash mob to date. According to the *Wall Street Journal*, more than 5,000 participated in New York City, overtaking

London's 2006 Silent Disco gathering as the largest recorded flash mob.' Other notable significant flash mobs included a Michael Jackson tribute in Stockholm, a *Sound of Music* routine in Antwerp railway station and a multi-country dance as part of Eurovision 2010. While some see these as increasingly commercial gimmicks, others highlight them as phenomena that show that people increasingly want to be part of something.

Social commentators have expressed many views on why these varied live experiences are growing in importance to us – from needing to feel part of the story to having something to discuss with friends through to believing that they are involved are all perspectives. However, several people have commented about the role of live experiences, and especially TV-based ones, in connecting lonely people with a surrogate family. In a comment reminiscent of the *Truman Show*, one workshop participant mentioned anecdotal evidence that one of the peak times for viewing of a recent series of *Big Brother* was at 3.00 am in the morning when everyone was asleep: people simply had the show on for company. Given that more of us live alone, so the argument goes, more of us will embrace the opportunity for being part of the live experience no matter how dull that may be.

Living alone, and therefore the possibility of loneliness, is certainly something to consider. In the UK, already more than 10% of people aged between 22 and 44 live by themselves, compared with 2% in 1973, and over 37% of all UK households are expected to be 'solo' by 2020. Interestingly, young men are more likely to live alone than young women – 15% of men aged 25 to 44 compared with 8% of women. Women generally tend to live alone when they grow older. About 27 million Americans lived alone in 2000, accounting for about 26% of all households and nearly one in ten of the overall US population. By 2020, solo living in the US will account for nearly 30% of homes. In Japan over one-third of households will be composed of people living alone by 2020. Even in Australia, forecasts predict up to 20% of the population living alone. These shifts, it is argued, will increase the need for more people to connect with others at key points and hence the rise in more live moments.

Today we can already see the crossover between live and virtual experiences. As we move forward, many expect that these will blur to a point where the two become merged. 'Live experiences will be the moments when brands come to life and touch people in new ways.' So seeking to create a live experience to drive the brand will be a key challenge for many companies and not just those within the entertainment sector. More organisations will seek to monetise this and, following on from the precedents in the music sector, business models will be reinvented to make live the exclusive premium pay-for event supported by free 'virtual' access for those who can't be there.

Related insights

Page 129

Page 141

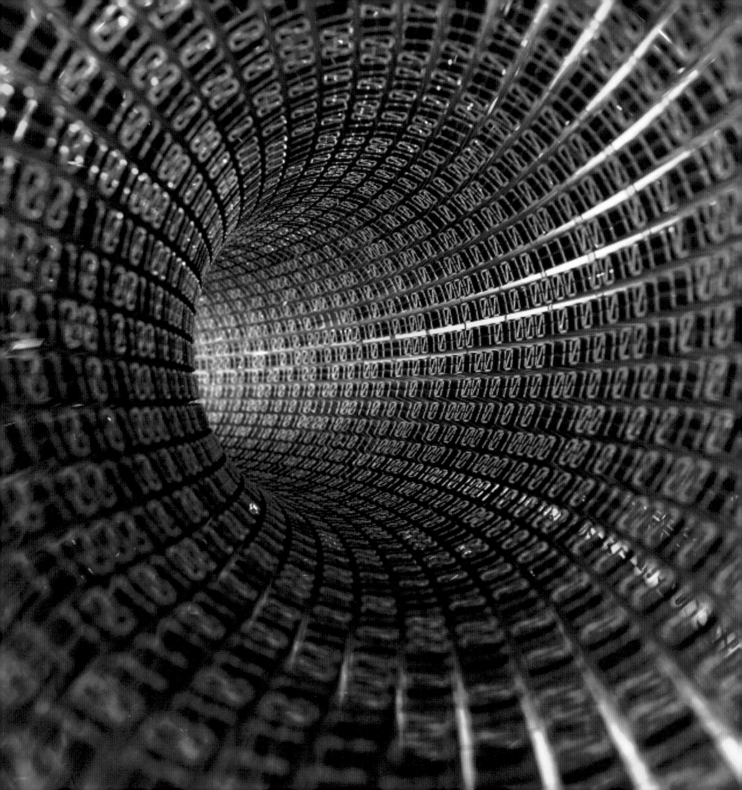

Seamless media consumption

Multiple media sources are instantly integrated at the point of consumption to provide us with immersive access to tailored, bite-sized content.

How we access and consume information has undergone rapid change over the past few years. The rise of platforms including Google, YouTube, Netflix, Facebook, Twitter and the BBC iPlayer as well as the introduction of new devices such as net-books, IPTV, the iPhone and the iPad have all fundamentally affected how many of us now use and interact with media. Given that all of these appeared in the last decade, as we look forward to 2020, many expect even greater change as the acceleration of new technologies increases.

While some of the new platforms and devices that will have an impact are yet to be invented, many others are already in development and being planned for mainstream rollout. As such, there are several impending shifts already visible as we look at the future of media creation, sharing and consumption. How quickly they will occur and in what specific areas are open to debate and potential influence by existing media organisations, but the effects they will have over the next ten years are becoming clear. In recent times, the concept of seamless consumption has been much hyped as an impending reality but has yet to be delivered. It now appears that many of the key technologies and business models to enable it to happen are all starting to align: the *Wired* magazine app on the iPad, which allows intuitive browsing between text, video and image manipulation, is a leading signal of where we are heading. Research at MIT's Media Lab and multiple TED presentations also focus on how options for consumption are changing.

A future in which we can all access a host of alternative media sources as we switch between many different devices from multiple sources in a smooth and seamless manner is increasingly evident. By 2020, this will be ubiquitous and the norm for many of us: our PCs, mobiles and TVs will have merged and become integrated with a host of new devices that allow us to access a global library of information and data. Everything that has ever been filmed, written, created or captured will be organised and indexed automatically and be available to us all. All content, including that which has just been created, will be tagged and available to be shared by anyone and everyone through fully open data archives. Initially

All content, including that which has just been created, will be tagged and available to be shared by anyone and everyone through fully open data archives.

led by public broadcasters but capitalised on by new text, image and video search engines, the web will automatically organise the most relevant material for us. TV feeds, amateur video, relevant text and data will all be auto-assembled for us and around us with the final edit taking place at the point of consumption. Everyone will have a continuously updated, unique and tailored mix of different media that gives each of us exactly the information we want.

Talking to the experts in the space, not only will we be presented with this constantly evolving mix of content, but augmented video and text will provide additional information as a layer on device screens and within holographic projections. Seamless media access and consumption will, it is predicted, be a richer and deeper, more tailored experience. While a good proportion of us will still want the sit-back-and-relax passive consumption as opposed to the more interactive and participative option, how and what we consume will become more sophisticated and less linear. Your TV will instinctively know your preferences (and favourites) and so sense and suggest similar and new material to best fit your mood. We will access information not via a remote control, touch pad or mouse, but by using gestures very similar to those seen in the movie *Minority Report* and already being introduced in a simpler form by Xbox. Images, video and data will be gathered, selected, explored and shared intuitively in 3D and provide you with a fully immersive experience – if you so desire. In many ways the distinction between content forms will break down completely as all media sources, from TV, film and radio to news, blogs and networks, are integrated and cross-linked. Bite-sized, tagged segments of video, audio and text will be reassembled for you and by you around topics of interest.

The role of media companies will shift from one of being creators, commissioners, editors and schedulers of their broadcast content to being curators of everyone's material.

As all this technology is integrated to allow the constantly evolving and seamless access to information of all sorts, the business models of the organisations which provide the source material will be radically altered. Just as the fundamental dynamics of the music industry were reinvented in the past few years, so over the next few will many parts of the rest of the media industry. In the TV industry, the role of media companies will shift from one of being creators, commissioners, editors and schedulers of their broadcast content to being curators of everyone's material. They will provide viewers with access to a recommended repertoire of constantly evolving content drawn from their own and other companies' catalogues and mixed with increasingly sophisticated user-generated content. In many areas, the co-creation of material – where fans and the media industry reuse and reinterpret each other's content – will expand the 'pro-am' arena. Just as traditional A&R in the music industry has been replaced by the main labels tracking MySpace activity and signing up those acts that get 50,000 hits, so the wider media industry may shift its modus operandi. At the same time, increasingly demanding viewers will want guaranteed quality and relevance and so be prepared to pay for access to personalised sources for 'just the gems' – they will want all the highs and none of the lows and so the ability of many broadcasters to fill in the gaps between peak programmes with lower quality material will be taken away.

As the next generation of consumers becomes the focus and also takes control of the media industry, gaming will increasingly set the standards. The expectations set in the multi-player, highly participative, interactive $100 billion gaming industry, where integrated decision making, alternative outcomes and cross-referenced materials are the norm, will influence how the rest of the media industry thinks and behaves. Already we can see the influence of *Call of Duty*, *Grand Theft Auto* and *Halo* extending beyond the PC, PlayStation and Xbox into parallel worlds online as well as comment in the real world.

Gaming will increasingly set the standards.

By 2020, the gaming experience will be a standard expectation for many. Adverts will no longer be found in breaks or in separate areas but will be fully embedded into media content. Enabled by new digital platforms, personalised product placement will occur within, not outside, core media and so the business models for many media companies will fragment. Many see that the next decade will be a time of reinvention for the media industry and traditional players, mobile operators, new platforms and globally open sources of material will all compete and coalesce in new ways. One way or another 'seamless consumption' will be the way ahead.

Related insights

Page 91

Page 137

Page 145

Switching off

Being disconnected in an always connected world is a desire met by virtual cocoons at home but real physical solitude becomes an option only for the rich.

In one workshop it was highlighted that, in an ever-present always-connected world, people will sometimes want to disconnect, to switch off and be, for a time, not available. In another it was mentioned that for many professionals today, rather than talk to their spouse, the last thing they do at night and the first thing they do in the morning is check their mobile for messages. While some find this lifestyle attractive and in many ways addictive, for others it has become apparent that it is not healthy and there must be an alternative.

For numerous professionals and knowledge workers, being able to temporarily become isolated from the always-on world is therefore seen as a significant backlash against some of the technological and social advances of the last decade. Whether virtually or in real life, the ability to have a moment or two of solitude is destined to become a prized commodity – but one that, given current trends, becomes less available for many in 2020. As such, for those that can afford it, solitude becomes a luxury.

According to the OECD, the average South Korean works 2,074 hours each year or over 44 hours a week. While this is the extreme, in many countries we typically work over 40 hours and even in France, a country well known for its high living standards, there is a shift to increase the average up from their

We are filling our lives with more and therefore the option to have less is becoming a treasured ambition.

target 35 in order to improve productivity. The EU working time directive imposes a maximum working week of 48 hours everywhere except the UK, which opted out. Overall, the global picture is one where official data shows a slow decline in the time spent working, but in many of the knowledge-based service sectors off-the-clock emails, conference calls and weekend working are considered normal. What is surprising to some is that, even in our leisure time, many of us are choosing to be always connected. According to Nielsen, the average internet user in the US now spends over 70 hours a month online while the average Facebook user is on the site for over 7 hours per month. Generally speaking we are filling our lives with more and therefore the option to have less is becoming a treasured ambition. Time to stop and get away from things is consequently steadily rising up the work–life balance wish-list.

Although economic pressures in many countries mean that earning an income is not an option to be toyed with, there is mounting evidence that, given the

Time poverty is becoming as much a problem as money poverty.

choice, many workers would prefer extra holidays over extra money. Clearly this is not common globally across every demographic, but in many areas of the economy where the 'money rich/time poor' are present, this is a growing issue. For those who have high disposable incomes through well-paid employment but relatively little leisure time as a result, time poverty is a growing concern. But it is not only the rich: for some of those on low incomes who also endure long working hours, time poverty is becoming as much a problem as money poverty.

Looking ahead, to keep the best talent, some commentators feel that many companies' motivation and reward policies are being challenged to give hard-working employees extra time to be away from the office rather than a bonus to keep them at it. Some organisations predict that over the next decade we will increasingly see time traded for money: workers with unused holidays will sell them to those who want more time and open but informal trading of time off will increase – time itself will become a commodity. The hope, of course, is that this will lead to a healthier, happier and more committed workforce.

When those with the time and the money do go on holiday, the preferred options are increasingly either spa-based resorts or retreats where activities take you away from it all. With cheaper flights, access to centres of relaxation has become easier and visiting a spa has become an increasingly mainstream vacation ingredient – for men just as much as women. Several mainstream men's magazines and websites regularly feature top 10 spa lists and many see that this popularity is driven primarily by the desire to fully disconnect for a while.

However, for those times when a vacation is not an option and the desire for disconnecting for an hour or two rises, some notable developments are taking place. Second Life's virtual world, for example, provides approximately 18 million people with a means of escaping the real world for a while. Equally, and more significantly, there is the huge popularity of gaming. Online role-playing games like *World of Warcraft* regularly have over 10 million participants and also offer a way for many to switch off. Although relaxing for some, others see that these and similar high-impact virtual options are less about solitude, disconnecting and tranquillity and more about getting even more connected in a different world.

For those after controllable, real isolation, there are other options. A Faraday cage is an enclosure that cuts out electrical signals. It is often made from a perforated metal sheet or fine wire mesh that is part of an electric field that cuts down electromagnetic interference within the cage – either stopping outside signals getting in, or inside signals getting out. Traditionally used for computer test facilities and microwave ovens, over the years they have also been built into buildings where having communication with the outside world is undesirable. Dealing rooms and casinos are probably the most well-known applications but, as discussed in one workshop, they are also finding new ones closer to home. A number of private homes around the world are including rooms with in-built Faraday cages that can be switched on to create a space where no electronic communication can get in. Wifi, mobile connections as well as radio and TV signals are all blocked so that, within the room, occupants can really switch off. Not only are such rooms being built into new homes but do-it-yourself advice for building Faraday cages is starting to appear more and more on the internet. Although some may see this as a poor reflection on others' ability to simply switch off their mobile, it is notable how many recognise the issue and are being attracted by the opportunity to have an accessible sanctuary within the home.

Underlying this, one has to recognise that for many the ability to switch off and be temporarily alone is an increasingly scarce luxury. From an economic perspective, as highlighted above, some people do not have the money to be able to disconnect. From a social perspective, we are also seeing the growth in some regions of the multigenerational household: as lifespans are extended and out-patient care is improved, grandparents are around for longer. Equally, as rising house prices in many countries align with increasing costs of higher education, students

For many the ability to switch off and be temporarily alone is an increasingly scarce luxury.

are staying at home for longer. After half a century of families becoming more geographically dispersed, in some areas cohabitation in more crowded homes is increasing and, with it, fewer opportunities for solitude.

Whether through such physical alternatives as electronic isolation or seeking more so-called 'quality time', it is clear that a good proportion of the working population want a bit more solitude. Whether people want more privacy, to be fully alone or to be with family and friends, it is evident that the desire to be disconnected in an always-connected world is on the increase. How far we will have gone by 2020 is open to debate, but the ingredients for change for some are all becoming aligned.

Related insights

Page 125

Page 129

Page 141

The future of mobility

There is little doubt that over the next decade there will be increased mobility. Although in some areas less travel is possible, people and things overall will be moving around the globe further and faster. The future of transport and the future of migration were two of the initial perspectives in the Future Agenda programme that attracted a great deal of discussion and feedback from all over: from Brussels to Melbourne, from Shanghai to Rome and from Delhi to Washington, everyone has strong opinions about what should happen. However, what will happen in the future of mobility over the next decade will, for some, not be the end point but more of a transition. Especially in the transportation arena, the future of 100% clean mobility is considered to be further out than 2020, but some of the main ingredients of this are coming together and will be increasingly evident in the next few years. One notable feature of some of the probable futures explored here is the pivotal role of China – in planes, trains and automobiles. In addition, there is an underlying driver of economic wealth that will be both enabling investment in new systems but also causing increasing migration and mobility of people. Within the myriad conversations, the eight probable futures selected here were the ones that had the greatest potential impact for the next decade.

The topics covered in the following pages are:

Asian aviation

Chinese trains

Clean shipping

Electric mobility

Intelligent highways

Muslim Europe

People tracking

Urban (im)mobility

Asian aviation

Led by more tourists and steady growth in cargo transportation, Asian aviation places more orders and becomes the largest air market in the world.

In terms of flying, we live in a world at a point of significant change: around half of us have just started to recognise that we need to travel less at the same time as the other half want to travel more. Overall, rising demand from both low-cost and premium passengers keen to fly more shows little sign of abating in the next decade. Add in increased air freight and there is little doubt that the number of passenger and cargo air miles flown will rise year by year through to 2020 and beyond. The International Air Transport Association projects that the number of passenger departures each year globally will rise from 2.3 billion in 2009 to 16 billion by 2050. Although much of this growth can be seen to be global, with the US continuing to play a major role, Asia will be the most significant source of air transport expansion – and many of the orders for the planes that will deliver this have already been placed.

While the aviation industry has been under scrutiny in many countries on account of its carbon emissions, as a sector it is only responsible for around 2% of the carbon released into the atmosphere. Despite the industry's stated ambition to cap emissions by 2050, the reality is that very little of note can actually be done by 2020. This is because, firstly, the average plane is in service for around thirty years and so the cycle time to change the fleet is too long – both Airbus and Boeing are already selling more efficient planes, such as the A380 and the Dreamliner, but it will take several decades before all of the old models have been replaced with modern ones. Secondly, there are currently few technology options open to the aviation sector for reducing emissions. Any major innovation in aircraft propulsion units is many years away, so the only change that can be implemented during our time horizon is to introduce bio-fuels into the aviation fuel mix. Even with this shift, it is very unlikely that aircraft across the whole sector will be run on 100% bio-fuel any time soon, so most experts in the industry are planning for an extremely gradual shift – and hence the 2050 targets. Unlike other modes of transport, it is therefore unlikely that there will be any significant platform change by 2020.

The major difference we will see a decade from today will be the sheer number of planes in the skies, moving ever more people and goods around by air between growing numbers of airports. Given the nature of the lead times in the aviation sector, this can be guaranteed – the orders for the next decade are already with the manufacturers.

Both Airbus and Boeing release twenty-year projections for the sector which provide some salient facts. Globally, Boeing forecasts an average growth in passenger numbers of around 4% per annum but 'air travel for the Asia-Pacific region is expected to grow at an average rate of 6.5%'. As a consequence, over the next twenty years, 'the Asia-

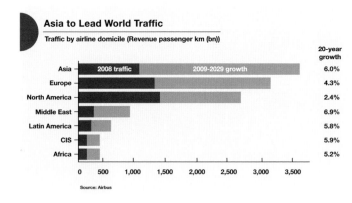

Asia to Lead World Traffic

Traffic by airline domicile (Revenue passenger km (bn))

	20-year growth
Asia	6.0%
Europe	4.3%
North America	2.4%
Middle East	6.9%
Latin America	5.8%
CIS	5.9%
Africa	5.2%

Source: Airbus

This Asian market growth is the result of a rise in regional tourism and an increase in cargo.

- The desire to travel for a younger, wealthier and increasingly middle-class Asian population will lead to significant intra-regional and international tourism. China alone is expected to produce 100 million outbound tourists a year by 2020 and, across Asia, real GDP in tourism is forecast to grow at an average of over 8% per annum over the next decade, adding an extra 10 million jobs.

- From a cargo perspective, Chinese flights dominate international traffic. New links between China and Africa, especially, are growing rapidly with new routes opening between key hubs such as Nigeria on a regular basis. Airbus expects India's fleet to grow 13.5 times by 2028. Over the next twenty years, 'the overall Asia-Pacific freighter fleet is expected to increase five-fold', rising from 16% of the global fleet in 2009 to nearly 40%.

Pacific fleet will grow from 3,910 to 11,170 planes' and, by 2020, 'Asia-Pacific will easily be the largest air travel market in the world'.

Airbus sees that 'global air traffic will triple over the next twenty years and, as average aircraft size will grow steadily, airlines will more than double the size of their fleets'. Like Boeing, Airbus identifies Asia as the major growth area, with over 30% of new aeroplane deliveries planned for the Asia-Pacific region. At the 2010 India Aviation Show, the Indian Civil Aviation Minister announced that he expected India to need another 3,000 aircraft over the next decade just to keep pace with economic growth. Also over the next decade, China's domestic market is expected to grow towards the size of the US and international flights between these two countries are forecast to represent more than 15% of all flights by 2028.

Asia-Pacific will easily be the largest air travel market in the world.

On top of this, many Asian countries are relaxing regulatory restrictions to stimulate air travel and are rapidly upgrading their airports. Whereas the likes of Kuala Lumpur, Singapore, Hong Kong and Shanghai led the region over the past decade, other cities are rapidly catching up. Over the next ten years, China plans to invest $64 billion, including numerous upgrades and nearly one hundred totally new airports. With expanding international operations in Beijing, Shanghai, Kunming, Guangzhou and Nanjing, China will have 244 major airports by 2020. In India, the current five-year investment plan has earmarked nearly $7 billion for airport expansion, including upgrades that have started in New Delhi and Mumbai

China will have 244 major airports by 2020.

and new green-field construction that has been led by Hyderabad and Bangalore. As many as thirty-five airports are being improved and expanded in the country. Half of all intra-Asian future demand will be between just eleven cities. These will become tomorrow's major aviation hubs.

Although the scale of change within Asia alone is significant, there is additional growth in aviation directly linked to the Asian expansion. Many of the new orders for planes in Europe, the Americas and, especially, the Middle East are for planes that will fly into Asia. For example, the expansion of facilities at Dubai International Airport means it already caters for the third largest number of international passengers (after London Heathrow and Hong Kong). By 2020, it is planning to accommodate 90 million passengers a year, with Emirates carrying just less than 80 million of them. Adding in Doha and Abu Dhabi, and their associated airlines, well over 200 million passengers will fly to and through the Gulf by 2020 – with over 40% of them heading to and from Asia. When these projections are combined with the Asian airline figures, the scale of growth is astounding.

Whether through more internal domestic flights, more intra-Asian flights or more long-haul passenger and cargo services to and from the rest of the world, there is little doubt of the impact of Asian aviation on the world landscape over the next decade or so. The investment is already being made and so now it is just about execution of the ambition.

Related insights

Page 69

Page 155

Page 231

Chinese trains

China, the pacesetter for change in inter-urban transport, is investing over $1 trillion expanding its rail network to 120,000 km by 2020.

In a world where city-to-city, inter-urban transportation is increasingly seen as the major growth area for mobility, competition is rife between air, road and rail. Around the globe, cities, countries and regions have been talking about the benefits of speed, efficiency and convenience of the relative options and are variously making some serious commitments. While low-cost airlines continue to grow in many markets and car ownership is rising steadily, many governments are investing heavily in rail as the future of inter-urban transport. Having observed the advantages of high-speed rail travel in Europe and Japan, which have been largely ignored in the US, China is now considered by many to be the pacesetter for change.

A hundred and thirty years after the invention of the railway and its growth as the primary form of mass transport, the introduction of the first high-speed trains in Japan caught the imagination of many around the world. To help overcome capacity constraints on the existing networks, the Toyko to Osaka Tōkaidō Shinkansen line opened to coincide with the Olympics in 1964 and its 'bullet trains' ran at speeds of over 210 kilometres per hour (130 mph). Since then, newer, faster trains have cut around an hour and a half off the usual four-hour journey. Looking ahead, the Chūō Shinkansen maglev line planned for launch in 2025 will cut the time down to just one hour as trains travel at over 580 kilometres per hour (360 mph).

In Europe, high-speed train development is lagging behind. Supported primarily by the state railways of France and Germany, a network of TGV and ICE trains has been growing for the past forty-five years. Starting with the Paris-to-Lyon TGV, investment in high-speed trains across Europe has now extended the network beyond just France and Germany into Spain, Switzerland, Belgium, the Netherlands, Italy and, most recently, via the Eurostar to London. Regularly operating at speeds up to 350 km/h, travelling around Europe by train has for many become the ideal. Faster than the car and more comfortable than the plane, both business and leisure travellers have increasingly opted for the train as the preferred mode of city-to-city transport. Today, with over 2,400 km of high-speed track in Japan, 1,700 in France and 1,200 in each of Germany and Spain, the routes have been expanded, and clean, high-speed electric rail transportation continues to secure more investment from the varied governments.

By comparison, the impact of high-speed trains in the US has been minimal. Although the US freight trains are amongst the most efficient in the world, they typically run at only 50 mph and slow down passenger trains to around 80 mph. Today, with just one high-speed rail line in operation, there is only just over 700 km of track. The Acela Express, which was opened in 2000, runs between Washington, DC, and Boston via New York City and typically hits its target

China has seen high-speed trains as an opportunity not only to efficiently connect its cities but also to invest in an infrastructure for the 21st century and further drive economic growth.

operational speed of 150 mph (240 km/h) on around 50% of journeys. Given the size of the country and the history of the American railroads, the US has to date gained surprisingly little advantage from high-speed rail. However, this situation is beginning to change. In 2009, the White House announced a strategic plan for high-speed rail and a budget stimulus of $8 billion. This identifies ten high-speed rail corridors as potential recipients of federal funding. Those lines are in California, Pacific Northwest, South Central, Gulf Coast, Chicago Hub Network, Florida, Southeast, Keystone, Empire and Northern New England. Of these, only the California line has so far gained much traction, with the California High-Speed Rail Authority planning lines from San Francisco Bay and Sacramento to Los Angeles and Irvine via the Central Valley, as well as a line from Los Angeles to San Diego via the Inland Empire.

In contrast, China has seen high-speed trains as an opportunity not only to efficiently connect its cities but also to invest in an infrastructure for the 21st century and further drive economic growth. Having only opened its first TGV-like conventional high-speed route between Qinhuangdao and Shenyang in 2003, China already has a high-speed train network of over 6,500 km, the largest in the world by far. Average speeds of 312 km/h (194 mph) on the 922

km route from Wuhan to Guangzhou North make this currently the world's fastest commercial train service. As well as these conventional high-speed tracks, China also has the world's first commercial maglev route, from Shanghai airport to the city, which was opened in 2004. Trains on this line already run at over 430 km/h.

China has urbanised far more rapidly than India and has built new infrastructure ahead of demand. Recognising both the challenge and the benefit in increasing the speed of travel across the country, China is now investing over $1 trillion in expanding its rail network to 120,000 km by 2020 – the second largest public works programme in history. Just as the US invested in the highways after the downturn in the 1930s and helped drive growth in automobiles, China has used the opportunity for well-targeted economic stimulus. Like Japan, South Korea, France, Spain and Germany before, China is reshaping its landscape around train services by investing in a mix of both very high-speed rail (350 km/h) and high-speed rail (125–150 km/h) that will be the global benchmark for mass transit systems. Cargo and passenger transport are being separated, double track artery lines are being electrified and transport hubs are being built in 196 cities. The decisions have already been made and the ambition will be implemented. China has become the new test bed for the world's high-speed train technologies and the country is moving forward fast. As a recent article in

Like Japan, South Korea, France, Spain and Germany before, China is reshaping its landscape around train services.

Time magazine put it: 'At a time when infrastructure in the US and Europe is ageing fast, China's railways may give it a competitive edge over the world's leading economies.'

In a world of rising demand for mobility, increasing city-to-city travel and escalating concerns about fossil fuel-based road and air transport, electric high-speed trains are seen as the best option. However, it is clear that many other nations are yet to take such bold steps forward and probably will not be able to deliver material change by 2020. Japan, France, Spain and Germany are continuing to invest and build

At a time when infrastructure in the US and Europe is ageing fast, China's railways may give it a competitive edge over the world's leading economies.

upon existing networks but, while there is much talk of new high-speed lines, there is little action and their expansion is certainly not guaranteed. China is the clear pace-setter for change in inter-urban transport over the next decade. Will America follow?

Related
insights

Page 151

Page 167

Page 231

Clean shipping

Under increasing pressure to improve efficiency, growing freight shipping adopts a range of alternative policies and power systems.

Shipping already accounts for nearly 4.5% of the world's greenhouse gas emissions and, as the volume of global trade continues to grow, this proportion is also set to rise. According to the UN, annual emissions from the world's merchant fleets exceeds 1.2 billion tonnes of CO_2, twice that of the aviation sector. While planes and cars have been a common focus in the popular media, in the think tanks and transport forums around the world, ships have been rising up the agenda. Not surprisingly, then, this is now a growing concern for many governments seeking to take steps to reduce not only CO_2 emissions but also other environmental impacts such as waste contamination. As a result, people are turning to the concept of clean shipping and the benefits that it can potentially provide.

Shipping is a vital cog in the world's trade machine. Most people are unaware that almost every product is transported by sea at some stage. Put simply, when it comes down to shifting material around the planet, ships offer the best option, particularly when it comes to bulk transport of ore, coal, oil and cereals for which there is no alternative. For consumer goods and foods, the only option is the far more costly one of air freight. As a result the global shipping industry is booming.

Currently, maritime transport is handling around 90% of all world trade and is rising steadily. Over the

Most people are unaware that almost every product is transported by sea at some stage.

past decade, the number of cargo miles has doubled from 20,000 billion to around 40,000 billion tonne-miles. With the world economy set to continue to expand steadily through to 2020 and beyond, many see that this figure will again double over the next decade. In addition, from an economic perspective, since freight rates are very competitive, companies tend to keep old ships in service for longer than originally planned. This means that while some ship owners are trying to improve efficiency, many others operate their ships as cheaply as possible and just follow the minimum regulations.

Comparing air and sea transport is an issue that several people have been focused on in recent years. In his book *Sustainable Energy – Without the Hot Air*, David Mackay, Professor of Physics at Cambridge University, makes some highly relevant points on the movement of people: 'For a time, I thought that the way to solve the long-distance transport problem was to revert to the way it was done before planes: ocean liners. Then I looked at the numbers. The sad truth is that ocean liners use more energy per

The sad truth is that ocean liners use more energy per passenger-kilometre (pkm) than jumbo jets.

passenger-kilometre (pkm) than jumbo jets. At a typical 85% occupancy, the energy consumption of a tourist class liner is 121 kWh per 100 pkm – more than twice that of the jumbo jet.' He also sees that, in the freight world, 'international shipping is a surprisingly efficient user of fossil fuels. But fossil fuels are a finite resource, and eventually ships must be powered by something else. Bio-fuels may work out but another option will be nuclear power.'

Others, however, see that there are major efficiency improvements to be gained in shipping beyond just a switch of power source. Better navigation, new fuel consumption software and advanced materials are in the repertoire, but clean shipping is increasingly seen as a key part of the solution. A clean ship is one designed and operated so that it maximises the opportunities for improved energy efficiency and reduced environmental impact. Over the past few years, momentum for change has been building and specific areas for new approaches are being addressed: slower speeds, better hydrodynamics and new power generation technologies are being adopted to improve overall fuel efficiency; low sulphur fuels are being introduced to reduce exhaust emissions to the air; waste reduction and onboard recycling is increasing to reduce to zero the refuse, sewage and cargo discharges to the sea.

Companies and governments around the world are planning to change the status quo and are adopting clean ship strategies. For example, twenty-seven countries in the North Atlantic have signed the Paris Memorandum of Understanding and agreed to control visiting ships in their ports. In addition, the International Maritime Organization, the UN agency responsible for ship safety and environmental protection, is introducing higher regulatory standards.

A clean ship is one designed and operated so that it maximises the opportunities for improved energy efficiency and reduced environmental impact.

Cargo owners are starting to specify environmental performance targets for ships that are used to transport their goods and cradle-to-grave environmental footprinting is bringing wider consumer attention to the shipping issue. At the same time, financial incentives – such as lower insurance costs for clean ships – are being introduced and several governments and port authorities are planning larger fines for polluters. In June 2010, Lloyds Register, the London-based ship classification and risk organisation, announced that it is working on providing a verification service to ship owners that is approved by the Clean Shipping Project,

Cargo owners are starting to specify environmental performance targets for ships that are used to transport their goods.

the organisation that developed the Clean Shipping Index, which analyses the environmental impacts of shipping – another structural shift for the maritime industry that is nudging it towards its own ranking of ships by environmental performance.

So, what will shipping look like in 2020? More organisations now forecast that, by 2015, a significant number of clean ships will have been built and will be being introduced. By 2020, the nature of the overall merchant fleet will be changing. Most significantly from an overall emissions perspective will be the adoption of new fuel and power options that are already available or coming on stream soon: nuclear-powered vessels are common in the navy and are increasingly being adopted for merchant fleets; more ships are using liquefied natural gas (LNG) to fuel their engines, which are significantly cleaner than marine diesel ones; fuel cells are being developed for marine applications; solar power is being used

By 2020, the nature of the overall merchant fleet will be changing.

for onboard equipment; wind-assisted propulsion is being reinvented, ranging from the use of large kites to pull vessels along to the reintroduction of high-tech sails that can work with other power options and provide 30% of the energy required.

At the same time, new designs of ship hulls are being introduced that reduce friction and so reduce energy consumption. Low-friction paint coatings are also becoming available. We can also expect to see pentamarans – fast cargo ships with five hulls that fill the gap between expensive air transport and slow traditional ships. Clean ships will become a common point of discussion, and not just in specialist transport forums.

Related insights

Page 95

Page 219

Page 223

Electric mobility

With France and Germany taking the initial lead roles, electric cars take off and form up to 10% of the world's vehicle fleet by 2020.

It is has been a long time coming, but thirteen years after the global launch of the Toyota Prius hybrid, a host of companies all have electric vehicles scheduled for introduction over the next few years. The alignment of technology development, targeted incentives and economies of scale together with a fundamental change in consumer sentiment has started the shift towards a future where electric mobility has a significant role to play in global transportation. By 2020, experts predict that nearly one-third of all cars being sold will be electric and that electric cars will form up to 10% of the world's vehicle fleet.

Electric mobility is not new: in the late 19th century, many of the first cars to be produced were electric. Before the internal combustion engine took over, electric cars were making a mark, breaking the 100 km/h barrier in 1899. A fleet of electric taxis first appeared in New York in 1897 and, despite their relatively slow speed, electric vehicles had a number of advantages over their competitors in the early 1900s: less vibration, less noise and less pollution. However, with increasing competition from the internal combustion engine and sizeable support from the oil industry, gasoline and diesel vehicles became more popular and sales of the first generation of electric cars peaked in 1912.

One hundred years later, a second wave of electric mobility is gaining momentum, driven by a number of leading manufacturers and a massive swing of public support for more sustainable transport solutions. This step change has taken some time to make an impact. In 1990, General Motors announced its intention to market electric cars and introduced the GM Impact, but, over the following two decades, little was achieved and most of the concept cars never made it into the showroom. However, the past couple of years have seen the arrival of some notable catalysts for change.

Although in many eyes electric cars are epitomised by the small, Indian made, G-Wizz and similar vehicles, high-speed electric sports cars have come out of the shadows, most notably those being produced by California-based Tesla. The notion of 125 mph electrically powered cars that can go for 240 miles or more between recharging has captured the imagination of many, resulting in a surge of investment. In comparison to traditional competitors, electric vehicles offer a number of advantages: they are quieter, accelerate faster, require less maintenance, cost less on a per-mile basis and in many ways are more sustainable because, in certain locations, they can run on clean energy. At the same time, they have the potential to be lighter.

However, while electrically powered transport for personal use dropped off the agenda for around one hundred years, public transport systems, particularly in cities, have often used electric mobility solutions.

Electrically powered trams, trains and metros running on fixed power supplies have long been part of many cities' transport infrastructure. In terms of independent road-based mobility, electric buses have been steadily introduced into many cities over the past twenty years or so and are now part of many a mayor's zero-emissions plans. Add in taxis and delivery trucks and the impetus for much technology development in electric mobility has come from public transport. Coupled with the success of early hybrids, a significant shift is taking place. Major advances have been made in efficiency, cost and weight in public transport, particularly for drive trains and battery technology. This knowledge is now being applied to personal transport. Although some, including several in a Shanghai workshop, question existing battery technology, many others are placing heavy bets on a breakthrough in the next few years.

In step with this burgeoning interest, over the past year or two, more manufacturers have made announcements about their plans for electric vehicles: in 2009, BMW did field trials of the electric version of its Mini, the Mini E, in Germany, the UK and the US, and these were followed by China and France in 2010. While GM has just launched the 2011 Chevrolet Volt/Opel Ampera electric hybrid, Nissan has gone a step further with the introduction of the Nissan Leaf, an all-electric vehicle, with full global rollout planned for 2012. In addition, companies like Better Place are earning attention for alternative solutions such as its battery swap system which allows batteries to be exchanged automatically for fully charged ones in less time than a traditional refill at a petrol station.

Although some question whether it will be in other regions where the early breakthroughs take place,

The German car industry has signed up to a government push to get a million electric cars on to the roads by 2020.

much of the debate on the future of electric mobility in the media has been focused on the US and China. In August 2009, an article in the *McKinsey Quarterly* argued that 'a global electric-car sector must start in China and the United States, and it must begin with the two countries creating an environment for automotive investors to scale their bets across both nations'. It suggested that, although private companies will compete to provide the technologies, charging stations and the vehicles, 'the two governments can no doubt create the conditions for them to succeed – for example, by setting standards, funding the rollout of infrastructure and sponsoring joint R&D initiatives'. This was supported by facts and figures that show that if penetration of electric vehicles rises above 45% by 2030, oil imports and CO_2 emissions would fall dramatically. To achieve this, China needs to spend $28 billion and build 700,000 charging stations; the corresponding figures for the US are $50 billion and 1.2 million respectively.

While this sounds promising, some workshop participants highlighted two issues that might mean this US/China leadership should be questioned. The first one concerns the fact that other countries have already made the necessary decisions and are acting on them. Electric car recharging networks are already being built in Denmark, Israel and, most significantly, France. We emphasise 'most significantly' for France because it is there where government, the car industry and the energy sector appear to be most aligned: the Renault Fluence ZE, the world's first switchable battery electric car, is being launched early in 2011; at the same time, Renault and EDF are building a nationwide electric car-recharging network across France in 2011; and €400 million of initial state backing was guaranteed by President Sarkozy in October 2008. So, the alignment of significant market potential, the technology, regulation and finance required to establish a suitable environment for a breakthrough change seems to be coming together pretty well in France. Indeed, as many other manufacturers focus more on hybrids and hydrogen options, Renault is taking ambitious steps forward into full electric mobility. Carlos Ghosn, boss of both Renault and Nissan, sees that: 'By 2020, purely electric, zero-emission vehicles will take 10% of the global car market.' What is more, he wants such vehicles to account for 20% of Renault-Nissan's sales by then.

The second issue concerns the CO_2 reductions being claimed versus those being delivered. In many countries, the switch from hydrocarbons to electrons for transport is a diversion because they will still be largely relying on oil, gas and coal to generate the electricity in the first place. So, the point of CO_2 production shifts from the vehicle to the power station, but significant breakthroughs are still required before effective and economic carbon capture and storage (CCS) technologies are retro-fitted to the existing energy base. If electric mobility is going to have significant impact within the next decade, some argue that it needs to be aligned to major sources of renewable, clean energy. So, looking at the current leaders in this field, it is no surprise that Denmark (wind), Israel (solar) and France (nuclear) are seen as front-runners. These locations have high renewable supplies of electricity already installed or being installed and, as such, they will gain most from the associated carbon credits from the introduction of electric mobility.

Also of great significance is Germany, the global centre of automotive development in many people's eyes. The German car industry has signed up to a government push to get a million electric cars on to the roads by 2020. Industry commentators say that: 'If they manage it, we're talking about one in four new cars sold in that year being electric, which is a staggering change in just the next ten years.' In cooperation with E.On and other energy firms, who are building the charging infrastructure, the likes of VW, BMW and Mercedes-Benz are all planning a host of new electric car launches over the next couple of years. German government support and commitment to electric mobility is strong and growing.

Only 1% of the 50 million cars sold in 2009 were hybrids, the rest having petrol or diesel engines. By 2020, several predictions indicate that up to 20% of the world's car fleet will be hybrids but 10% will be electric powered. A century after the electric car gave way to the internal combustion engine, the combined action of many governments, companies, NGOs, investors and entrepreneurs is bringing about a renaissance that is on course to produce a major global shift in the way our mobility is powered.

Related insights

Page 95

Page 179

Page 205

Intelligent highways

Mesh networks and ubiquitous mobile connections deliver the automated highways to improve safety, increase capacity and reduce congestion.

The intelligent highway is a term used by many in the automotive industry and government bodies to describe a world where cars don't crash, congestion does not occur and there are no accidents; a world where cars automatically detect a problem ahead and avoid it through either slowing down or taking alternative routes. Intelligent highways, when they arrive, will significantly reduce the number of deaths on the road and make travel smoother and faster, which will also mean that we use less energy for mobility. This ambition of the transport professionals has been much discussed and has been the focus for numerous programmes over the years, but these efforts have only led to many false starts. However, in the opinion of many commentators, realisation of the intelligent highways concept is on the horizon. With forthcoming regulation, technology deployment and cooperation between manufacturers, they look set to be part of our world by 2020.

Although private cars are a primary focus, commercial vehicles are equally as important. As intelligent highways expert Richard Bishop commented on the Future Agenda blog:

"In the USA new truck-exclusion roads are being studied for construction in parallel to major interstate highways to relieve congestion. I think this will become reality – and, when it does, trucks can start to cooperate with each other for greater fuel efficiency and lower emissions. This is the platoon idea, and in its fullest form you have roadways full of nothing but robotic trucks. This will be very much within our reach within ten years and the implementation issues revolve solely around the business case, road facilities, and such like."

At the extreme, intelligent highways enable the introduction of the driverless car – an autonomous vehicle that drives itself from point A to B, selecting the best route, avoiding congestion and choosing the speed and distance from other vehicles to ensure that there are no accidents. This is what you see played out in science fiction movies from *Batman* and *Total Recall* to *I, Robot* and *Minority Report*. Over past decades, there have been numerous research programmes focused on this goal, including the ARGO project in Italy, the FROG project in the Netherlands, the DARPA Grand Challenge in the US and, most notably for the media, the 1997 San Diego Automated Highway demonstration in which a number of driverless cars followed each other down a 12 km test track. In 1995, on the open road, a Mercedes Benz drove from Munich to Copenhagen and back using saccadic computer vision and achieved speeds of over 175 km/h over distances of up to 150 km with no human intervention; the ARGO project used stereoscopic vision algorithms to follow the white lines in the road for 2,000 km, with the car in fully automatic mode over 90% of the time; and, after previous competitions in the desert, in the 2007 DARPA Grand Challenge, a team from Carnegie Mellon University won the prize for a car that autonomously navigated through

By 2020 no one will be killed or maimed in a Volvo.

an urban environment. In 2008, GM announced that it would start testing driverless cars by 2015 ahead of launching in 2018. In Europe, autonomous vehicle demonstrators are being built in several locations including Rome, Vienna, Trondheim and Heathrow Airport.

At the next step down from fully autonomous vehicles, assisted driving is increasingly common in cars of today. Adding to the long-standing cruise control capability, manufacturers have variously introduced lane departure warning systems, anti-lock braking, traction control, night vision, rear view alarms and automatic parking. Additional developments such as automatic emergency braking, intelligent speed adaptation and predictive cruise control are also on the horizon. All of these technologies help the driver to control the car more efficiently and so are proven ingredients for the overall intelligent highways ambition. As Volvo, one of the leaders in automotive safety over the years, puts it: 'In principle, a future Volvo will be able to "speak" to an oncoming vehicle, potentially communicating: You and I are about to collide head-on. If our drivers don't react, we have to do something to avoid the danger.' A stated company aim is that 'by 2020 no one will be killed or maimed in a Volvo'.

There is, however, a missing link, namely, the integrated systems needed to allow cars to communicate seamlessly with each other and the ecosystem through which they are moving. This is the key network that will allow interaction between the moving and fixed nodes (ie, vehicles and traffic signals etc). While some of the initial experiments focused on embedding sensors into and alongside the roads, thinking has quickly evolved to take advantage of GPS and 3G/4G mobile systems. With vehicle infrastructure integration, as some are calling it, standard wireless protocols will allow cars to communicate with each other and with traffic signals; at the same time, government agencies, car manufacturers and traffic control systems will be able to communicate directly with every vehicle.

In the US, there has been significant focus on intelligent highways as a means to reduce the 42,000 traffic fatalities that occur every year as well as the $230 billion of losses from wasted fuel, emergency response costs, 6.3 million insurance claims and medical bills. Aiming at connecting 150 million vehicles to the internet, companies such as Google, Cisco and Microsoft have all announced plans for advanced transportation communication networks.

In the UK and Canada, Aviva, the insurance company, launched a product that paves the way for consumer acceptance of some of the key technologies: the 'Pay-As-You-Drive' insurance system. This uses standard mobile SIM cards within cars to allow them to be tracked continuously. The upside for customers was cheaper insurance depending on where and when they drive. The system also proved that, on a large scale, vehicle tracking is already fully practical. This type of technology is being implemented in Europe over the next couple of years under the eCall in-vehicle programme for emergency assistance, but also allows other options such as road pricing without toll-booths to come into place. Other systems use radio frequency (RF) tags to communicate with and between cars (Zipcar uses this system to allow people access to its car-sharing services). Meanwhile, countries like Singapore, which were early adopters of road pricing, are now looking at wider GPS-based systems. Together, these innovations not only enable safer driving but are also the gateway to a wider shift in the currency of travel. Some Bangalore workshop participants contended that new payment mechanisms – where fuel, insurance, vehicle use and travel overall are charged by distance – are already operable within a short timescale.

While Western economies to date have invested most in the concept and testing of intelligent highways, several workshop participants felt that the breakthrough in terms of implementation of a viable, scalable system may first occur in India. With companies like Tata having a significant interest in both the automotive industry and the ITC sector, it is possible that a partnership between Tata Motors and Tata Consulting could be the catalyst for a mesh network approach to greater assisted-driving and eventually the intelligent highway.

With many different systems in development around the world, a critical issue for widespread implementation will be the adoption of a common platform. A recent comment by Booz & Co highlighted that 'from a policy perspective, there is little question but that an open standards approach, which would allow all to use the same technology, would be best'. Ford has already taken a step towards this by adopting an in-car WiFi system turning the entire car into a hot spot – which, in the words of a workshop participant from the communications sector, 'paves the way for the car to be the fourth space for mobile connection'. For the mesh networks that many see as being the foundation for the next generation of intelligent highway design to deliver the goods, all cars, traffic signals and integrated infrastructure have to use the same system to enable fast and free transfer of data. Just like the internet itself, no one will own this system-wide network but everyone's and everything's participation will make it work.

The other big hurdle is social acceptance of intelligent highways and, by implication, autonomous vehicles. The UK government, for example, sees that, while much of the technology and systems are available and proven, it will be 2015 before many of the legal and consumer issues are agreed: trusting the system rather than the driver to control the car is no easy step. As Markus Armbrust, manager of advanced driver assistance at GM, was quoted as saying: 'Drivers will not want to give up all the fun.' Equally BMW want to continue to provide the 'ultimate driving experience'. Many, however, are confident that once the benefits of safer, quicker travel are evident, for the majority of drivers, the option of joining a smooth intelligent highway system rather than the usual nose-to-tail commute will become increasingly attractive. There are clearly a number of outstanding issues to be dealt with but, given the impetus and the number of vehicles being added to the global infrastructure every day, the world in 2020 could well see us travelling on intelligent highways.

Related insights

Page 87

Page 155

Page 175

Muslim Europe

With increasing economic migration the total Muslim population of Europe is similar in size to that of Germany and has a rising cultural/political influence.

Migration has been a contentious subject for a number of years and, as politicians continue to avoid the heart of the issue and media misrepresent many of the arguments, the real implications are misunderstood. Yet, in terms of impacts on other issues, migration is perhaps the archetypal cross-cutting issue. In his initial perspective on the future of migration, Professor Richard Black stated that 'immigrant integration and increasing diversity in Europe and the North are significant questions for today's societies'.

From the varied discussions around the topic it is clear that in Europe there is a mounting population challenge that will lead to a shift in society. 'The low white birth rate in Europe, coupled with faster-multiplying migrants, will change fundamentally what we take to mean by European culture and society,' is one pertinent view. Many increasingly see that, to sustain competitive growth in the face of declining fertility, Europe will support increased migration – and this will largely come from North Africa and the Near East. Although raw data is highly sensitive and hard to come by, leading commentators see that, by 2020, economic migration will have started to change the multicultural balance in a new direction. Europe will become increasingly Muslim and, if current trends continue, over 10% of European nationals will be Muslim by the end of the decade.

There are a number of different scenarios being discussed regarding Europe's overall future population.

UN figures predict a 6% decline by 2050 but also that, having peaked in 2015, by 2020, the total number of Europeans will be around 730 million, which is largely the same as today. In several projections, bearing in mind the impact of Germany's low birth rate, some analysts expect that the UK will be Europe's most populous country by 2060, with nearly 80 million inhabitants. While fertility rates and life expectancy in different countries can be used for base-case models, a big uncertainty is the impact of migration within and immigration into Europe.

In an early comment to the Future Agenda programme, Professor Robin Cohen, Director of the International Migration Institute at Oxford, commented that 'the major challenges are to predict the size, direction and character of global migration flows and to manage the social and political consequences' and that 'the level of irregular – undocumented, trafficked, illegal – migrants is likely to remain high and probably increase as a proportion of the world's mobile labour force'. That said, some trends are becoming clear: according to recent EU reports, 'since 2002, net migration into the EU has roughly tripled to around 2 million people a year' and 'migratory pressure at the EU's borders … could increase in the future'. Eurostat data from 2008 suggests that, within the EU, from 2015, deaths will outnumber births and so natural growth will cease. From that point on, positive net migration will be the source of population growth. 'Migration from other

World Muslim Population (%)

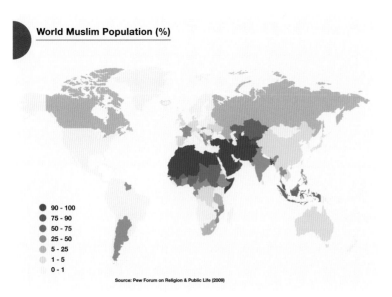

- 90 - 100
- 75 - 90
- 50 - 75
- 25 - 50
- 5 - 25
- 1 - 5
- 0 - 1

Source: Pew Forum on Religion & Public Life (2009)

regions, through northern Africa to reach Europe, is likely to intensify.' Although Europe has a long history of welcoming migrants, over recent years immigrants have increasingly come from developing economies and in accelerating numbers. By 2020, there will more international migration than ever and Europe is expected to be a primary destination. As Robin Cohen stated: 'The economic case for migration has always been strong. Migrant labour is often cheaper, more reliable and (in certain cases) flexible.'

Islam has been part of Europe's culture for many years. From the conflicts between Arabs and the Byzantine Empire in the 7th and 8th centuries to the conquest of Russia and the Ukraine by the Golden Horde in the 14th century and then the expansion of the Ottoman Empire, Eastern Europe has included a Muslim population for many years. Equally, on the Iberian Peninsula, from the 8th century, Muslim

forces exerted influence across Spain and even into France. However, it has been in the past fifty years that the numbers of Muslims in Europe have started to grow steadily. As 'guest worker' immigration to support growth drew in people from the former colonies of France, Germany, the Netherlands, Belgium and the UK, the Muslim population in the EU has risen, doubling in the past thirty years to around 20 million today. According to a 2008 Brookings study, the countries with the largest percentages of Muslims are France at an estimated 8%, the Netherlands at 6%, Germany at 4% and the United Kingdom at 3% of the population. Significant numbers of Muslims have congregated in a numerous urban areas and many observers are aware that certain neighbourhoods in several European cities are becoming more Muslim, and that the change is gathering pace. According to Karoly Lorant, a Hungarian economist, 'Muslims already make up 25% of the population in Marseilles and Rotterdam, 20% in Malmo, 15% in Brussels and Birmingham, and 10% in London, Paris and Copenhagen.' Taking Europe as whole into consideration, beyond the boundaries of the EU, the German Central Institute Islam Archive calculated that the total number of Muslims in 2007 was about 53 million.

An EU report from 2008, stated that:

"Europe's immediate neighbourhood, the Middle East and North Africa region, has the world's second fastest growing population, after sub-Saharan Africa. Future migration flows towards the EU will mainly arrive from the Mediterranean region, in view of differences in living standards and population trends exacerbated by natural resource constraints."

Over the next decade, there will be continued change in the European populace, with the largest shift coming

Muslims already make up 25% of the population in Marseilles and Rotterdam, 20% in Malmo, 15% in Brussels and Birmingham, and 10% in London, Paris and Copenhagen.

from the possible entry of Turkey into the EU. This alone would increase the Muslim population by around 70 million. Several commentators expect that, excluding Russia, Europe's Muslim population will easily double by 2020 and that, by 2050, one in five Europeans will probably be Muslim. Even without Turkey in the EU in the next decade, with a Muslim population equal to that of Germany, this will have a significant impact on not just Europe's culture and societal make-up but also in how the region operates on the international stage. For example, in 1999 Germany started to reform its voting laws, granting certain franchise rights to the large Turkish population.

In the short term, we can possibly expect more cultural conflict as, since 9/11, Europe's growing Muslim population has been the focus of debate on many issues. Several incidents in recent years have increased tensions between some Western European states and their Muslim populations: the 2004 Madrid and 2005 London attacks, the 2004 ban of the hijab veil in schools coupled with 2010 regulation to ban the niqab and the burqa in France, the 2005 Paris riots, the 2006 Danish cartoon incident, and several high-profile murders. However, while today most of Western Europe's Muslims are still poorly integrated into society and are self-segregated for reasons such as language barriers and different cultural norms, like prohibitions against drinking, the reality is that, despite the anxiety, Muslim integration within Europe is improving. Going forward towards 2020, several analysts see that there is hope that a stronger Euro-Islam identity will emerge as Muslims continue to grow into European culture. Some experts believe that middle-class Muslims are much more likely to favour assimilation: 'Muslims in Europe are working hard to try to find ways to educate their own communities and talk about the balance between being Muslim and Western, not Muslim or Western'. There are clear unemployment, cultural and political challenges to be addressed, but with overall economic growth in Europe dependent on sustaining its population, and an increasing recognition that this can only occur through immigration from Muslim countries, the reality of a more Muslim Europe is on the horizon. As the Muslim population grows – most likely concentrated around twenty to thirty key cities across Europe – we can expect multinationals to start to focus on this group as a new segment. Previously a niche marginal market that was largely uneconomic to support due to size or dispersion, improved connectivity and declining costs of access will make the 80 million European Muslims an increasingly addressable mainstream.

Related insights

Page 107

Page 121

Page 247

People tracking

The acceptance of being tracked by your mobile is accelerated by ticketless transport systems, increased surveillance and successful location-based services.

Anyone who has used an iPhone will be aware that location services are now embedded in most smart-phones. By the start of 2010, there were over 6,000 location-based iPhone apps, with 600 new ones being released every month. Equally, those who make use of Google Latitude will know how easy it is to see where their friends are, in real time, on the basis of where their phones are. Facebook Places similarly allows you to openly share your whereabouts. For many, the ability to be located via the position of our mobile phones can seem like a new development but it has actually been used for quite some time.

From a security perspective, when needed, and with the cooperation of the mobile networks, security services in many countries have been able to locate suspects to within a meter or so by triangulating signals from a mobile phone to the communications masts and this has been a key asset in the police's toolbox for over twenty years now. More specific location of people has been possible in recent years, even when a phone is switched off. As long as there is a battery in the phone, it can be remotely turned on, located and turned off in milliseconds and this

As long as there is a battery in the phone, it can be remotely turned on, located and turned off in milliseconds.

too has now become an additional security issue. Especially with products like the iPhone, where the battery is integrated into the product and cannot be removed, this essentially provides 24/7/365 tracking potential of phones. This capability is now also being exploited in the commercial world. Services such as Loopt, Venti Coffee and Njection are using this information to respectively broadcast your whereabouts, find the nearest Starbucks and notify you of speed traps.

Moving forward, as phones are used to enable ticketless travel through charging the owner when the phone rather than the person gets on and off public transport networks, the use of the location of a personal mobile device as a reliable surrogate for the individual is stimulating new applications in healthcare, financial payments and social networking, to name just a few. However, it is not all just about your mobile.

In the US, the On-Star in-car communication system has been around for several years now and provides drivers with a back-up whereby emergency services can be called and locate a vehicle in case of a breakdown or accident. As this technology has become more widely adopted, the ability to use it to track vehicles has also evolved. Car hire companies have for some time had the capability to actively track where you drive and make sure that you don't cross state and national borders without prior agreement

The use of the location of a personal mobile device as a reliable surrogate for the individual is stimulating new applications in healthcare, financial payments and social networking.

– or, if you do, then they charge you for the privilege. Although there was a privacy backlash initially, today there is widespread acceptance of this capability. The EU is also mandating the incorporation of this type of technology into every new car from 2012 and so soon the whole vehicle fleet, and hence its drivers, will be able to be tracked. Not only does this allow for better emergency assistance, it also facilitates the introduction of pervasive road pricing and similar schemes – without the need for toll booths.

Moving away from device-enabled tracking, but on similar lines, many of us are already being clocked in and out of transport systems and many public and corporate buildings. In the UK, the Oyster Card on the London Transport system is increasingly linked to an individual credit card holder and so can tell the system where you enter and exit the tube or get on and off buses. Similar systems in Hong Kong and Melbourne provide the functionality and so, as non-contact payment is adopted more widely, this tracking of us in and out as well as within transport networks will increase.

While passes are common for many corporate employees and visitors, the introduction of biometric entry systems – whether based on fingerprints, voice recognition or iris scans and which are a common feature at many airports – are adding an extra layer of traceability. While the security benefits are clear, major issues around privacy are bubbling under the surface.

In addition, the ubiquity of security cameras in many urban centres and transport networks also allows for the monitoring of people and their movement via facial recognition software. In London, the most monitored city in the world, with over 7,500 CCTV cameras, the average person is photographed over 300 times a day. After being refined, again in the first instance by the security services for national security and counter-terrorism surveillance, this is now going mainstream in the commercial world. Although the subject of some concerns about privacy, after trialling in Picassa, Google's Goggles project is bringing facial recognition to a wider audience to allow them to search for something on the internet simply by taking a picture of it on a mobile phone.

Privacy campaigners have cautioned that adding facial recognition to Goggles allows users to track strangers through a photograph, making it into an ideal tool for stalkers and identity fraudsters. But as other companies, such as Israeli start-up Face.com, are also developing face-recognition tools, a global rollout is not far away. Although a privacy invasion backlash is possible in some areas, most see that with more customer-focused applications coming on-line every day, providing new information to all, consumer resistance will be marginal.

Car hire companies have for some time had the capability to actively track where you drive.

Looking ahead to 2020, we can therefore see a world in which, whether we want it or not, and whether we seek to avoid it or not, we are no longer just monitored by border control when we leave and enter countries but are all constantly tracked for both security and commercial applications. Pervasive people tracking will fast become the norm in most regions.

Google's Goggles project is bringing facial recognition to a wider audience to allow them to search for something on the internet simply by taking a picture of it on a mobile phone.

Related insights

Page 87

Page 167

This is to Cert

Page 209

Urban (im)mobility

Informed choices, growth, congestion and regulation impact the world's cities to drive a shift to more sustainable and efficient transport options.

Although all cities are in many ways different in terms of layout and structure, and consequently have different transport options, many share similar issues and challenges around sustaining growth without gridlock setting in. With increasing recognition not just of the efficiency and emotional problems resulting from congestion but also of the environmental implications, many leading mayors and supporting administrations have been taking steps to encourage citizens to make alternative choices. In many developed-world cities, primary challenges include encouraging people to change their existing habits and behaviours, while in the developing world it is often a case of encouraging people to make different choices about mobility than others have made in the past. With car ownership rising steadily in many nations, this is no easy task.

The challenge of future urban transport was examined in a number of different workshops within the Future Agenda programme – in Bangalore, Brussels, New Delhi, London, Melbourne, Shanghai and Singapore. Across all these discussions it is clear that the answer 'is not simply about stopping people using cars, but is about improving the efficiency of car usage and providing viable alternatives'; nor is it just about 'encouraging people to travel less by better co-locating home, work and leisure' or 'developing wider eco-literacy'. It is actually about all of these and more: urban transport is a complex issue driven

The key challenge is that as London in 2020 seeks to be more like Shanghai in 2010, can we stop Shanghai becoming more like London?

by many different factors on top of the geographic and cultural differences present.

There will be an additional 300 million car drivers added to the world over the next decade, most of them in cities in the developing world. According to a recent Shell/Transport Research Laboratory study: 'Today in London, car journeys account for 40% of journeys and cycling 2%. In Shanghai, car journeys account for 5% with cycling accounting for 33% of journeys.' In comparison with many US cities, London is a relatively good example of sustainable developed-world urban transportation, albeit not as good as places like Munich, Amsterdam and Vienna. At the same time, Shanghai today is by no means an exemplar. In many ways, London and Shanghai can be considered as typical, average examples of developed- and developing-world urban mobility. The key challenge is that as London in 2020 seeks to be more like Shanghai in 2010, can we stop Shanghai becoming more like London? As was mentioned in a Singapore event: 'In Asian cities, the car is more

Urban Mobility Comparisons

Transport Parameter	Asian Cities	European Cities	US Cities
Car ownership (per 1000 persons)	109	392	608
Specific road length (m per capita)	1	2	7
Road density (m per urban ha)	122	115	89
Walking/cycling/pedicab (% of work trips)	19	18	5
Role of public transport (% of all km)	48	23	3
Car use per person (km per capita p.a.)	1,397	4,519	11,155
Energy use per person (MJ per capita)	6,969	17,218	55,807

Source: TRL / Shell

than just about transportation. It is a status symbol. Especially in India and China, even though people don't need a car, they aspire to owning one.' In a world where access to personal transportation is a cultural ambition, a status symbol and, in many places, a major advance, many of the discussions in the Future Agenda programme looked at how this conundrum can be accommodated.

Any global blueprint solution has to consider the range of already defined constraints such as city design. For example, with the benefits of its high density, Hong Kong can spend around 5% of its GDP on its transport systems, with people typically spending between thirty and sixty minutes a day on public transport, whereas in Houston, where 15% of its GDP (so, three times as much pro rata) is spent, daily transportation time in cars is up to three hours for each person. As Europe and the US are focusing more on regeneration for city planning, Asia is creating brand new cities and extending existing ones, but 'in several Asian cities, urbanisation is happening at a rate that is much faster than transportation can cope with'. Urban design is clearly both a constraint and an enabler of more effective urban transport. In Singapore (an often cited example), one important

realisation early on was that 'urban transport planning has to be integrated with the urbanisation policy to create efficient and sustainable cities'.

Given that the majority agree that 'cities should be focused on people, not cars', one much-debated solution is clearly to regulate against the car. While congestion charging, road pricing and lane prioritisation for multi-passenger and low emission vehicles has become increasingly popular in many cities, others have tried alternative approaches. For instance, a reduction of the number of car parking spaces is under way in London and Beijing. However, if this happened in India, a place where labour is still cheaper than land, according to one workshop comment, 'the result would be more cars on the road as people's chauffeurs merely drive around while their employers attend a meeting or go shopping'. In a world of such variety, legislating against cars has severe limitations, even though more people are recognising the issues including 'the negative health aspects of cars in cities'.

In terms of alternatives, many in Europe advocate walking and cycling and so, over the next decade, we can expect ever more dedicated cycle lanes within and around cities. However, in Delhi many of the pavements are in a dangerous condition, while in a number of US cities they are non-existent. Cycling might be an attractive option in places like Amsterdam, Bogotá and San Francisco, but, in temperatures of 40°C and high humidity, persuading people that it is a progressive option for transport can be an uphill struggle. What many agree upon is the role of an integrated public transport system that fits the purpose. However, whereas in such places as Copenhagen, Shanghai, Bangkok and Melbourne this may mean buses, trams and trains, in other places

In several Asian cities, urbanisation is happening at a rate than is much faster than transportation can cope with.

there may already be better answers: tut-tuts are perfectly suited to India just as rickshaws are to Vietnam and Indonesia. Several people in workshops argued that with perfectly flexible, efficient solutions already in place, the need for monorails and metros could be questioned. Although many cities are investing in high-profile urban transit systems, there is still the 'last mile' challenge for those not directly on the network.

Looking forward over the next ten years, it is clear that 'the solutions must be different for different countries'. In Asia, a common aspiration is to create a multilevel approach where underground transit systems move people around the cities quickly, cars are put up in the air on flyovers and the ground is for people. In many of the new cities being built, and some of the existing ones that are being upgraded, this option has many supporters and will, de facto, become the future. The new Chinese cities of 2020 have already been designed and so have their transport options. However, elsewhere, many commentators see that a more sustainable urban transport future can only be achieved if more informed choices are made by governments and organisations as well as individuals.

The recognition that 'in most OECD countries, transport usually accounts for over 25% of total greenhouse gas emissions' is increasingly influencing planning policy for regeneration as much as new-build. As such, pedestrianisation and cycle routes, for example, are both on the increase. However, while 'policymakers believe that car users are able to reduce their car use, many are unwilling to do so'. As it seeks to break the vicious circle of transport growth and decouple the linkage between it and economic growth, mobility management has to therefore consider structural and attitudinal change. In terms of influencing personal behaviour, the recent Shell/TRL analysis highlighted the impact that smarter choices can have – from better travel plans, improved taxi services, changing access to vehicles through car clubs and car-sharing schemes and increased awareness of alternatives to the car, a reduction in car use in the UK of up to 20% was forecast. Whether or not they start with transit system plans or shifts to cycling, all discussions on future urban transport ended up highlighting the need to reduce car use. In the developed and the developing worlds, in new and old cities, the big push that is evidently building momentum is to use manifold means to constrain movement by car and reward alternatives. By 2020, although globally we will clearly have more drivers in the world, the hope of the planners is that the overall miles travelled by car will be stable and that the increase in numbers will be offset by a reduction in distance.

Related insights

Page 163

Page 223

Page 231

The future of security

Security is considered one of the core human needs and is an area that is under increasing pressure. For some, this is more evident than others. However, around the world, with increasing ease of communication and connectivity, more people and the certainty of key resource constraints, we will all get used to more coverage of security-related topics over the next ten years. These will not be just issues about military or national security, although this is evidently an important topic where changes are taking place. The eight probable future changes covered in this section also cover food security, health security, energy security and water security. They deal will fundamental concerns that nations and cities have about securing supplies of the resources to feed their populations, protect their health and access the resources to grow. In addition, some of the issues addressed cover topics related to data security. In the always connected, data-intensive world that more of us will be part of by 2020, which data we trust, how identity is verified and how organisations manage the control of their corporate data are all areas where significant change is possible. Touching all these elements, the probable futures in this section hopefully stimulate some new perspectives on the world we are moving into.

The topics covered in the following pages are:

Alternative proteins

Bio-surveillance

Corporate LEGO

Credible sources

Drone wars

Solar sunrise

Virtual authenticity

Water management

Alternative proteins

The shift in global diet from rice to meat brings new sources of protein including lab-grown manufactured meats and high protein vegetable combinations.

One of the common challenges with rising economic growth is that of increased resource consumption. As highlighted in the first section of this book, as GDP per capita increases so does food consumption: once people have more money available, one of the first things they do is to seek to improve their diet. Whether this involves an incremental shift to higher quality or more tasty foods or a more fundamental shift from, say, a rice-based diet to one with more meat, the well-recognised global impact of increased wealth is a higher calorie and, ideally, higher protein lifestyle. Just as individuals climb what is seen as the energy ladder, so they also climb the calorie and protein ladders. The more money we have, the more or better foods we eat and this is pretty well a linear relationship until the point when enough is enough. Wrap all this together with an increasing population and steadily rising economic growth worldwide and we face a significantly growing world protein demand. The big issue here is that complete protein commodities are becoming increasingly scarce and alternative sources will be required.

Even without all the growth on the horizon, we already have some problems with protein deficiency. In developing countries, where food is based on plant fibres, protein deficiency is a major cause of ill health. In developed economies, protein deficiency is relatively rare but can still be found in the poorest communities where poor diets are the most common. On average, we all need around 50g of protein per day to avoid a deficiency and in the US the recommended daily intake (measured as intake per body weight) is 0.8g/kg – so, 80 to 100g for the typical male. In terms of sources, an egg provides 6g of protein, 1 pint of milk, 19g, and 100g of chicken contains 25g of protein. Red meats contain more protein but also have a lot more fat. Excess protein cannot be stored in the body so over-consumption has no benefit and is effectively a waste.

Considering the number of people on the planet, the rise of many up the protein ladder and the availability of protein, the problem we face is that we are fast running out of natural sources. Yes, we could all farm and eat more meat but the environmental impact of that in terms of land use, water consumption and carbon emissions, to name just the obvious ones, is unsustainable. Food security is an increasing issue for many governments as they seek to ensure that they have enough food for their populations. Several nations are now developing food supply strategies that will secure supplies in times of scarcity or higher prices. The 2008 food price spike caused riots and civil unrest in a number of countries, including Yemen, Somalia, Senegal, Pakistan, Mozambique, Indonesia, India, Egypt, Ivory Coast, Cameroon, Burkina Faso, the Philippines and Bangladesh. If we are going to satisfy the growing protein demand without resorting to protectionist behaviours that lead to hoarding of supplies, we need alternative sources.

The problem is that more and more of us want to eat meat and less of us are prepared to be vegetarian, even just for a day a week.

If we were prepared to eat more of them, then beans, whole grains and nuts are all good options because animal protein and vegetable protein have the same effects on health. The problem is that more and more of us want to eat meat and less of us are prepared to be vegetarian, even just for a day a week. Added to that, the demand for soybean, a staple diet for animals, is rapidly getting out of balance with supply. China already buys more than half of globally traded soybeans and, according to Cargill, the world's largest food supply company, 'the country's annual soybean consumption will rise as much as 8% for the next three to four years'. Others see that, by 2020, global demand for soybeans will be double that of 2008.

One very good, low-fat source of protein is fish, which provides around 20 g of protein per 100 g of fillet. However, according to organisations such as the International Food Policy Research Institute, the ability to meet world demand for fish from natural fish stocks has reached its peak and now is declining. Over-fishing has depleted global stocks to such an extent that we can no longer rely on this resource and the world will have to 'turn increasingly to aquaculture or fish farms, managed natural fisheries, and genetically improved, fast-growing fish if it is to meet future food needs without ruining global aquatic resources'. The EU's view is that, 'As global fish stocks continue to plunge, fish farming is seen as a way of contributing to food security', and according to the IFPRI, 'in 2020, fish production will rely less on natural stocks and more on aquaculture and enhanced stocks', but it will take at least another twenty-five years beyond that before aquaculture meets the majority of the world's fish needs.

The fact is, we need other alternatives and the main focus is on manufacturing proteins. As highlighted by Jim Kirkwood in the initial perspective on the future of food: 'The development of non-meat, high-protein foods as meat alternatives or acceptable protein vegetable alternatives could help us more efficiently meet the increasing world protein demand.'

The most progress in this area to date has been in the Netherlands where *in vitro* meat production is already occurring – albeit in a lab. '*In vitro* meat, also known as cultured meat, is animal flesh that has never been part of a complete, living animal.' To make *in vitro* meat, natural muscle cells are taken from a sample piece of real meat and proteins are applied to help these grow into large portions of meat. There are a couple of different approaches to this that have been tried in the field of tissue engineering and the greatest success has been seen in the Netherlands where a matrix of collagen is seeded with the muscle cells which are then bathed in a nutrient solution and induced to divide and multiply. In 2009, Dutch scientists, supported by government funding, grew meat in the laboratory using cells from a live pig and they are now also focused on using chicken cells. Other programmes are also under way in the US but at the moment the Dutch seem to be setting the pace. Although some fear such lab-based products, in reality they could be just as tasty as natural meats and may even be healthier by virtue of having a lower fat content.

Cost-wise, current estimates suggest that, with likely technology improvements, *in vitro* meat would be about twice the price of conventional chicken but with the advantage that only the bits that we want are grown rather than the whole chicken. The option of artificial chicken breasts is certainly on the horizon.

By 2020, with an extra 750 million or so people on the planet, many of whom will be higher consumers of meat, we can clearly see that natural proteins will more expensive. The possibility that lab-grown meat protein will be commonplace is increasingly supported by world experts. However, there are a couple of other options that should also be considered.

First, and highest on the agenda of many organisations including the UN, is that we all change our food consumption behaviour and become part-time vegetarians. Even if it were only for one or two days a week, if we could reduce all the world's consumption of meat proteins by 25% it would give us some breathing space before alternatives – such as increased fish farming and even vegetable proteins – can efficiently be brought into play to meet the world's increasing demand. In support of this, some are even advocating the rationing or premium pricing

The development of non-meat, high-protein foods as meat alternatives or acceptable vegetable protein alternatives could help us more efficiently meet the increasing world protein demand.

of 'natural' meat through the introduction of specific taxes on meat.

Second, and even more controversially, there is the option of simply creating designer food sources. Now that Craig Venter and his colleagues at Synthetic Genomics and the Craig Venter Institute have successfully created a synthetic bacteria cell, the potential opportunities are endless. While the initial focus is on moving on from simple bacteria to creating algae that can play a major role in the bio-fuel arena, plants and animals are also possible avenues for this technological breakthrough. Designing new bespoke food sources as well as replicating existing ones is therefore increasingly moving from the world of science fiction into a credible future possibility.

Related insights

Page 73

Page 213

Page 239

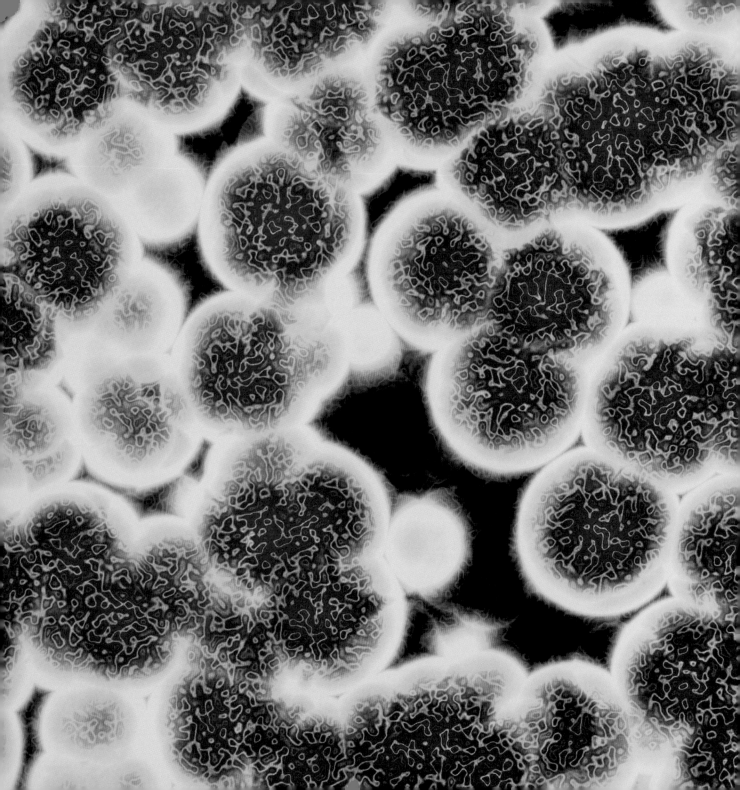

Bio-surveillance

Active gathering and interpretation of data related to threats to human and animal health delivers faster early warning and situational awareness.

In an era of increased globalisation, public health and surveillance are playing an increased role in bio-security. Protecting us from the outbreak of disease has become an increasingly hot topic in healthcare circles and is a focus for major investment. As part of global and national health security systems, public health surveillance is widely used for such activities as detecting new cases; estimating impact; modelling the spread of diseases; evaluating prevention and control measures; and strategic prevention planning. To achieve these ambitious objectives involves ongoing and systematic collection, analysis, interpretation and dissemination of a mass of health-related data on the population. An emerging field, known as bio-surveillance, has involved the expansion of the traditional public health surveillance into detecting and predicting bio-terrorist threats and disease outbreaks in animals and plants. This is far from easy and, as the world becomes more susceptible to the rapid spread of epidemics and pandemics, we face a challenge highlighted by Jack Lord in his view on the future of health – namely, that 'our ability to achieve global bio-surveillance for disease is limited because of unequal infrastructure, inadequate local investments and only limited global cooperation'. Successfully delivering and operating a reliable bio-surveillance system demands not just an alignment of multiple sources of data but the analytical capability to make sense of the data and highlight the critical patterns for disease detection and prevention. With

Protecting us from the outbreak of disease has become an increasingly hot topic in healthcare circles.

global health security increasingly high on national agendas, many across the healthcare system see bio-surveillance as a priority and one that could be fundamental in changing how we deal with public health in the future.

Bio-surveillance is presently defined as 'a systematic process that monitors the environment for bacteria, viruses, and other biological agents that cause disease; detects disease in people, plants, or animals caused by those agents; and detects and characterises outbreaks of such disease'. It is a continuous process that encompasses not just data collection from myriad sources but also rapid, intelligent analysis and interpretation. It is by its very nature multidisciplinary, multi-organisational, data intensive, time critical, knowledge intensive and highly complex. As such, being able to bring together all the necessary ingredients in an effective manner is seen by many as one of the biggest challenges that we currently face. Improving the effectiveness of bio-surveillance programmes and the use of new technologies to enhance data collection and analysis

One major technological advance is the spread of DNA fingerprinting beyond crime-fighting into the tracking and detection of potentially harmful strains in bacteria, plants and animals.

are therefore high on the list of imperatives for many public health systems. Therefore, in recent years, organisations such the US-based Center for Disease Control (CDC) have been investing in projects like BioSense, which is 'designed to increase the nation's emergency preparedness through the development of a national network for real-time disease detection, monitoring, and health situational awareness'. Linking together data feeds from over 2,000 hospitals, it is a major step by the US in detecting diseases and is already seen 'as part of the nation's overall bio-terrorism and emergency preparedness strategy'.

One major technological advance is the spread of DNA fingerprinting beyond crime-fighting into the tracking and detection of potentially harmful strains in bacteria, plants and animals. DNA fingerprinting is, for example, now part of the screening process for fish catches to ensure that potentially dangerous bacteria like *E. coli* are not present. It is also being used to identify antibiotic-resistant strains to help doctors either to select an antibiotic other than the one to which the bacteria are resistant, or to consider choosing alternative treatments.

Although less sophisticated than the systems being run by the CDC, the World Health Organization a decade ago had a similar ambition for its Integrated Disease Surveillance Programme, which strengthened disease surveillance capacity in over forty African countries. Looking ahead, a major challenge lies in creating a global bio-surveillance system that will work equally well around the world. According to workshop participants, collecting reliable data from the field and connecting the sources in an effective manner itself requires 'a significant change in the current surveillance paradigm'. Add on the levels of intelligence required to be built into and support data mining of such a wide range of information and the barriers are clear. 'Integrated systems that use new data systems, analysis, visualisation and modelling as well as decision analysis tools are clearly required,' many of which are now in development.

At the same time, more open human-to-human communication is also a key ingredient for global bio-surveillance, and this is one aspect that is now more or less sufficiently advanced to have an impact. As the Chatham House Centre on Global Health Security puts it: 'With the advent of the internet and the blogosphere, there have been radical changes in the ways that public health risks are communicated by and to the public. These changes can influence national and international health policies that are designed to respond to threats to our collective health.' Non-traditional sources of health data such as news stories, unstructured real-time text messages between healthcare professionals and animal health reports can, if properly integrated, provide core elements of an effective system.

Looking ahead to 2020, the ambition of an international system that links together relevant sources of dispersed data from such sources as hospitals, animal health centres, local monitoring of water sources for biological agents and even remote monitoring of people and animals from space seems to be increasingly realisable. International agreements, legacy system integrations and open communication of data are already in place. Once these are matched up with the data analysis and visualisation software already in use in other sectors, the anticipated changes, it is argued, will occur. An increasing number of healthcare experts can see just over the horizon a future where 'as soon as an outbreak of disease occurs, whether in humans or animals, it can be rapidly tracked and analysed so that the appropriate responses can be activated.' With this, not only will we have faster early warning, detection and situational awareness of threats to public health, but we will also have the means to better plan for future disease scenarios from multiple sources. Whether

As soon as an outbreak of disease occurs, whether in humans or animals, it can be rapidly tracked and analysed so that the appropriate responses can be activated.

responding to ebola, avian flu or bio-terrorism, it is anticipated that 'linked overt and covert surveillance will protect the populace – ideally as well in the southern hemisphere as is likely in the North.' If everything goes to plan, whether you live in New York or the Rift Valley, improved public health will be underpinned by this type of global monitoring.

Related insights

Page 61

Page 73

Page 239

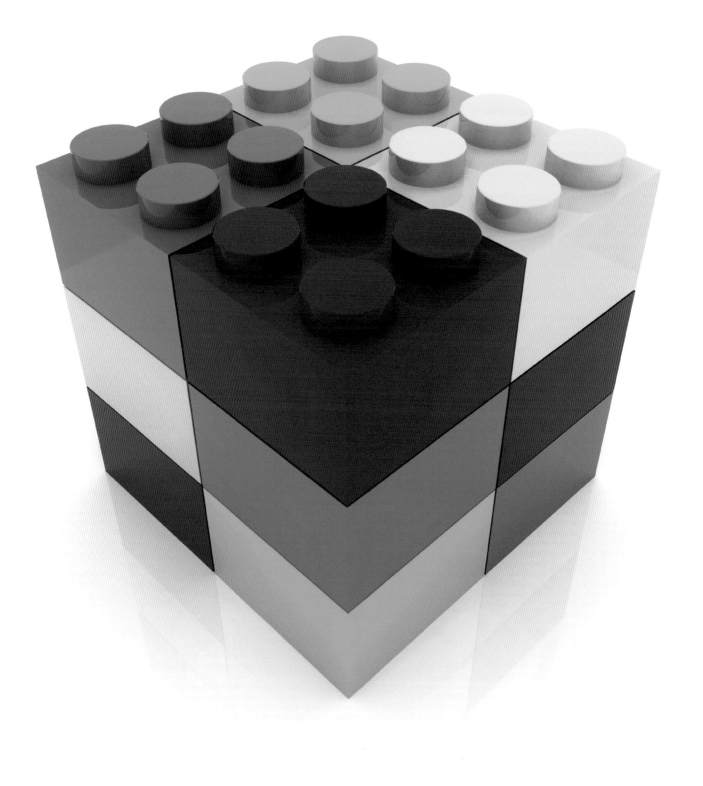

Corporate LEGO

With more free agents and outsourcing, non-core functions within organisations are interchangeable and easily rebuilt around value-creating units.

Organisations have already started to be more permeable and flexible. Increasing use of consultants, freelancers and other temporary staff has blurred the boundary between employee and contractor in many large companies. In addition, the outsourcing of such functions as IT, HR, finance and other so-called 'back-office' jobs, often to different countries, has saved money but also increased the complexity of the organisational framework. While many companies today still see themselves as entities with employees in control of a wide range of value-creating and support activities, by the end of the decade more and more organisations will be networks.

'While there will be a permanent core to the business, it will become increasingly small and more of a direction-setting and delivery-choreographing entity.' Businesses of 2020 will have fewer people managers in charge of cohorts of workers and more project managers ensuring that the right activities are undertaken in the most effective manner irrespective of whether the project team is internal or external to the organisation. Some examples of this shift are being collated in the world's business schools and associated organisations such as the Management Lab in California. What they are pointing to is a world where organisations are becoming increasingly unbundled and recombined around different tasks and issues. The ability of companies to manage a community, rather than employees with

Some organisations are now obliged to plug and unplug the leading-edge capabilities to meet ever more challenging local and global needs.

a clear reporting line, presents a challenge that will be difficult for many to deal with. Some business leaders are already learning how to play Corporate LEGO. In fast-changing markets and technology areas, more and more companies will have to learn to plug and unplug capability from inside and outside the organisation on a project-by-project basis.

The initial drivers for change in organisations are generally cost and efficiency. Pressure on costs, reach and access forced many firms to outsource or offshore many of their commoditised functions. Conversely, to date, most companies have generally kept their value adding, differentiating capabilities 'within the tent' – R&D, marketing and design have all been viewed as the key capabilities and so have been protected, nurtured and kept close to the strategic heart of the firm. However, as companies and brands are becoming increasingly more differentiated by the world-class expertise they can access to create and deliver their new products and services, some organisations are now obliged to plug and unplug

Open innovation has encouraged the heart of an organisation's future growth to become a network.

the leading-edge capabilities to meet ever more challenging local and global needs.

As Chris Meyer highlighted in his initial perspective on the future of work: 'Web 2.0 is teaching organisations about the power of collective work product, leading to Enterprise 2.0, an organisational form with porous boundaries, shared responsibilities, greater transparency, and fewer mandatory rules and practices.' Increasingly decentralised corporations are fast becoming a combination of amalgams of a series of independent capabilities that share common processes, systems and cultural norms but are structured as separate business units or profit centres with independent management and customers. Rapid changes in technologies, markets and strategic priorities are increasingly resulting in the separation and reformation of corporate structures using these independent units as organisational building blocks.

One major influence on, and catalyst for, this has been the widespread embracing of the 'open innovation' philosophy, where ideas flow into the organisation from an ever increasing ecosystem of partners, universities, consultants, customers and entrepreneurs. In firms such as P&G, which has staked a huge bet on the open innovation philosophy with its Connect + Develop approach, this has already meant a shift to engaging a wider, deeper supply base of innovation than was traditional with just internal marketing,

approved agencies and R&D as the focus. In a similar vein, Novartis has already relocated its R&D HQ from Switzerland to Massachusetts and is now well plumbed into the local biotech system; and the likes of Microsoft, IBM and Intel have all set up research labs in Beijing to access the local talent, especially around the field of speech recognition. These companies are, in their different ways, all demonstrating the ability to unbundle organisational capabilities from one part of the business and align them with a wider external ecosystem. Open innovation has encouraged the heart of an organisation's future growth to become a network. Going forward, several leading commentators see a similar shift on the horizon for strategy.

Over 30% of the US population are already 'free agents' working either independently or as subcontractors. Within ten years, around half of the Western workforce is expected to be self-employed, increasingly working on a project-by-project basis. This fundamental change is providing a plethora of experts and consultants available as subcontracted resources to be pulled in and out of firms as needs demand. At the same time, how we work is changing. The project team members of today, and certainly tomorrow, are increasingly people who have grown up in the connected world. As many of these 'digital natives' go mobile and become 'digital nomads', they will be looking to create value wherever, whenever, using whatever devices they like. In the 'always connected' world this becomes an accepted way of life for those who can contribute the most.

As Swedish academics Kjell Nordstrom and Jonas Ridderstrale forecast over a decade ago in their book *Funky Business*, we have a world in which there are 'people worth employing' and 'organisations worth working for' but by 2020 this will increasingly be on a temporary project-by-project basis. As such 'the heart of value creation for organisations will increasingly shift outside the traditional corporate boundaries to embrace people more interested in portfolio careers than company progression.' This places greater challenges for companies across the board, especially in managing risk.

With outsourced back-office functions, organisations can manage risk to delivery and support through contractual service-level agreements (SLAs) that set out exactly what needs to be done and to what standard. In the world where innovation, strategy and the best ideas sit outside the organisation and are developed by a group of individuals who are attracted by the challenge and opportunity for addressing them, the way companies manage corporate risk necessitates a fundamental shift from the past. Where business model discussions mean that know-how is freely shared outside the constraints and protection of intellectual property regulations, trust between colleagues and project teams becomes ever more important. As one workshop participant saw it:

"The ability of corporations to serve their customers is largely driven by access to and the use of data. Data integration is a growing challenge. The future will see more agile corporations, more decentralisation and new IT infrastructures."

At the same time, more organisations are seeing a future in which their brand can no longer be managed. In one workshop, old and new economy companies discussed how the ability to 'broadcast' your brand to customers and the outside world was already being replaced by participation in networks. Rather than brand managers, organisations are progressively having internal reputation managers – value-protecting professionals that mix traditional PR and investor relations with proactive participation in pivotal social networks. What is more, these individuals increasingly sit outside the corporate entity and work as consultants. Moreover, as highlighted by the foresight on differentiated commoditised knowledge, 'with the growth of the creative commons and open source movements, core components of corporate and institutional knowledge will increasingly be shared without restriction'. In a world where Corporate LEGO is the biggest game in town and companies continue to seek to grow globally through fast and more effective innovation, some pivotal business challenges for the next decade are already quite clear.

Related insights

Page 83

Page 111

Page 197

Credible sources

Greater information overload moves our focus from simply accessing data to including the source of the insight to distinguish what we trust.

As connectivity increases and the information being generated around the world rises, many of us will be faced with ever more data, insight and comment that we will have to try to make sense of. As was highlighted repeatedly in the Future Agenda programme, 'the biggest challenge is simply to manage the huge amount of data out there'. Many see that we already have too much data, are too dependent on information and this prevents us making decisions:

"Too much reliance on data to guide our views has meant that we have lost intuition. Going forward we need to rise above the mass of information so that once again we can make more focused decisions."

As a result, many organisations are seeking to help make sense of the information available. As pointed out by D. J. Collins at Google in his initial view of the future of data: 'Companies such as IBM, Oracle and SAS are making strides in data mining and database management. Their research shows that intelligent systems will become increasingly prevalent. Other organisations, like Amazon, Sun and even Google, are demonstrating the amazing benefits in scale and interoperability that come through moving data storage into the cloud.' The direction of travel is clear and many are focused on delivering the best answer ahead of the competition. However, there are numerous concerns over the impact this shift will have on how we use information.

"In many areas, knowledge is already a commodity — Wikipedia is one obvious example. If this trend increases, then where is the power? One could ask whether access to information really does empower the individual. I would say only if the recipient knows what to do with it. In the future we will move increasingly to wanting 'data we choose' to receive rather than just access to hard data. This could lead to a narrowing of opinions too early but clearly the successful recombination of the data received will lead to increased influence."

Many see that this information–power balance is currently in a state of flux and over the next decade could move significantly.

At a structural level, the migration of computer applications from the desktop to the web, the so-called shift to 'cloud' computing, will imply that more of our personal and professional lives will be spent using our web browsers. That means browsers will have to be stable, powerful and, above all, secure. In the initial view on the future of data, it was suggested that 'if we consider what has been achieved in the past ten years, over the next decade we have the opportunity to give more power to users. In the world of ubiquitous and uniform access, intelligent agents and the semantic web, we have the potential to enable even greater shifts in transparency and access to data than previous generations could have ever imagined.' From Google's perspective: 'If people are comfortable sharing their search history with us,

Opinion is of little value until you can authenticate it – so the challenge will be to identify credible (authentic) information.

we can use that as a valuable signal to provide them more relevant information more quickly.'

Within the next decade, some people see that there will be so much information shared and freely available that we will be able to create totally new information infrastructures. 'If, for example, we take the data sets associated with the human genome, then we can in principle create a complete world family tree – we can have a search engine of the world's DNA and we will be able to see how we are all individually related and so, as a consequence, how we seek to behave towards each other may change.' Greater sharing of data is seen by many as inevitable.

However, others disagree with this: 'We need more efficiency and greater relevance incorporated into the system as we focus on information not knowledge. Efficiency, timeliness and relevance are critical and having a sea of data is without value. We need more than search engine technology and to focus on information arbitration.' Or, in other words:

"The future will be about more efficient data use. If 90% of what we get from current search engines is useless, relevance is clearly a challenge. Therefore we have to apply more intelligent criteria to filter our information – and this is all to do with redundancy of information."

In effect, it is not that we need more information but that we need more credible information. To address this issue, those who are driving the web forward anticipate that it will be more powerful, flexible and useful in the years to come. 'The much-touted "semantic web" – in which the relationships between pieces of information will be both apparent and useable – may not be imminent, but it's certainly within sight. Its advent will drive further research, and it will also make the web more useful to people around the world.' Wouldn't it be good to have a system that asks questions as well as answers them? Others concurred with this: 'The semantic web will play a significant role in helping to align the key combinations of data we need to gain really useful information. Over the next ten years, semantic search engines will shift the intelligence behind search to a far higher level. The challenge will be in making the search engines more intuitive.'

One issue here is our increasing dependence on a single source of information – namely, the leading global search engine run by Google: 'If we are looking to capture more information, we need multiple sources, not just a single one. For real insights on the world we cannot trust just one search engine.' As Diane Coyle pointed out in the initial view on the future of authenticity:

"The most effective way to counteract falsehoods in the future will probably come from the pooling of many messages and reports so the people can see where there is a consistent story. The aggregation of different stories could be a powerful tool for verification."

However, some see that the growing gap between the wisdom of the crowd and the ignorance of the mob will increasingly create the demand for greater differentiation between believable views and more noise in the online world. Just having multiple sources is not enough: what people see as more important are credible sources, ones in which we have full confidence. 'We need to have trust in the medium as well as the data. We need to recognise the difference between fact and opinion — and so be able to see the credible from the incredible. The credibility of information is based on the profile of the person offering it and going forward this will become more significant. In addition, we need to be cognisant of the drivers of trust such as governance, stewardship and openness.' A complementary view was that 'opinion is of little value until you can authenticate it — so the challenge will be to identify credible (authentic) information. The definition of what is credible may have to change — in the future, credibility may be delivered through a ranking system based on trust.' Another added:

"With increased connectivity and sharing of data, we will need more trusted intermediaries. Choice agents will need to be trusted more and there will be a currency of trust appearing. Sources of information will be as significant as the information itself."

For many of us, decisions are emotionally driven, not data driven. Data are there to provide context and allow us to make informed judgements. Some see that 'if we are to be loaded with more data in the future, it will lead to slower judgement without

Sources of information will be as significant as the information itself.

depth of rigor. With too much data to process, we are increasingly being shallow and broad in our views rather than deep and narrow.' What people believe, who they trust and what they see as credible are judgements based on what information is available. This will increasingly be not just the information that companies and organisations put out into the media maelstrom, but also what people say about them.

In the parallel world of reliable sources for journalists, those who are seen as offering the most credible information will rise to the top of the stack of trusted brands, media organisations and individual commentators. Their opinions will be the most valued and the most used to inform decisions. The problem here is, however, that there is also a big question over the business models that will be able to work in the world of ubiquitous cheap data. As yet, it is unclear how the infrastructure will actually be financed over the next decade and whether people will be willing to pay for better information.

"We are increasingly accustomed to free access to free information and so shifting back to a pay-to-access approach will be no easy move — particularly for the younger generation. The question is, should access to information be monetised and, if so, by whom?"

Drone wars

Intelligent UAVs choose their victims themselves as the race for more focused military influence leads to the proliferation of assassination tools.

Over the past couple of years, Afghanistan and Pakistan have seen a significant increase in the use of drone aircraft by the US military and other security services. They have become the proving ground for a fundamental shift in how military power is exercised, how information is collated and used and, ultimately, how wars will be fought. With a military budget that accounts for nearly half of the world's military spend, the US has become increasingly attracted to drones, which cost a fraction of the price of a fighter but have the potential to provide equal if not greater presence. With over 7,000 unmanned aircraft already being used by the US military alone and as other countries scale up their arsenal, by 2020 the majority of both surveillance and conflict will be undertaken by increasingly sophisticated and intelligent unmanned aerial vehicles or UAVs.

Initially used for surveillance in Kosovo in the late 1990s and then armed from 2001, the Predator undertook one of its first CIA-controlled assassination assignments in Yemen in 2002. Since then the Chinese, Russians, Israelis, French and Pakistanis have all been using UAVs. In 2006, Hezbollah flew drones over Israel during the Lebanon War.

By 2010, the US Air Force was flying at least twenty Predator drones each day in Afghanistan. Much of their use has been for surveillance, with each drone

The US has become increasingly attracted to drones which cost a fraction of the price of a fighter but have the potential to provide equal if not greater presence.

providing up to ten video streams of footage back to their 'pilots' sitting either in Kandahar Airbase or, more likely, 7,000 miles away in secure facilities in Arizona or Utah. By 2011, an upgraded version of the more powerful Reaper drones will be carrying up to thirty cameras each. Alongside surveillance activities, drones also carried out over 200 missile and bomb attacks in the year – striking Taliban leaders and bomb-making factories. By comparison, at the peak of activity in Iraq, in 2008, seventy-seven missile strikes were launched.

In Pakistan, where drones are run by the CIA but launched from Pakistani airfields, there has been increasing coverage of their controversial use for the surveillance and assassination of both Taliban and Al Qaeda personnel. In 2009, there were sixty-nine recorded drone attacks in Pakistan. In the 'Af-Pak' region, where military ground action is complex, where exerting military power in no-go areas has

Thousands of hand-launched drones are used by soldiers to see what lies over hills and these are getting so easy to use that there are now even iPhone apps for controlling them.

become commonplace and where reports of US casualties have been an increasingly unwelcome item on CNN, the use of unmanned drones each equipped with four Hellfire missiles has been an attractive option and 'the weapon of choice'. Even though many see that these assassination machines are visibly provoking increasing anger in moderate society, their use is widely accepted and even promoted in the media.

It is not just the big Predator and Reaper UAVs that are being used. Thousands of hand-launched drones are used by soldiers to see what lies over hills and these are getting so easy to use that there are now even iPhone apps for controlling them. MIT's Human and Automation Lab has led the development of apps that use the iPhone's touch screen, tilting sensors and 3G data transfer to navigate drones and simultaneously view corresponding video feeds. Elsewhere, already in the final stages of development, are control systems that allow a single 'pilot' to control as many as three UAVs simultaneously while BAE Systems' Taranis drone is intended to

be completely autonomous, and so does not need human piloting. Scheduled for trial flights in 2011, the Taranis prototype shows the direction we are heading – a pilotless plane that can make its own decisions and even undertake air-to-air combat. As the world of gaming is integrated within military systems, the means of 'covert and overt engagement', as the military terms it, are changing rapidly.

What is more, the further disconnection of the 'pilot' from the 'action' is already making the emotional relationship of war weaker for some. Today's drone pilots in the US often live a 'normal life' where taking the kids to school is part of their daily routine: a shift flying drones over Afghanistan is just another high tech office job. Building on the increased automation of ordinance delivery that has gone before, the psychological implications of such decreasing contact between the source and recipient of action are raising some major questions in the military and beyond.

In ten years' time, many speculate that drones will be engaging in aerial battle and choosing targets for themselves. The US Defense Department is already financing studies of autonomous, self-governing,

BAE Systems' Taranis drone is intended to be completely autonomous, and so does not need human piloting.

armed robots that could find and destroy targets on their own. And as far back as 2002, initiatives such as the Autonomous Intelligent Network and Systems Program were planning to create an operational drone army by 2020. Going beyond autopiloting and pre-programming, these developments are preparing the way for a world where hordes of unmanned, unattended and untethered drones in the air, on the ground and under water reinvent the whole concept of a military structure. Linked together by an impregnable wireless mesh network capable of routing data between flying drones moving at 300 mph, this swarm approach to military operations is taking many countries rapidly into what was previously a world of science fiction. As one analyst quoted in the *New York Times* article said: 'The systems today are very much Model T Fords. These things will only get more advanced.'

In ten years' time, many speculate that drones will be engaging in aerial battle and choosing targets for themselves.

Related insights

Page 53

Page 197

Solar sunrise

Increasing governmental focus on energy security and climate change drives the uptake of large-scale solar as the leading renewable supply.

The combined pressures of rising global energy demand, increasing concern about climate change, greater focus on the advance of 'peak oil' and heightened awareness of the challenges around energy security are driving many countries to look for alternative energy sources. While long-term prospects rest on technological breakthroughs and the wider adoption of nuclear energy to decrease the use of fossil fuels, as highlighted in the first section, the next decade is still very much one in which oil, gas and coal are the major sources of energy. With India and China growing fast, and so requiring ever more energy to fuel this growth, with the US still very much 'addicted to oil' and with governments yet to agree a global way forward, the energy world in 2020 will, according to International Energy Agency projections, still be over 70% fossil fuel based.

However, by implication, over the next decade there will be a significant shift in the adoption of renewable, alternative energy supplies. Wind, wave, solar, nuclear, bio, hydro and geothermal generation are all pushing ahead, some with clear momentum and others with inertia yet to be overcome. As different countries are advocating different options, it is clear that there is no single global answer. Coastal locations favour wind turbines, mountainous districts favour hydroelectricity, Iceland is pushing ahead with geothermal, solar is the favourite of sunny regions and, while some countries want access to nuclear, many others do not. Talking

through the problem in our workshops, it is evident that, globally, the next decade is one in which solar energy is expected to make the most headway overall. To achieve change in the first place, however, many experts drew attention to two key issues.

Firstly, we are using the wrong business models. That is, we are trying to look at the potential future solutions through the lens of today's business models: 'The current economic models we use are not suitable for managing our future energy needs where the payback periods will be longer than the usual norms. We need to provide a framework to appropriate change in the energy mix and support the huge investment needed. The speed of transition that we need to address the energy challenge is out of sync with the established views on returns on investment.'

Secondly, 'it is not just about the technology; policy and markets are just as important'. This view is becoming increasingly clear as green stimulus packages start to take effect alongside the existing incentives already in place: Germany's 'feed in' tariff provides a long-term guaranteed price for renewable energy that has made it a leader in solar energy development while the US government's subsidies for bio-fuels have got the ethanol and bio-diesel market going across the Americas. Add in the failure of Copenhagen to agree any meaningful global targets, growing concerns over the environmental

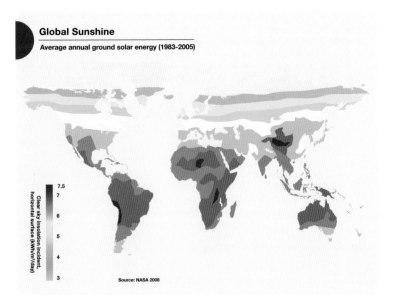

Global Sunshine

Average annual ground solar energy (1983-2005)

Clear sky insolation incident, horizontal surface (kWh/m²/day)

7.5
7
6
5
4
3

Source: NASA 2008

in the percentage of supply that nuclear provides during the next decade. We are also likely to see increased investment in proof-of-concept schemes for wave power, but again this will not have achieved a significant scale by 2020. Geothermal and hydro will continue to be limited to certain geographies and many scenarios increasingly expect that the fuel versus food debate concerning bio-fuels will have been exacerbated by more spikes in food prices and government U-turns on subsidies.

The fastest-growing area of renewable energy supply at the moment is wind. Xi Lu of Harvard has suggested that 'wind power in the US could potentially generate sixteen times the nation's current electricity production' – even when limiting locations to rural, non-forested sites and offshore. Moreover, 'worldwide, wind energy under the same constraints could supply at least forty times the current electricity consumption'. What is uncertain however, is the speed at which this capacity can be rolled out, at what cost and by whom. So, no one can say what the impact of wind power will be by 2020.

A pivotal issue in any assumptions about wind power is that of materials availability. 'In a world where telephone lines are routinely dug up so that people can resell the copper, using millions of tonnes of it in wind turbines seems unlikely.' Alternative materials such as high temperature superconductors are now in trial applications, but the likelihood of being able to scale these up substantially within ten years is low. So, despite the optimism shown by some, many others surmise that 'current growth in wind turbines will not be sustained'.

This brings us to solar energy – a virtually limitless clean resource. In its most common form, photovoltaic (PV) panels convert sunlight into

impacts of the Canadian tar sands and US government reaction to the Deepwater Horizon disaster and one can see a raft of new nationally focused policies on the horizon. As countries scramble to protect their supplies and gain individual energy security, and thereby steer away from what Shell sees as the 'blueprint' scenario of greater global cooperation, governments will seek to support the alternatives that are within reach from both a technological and economic point of view. Experience has shown that successful approaches work at many levels, so this combination of technology and economics also has to align with social acceptance and political will.

Together, these factors will mean that we are likely to see increased investment in nuclear energy for those that have access to the technology. As such, by 2020, in support of the traditional centralised view of supply, there will be more nuclear power stations coming on stream than ever but, given the overall dynamics of the sector, there is unlikely to be a tangible shift electricity. Typical current panels have an efficiency of around 10%, with more expensive ones achieving 20%. In the next few years, experts expect that this 'may rise to around 40%'. In 2009, PV installations grew by 20% to over 7 GW of new installations globally. While Europe, led by Germany, currently accounts for nearly 80% of global demand, over the next few years, many anticipate that more large-scale solar power systems will be installed across the world, from the US and China to Africa and India. As German subsidies decline in line with cheaper and more efficient technology, a tipping point of commercial viability will occur. According to the US Department of Energy's Solar America Initiative, PV solar energy will be competitive without subsidy by 2015. Just as with other technologies, increasing capacity will result in a steady cost decline and 'across the supply chain, manufacturers are increasing cell efficiency, using thinner silicon wafers and increasing power in low light levels'.

In the short term, the 2009 US Stimulus Bill, which included $60 billion in loan guarantees for companies building wind and solar plants, is giving a fillip to the US market. As Carol Sue Tombari of the US Department of Energy's National Renewable Lab points out in her recent book, 'Wal-Mart is aiming to meet 100% of its power needs from renewable energy' and, as part of this, is already installing solar power on its supermarket roofs in California and Hawaii. In addition, Google, a huge energy user, has announced a partnership with Sharp for PV roof systems. Elsewhere, China has also introduced a subsidy for solar energy installations and in 2009 the Qinghai province gave the go-ahead for the world's first 1 GW solar farm. More significantly, in January 2010 the Indian government launched its National Solar Mission, which is aimed at making India a global

There is little argument that, 'in the long term, all energy can be solar.

leader in solar energy and envisages an installed solar generation capacity of 20 GW by 2020 and 2,000 GW by 2050.

While some countries, such as those in northern Europe, could get around half their electricity needs from PV and solar farms within their national boundaries, if they had access to solar power from other countries, solar could meet nearly all electricity demand. According to calculations by experts, including Professor David MacKay of Cambridge University, 'a 100 km by 100 km square area of concentrated solar power (CSP) systems in the Sahara could provide enough power to meet Europe's current demand'. Looking ahead, organisations such as DESERTEC are promoting the adoption of CSP in Mediterranean countries and high-voltage DC transmission lines as a credible way to provide Europe with secure, clean energy. The same arguments clearly apply elsewhere in the world and some expect that they are likely to occur first in either India or China.

As was pointed out in the most recent Technology Futures programme hosted by Shell: 'Global energy consumption is around 470EJ per year. The sun delivers to the earth almost 4 million EJ of energy, so, theoretically, the sun could provide at least eight thousand times the energy we need.' There is little argument that, 'in the long term, all energy can be solar' and it looks likely that the next decade will be when the shift to solar truly starts gaining momentum.

Related insights

Page 95

Page 163

Page 219

Virtual authenticity

Trusting our digital credentials allows us to participate confidently in open global transactions to gain access to what we want when we want.

Proving what is real in an increasingly complex world is seen as a significant emerging challenge by many organisations. Although individual companies and even sectors have their own solutions to the problem of verifying what is authentic, there isn't a simple answer to this; nor is there likely to be. While this is a major challenge in the physical world, with the counterfeiting of everything from aircraft parts and pharmaceuticals to clothes and DVDs all on the rise, in the virtual world the problem is even greater. In the varied discussions relating to this topic during the programme, a number of alternative perspectives were shared and a significant proportion of them aligned around the crux of the issue: 'In a world where it is ever easier to make copies, the significance of authenticity is increasing, and gaining ever greater moral value.'

As Diane Coyle highlighted in her initial view on the future of authenticity, we are looking for verification across a number of different levels – from goods to information and from an experience to our identity. In terms of goods, 'fakes are proliferating in the online world. "Fake" music, films and software are sold to the benefit of customers but not of copyright holders.' The challenge here is that the fakes are just as good as the legitimate originals and valuing a fake is not new. As Wendy Schultz commented: 'The arts have a long traditional of valuing copies: Chinese painters traditionally learnt their craft by copying acknowledged masters, with the result that

The internet amplifies the questions of veracity and reliability which have always affected the mass media.

acknowledged masterpieces of Chinese art can themselves be copies.' Likewise, we can today point to the popularity of remixes in the music industry and fan-fiction, where high-quality literature can be created from substandard TV scriptwriting.

In terms of information, 'the internet amplifies the questions of veracity and reliability which have always affected the mass media'. Hence, as one commentator added, 'more people trust Wikipedia than CNN' – even though the latter is a professional news organisation. In one workshop, there was much discussion of how the Obama election campaign had used technology to create a seemingly authentic experience: 'The idea was that people could "get inside" the campaign and make a difference. The impression of being part of the network was certainly there even though the reality was probably different.' Technology, and especially the internet, was used to give people the sense of being closer to the heart of things than would otherwise have been possible, but at the same time it probably also exaggerated their perceived involvement.

Discussions with banks and data companies consistently highlighted the growing need for 'global secure identities' that could be trusted and used everywhere.

A lot of attention focused on how to authenticate identity – particularly online. The big challenge as yet unmet, it was largely agreed, is simply proving who you are in order to access information, purchase a product or a service or even gain entry to a building with excess process and complexity.

"Many of us now have multiple, real and virtual identities, and so can provide various sources of information that, pulled together, can give a rich picture of who we are. The question is, who can and should have access to it?"

As one workshop participant put it, 'authentication involves technological measures of verification … For example, biometric systems and digital rights management are two existing systems of authentication but, to date, and in spite of huge investment, digital rights management has been a complete failure.' Many existing attempts to create systems that work in the virtual space, and cannot be by-passed, have gained support but have not yet developed momentum to bring about global change.

As John Carr pointed out, in some areas, regulation makes identifying people a bigger challenge than it perhaps ought to be: 'For example, in the UK, mobile phones are not sold to people under 18 and so are designed, positioned and bought by parents and given to their children. However, in restricting access

to specific content, such as gambling sites and porn, a mobile operator in theory knows whether or not one of its customers is under the age of 18. Some companies have already said that they intend to achieve greater levels of granularity for the sub-18s so that young phone users could soon be stratified as sub-12s, 12–15s, 16–17s etc.' By comparing text patterns, phone usage and download behaviour, the differences between a 12-year-old girl and a 15-year-old boy are clear and steps could be taken to protect them from inappropriate content without having to know their name and address.

However, the big problem is global authenticity: having a system that works within certain national or regional boundaries or within certain sectors but not others is not the answer. Discussions with banks and data companies consistently highlighted the growing need for 'global secure identities' that could be trusted and used everywhere. While government-level authentication of identity via passport, biometric, iris scan or ID card is considered to be largely in hand for the next decade, the more open issue is that of proving who you are and so, for instance, how creditworthy you may be in relation to a specific transaction. This is not just about proving that you are who you say you are when at home using your PC, but doing so when you buy something from France over the mobile internet while you are in India. This second level of authentication of identity is relatively easy to achieve once you have the right data. However, the problem is that the existing data that retailers, utilities and airlines need is currently spread across many other firms: collectively sharing this so that, as a customer, you do not need to keep on providing name, address, date of birth, PIN number and password each time you want something is the core challenge and hence

A 'Google Identity' service or similar that allows us as customers to consolidate all our personal data in one place for sharing with whoever needs access to it to validate who we are could well be in common usage by 2020.

also an opportunity. Initiatives like Open-ID are a step forward here but many see a more integrated approach on the horizon.

Diane Coyle predicts that 'technological solutions will be commonplace in the next few years'. While some take the view that there is a role for the financial services players such as VISA, PayPal, Experian or a similar organisation to become the host of shared personal data to validate virtual authenticity, others see that right now the likely collator will be a company with a broader and established reach – namely

Google. Looking at the impact the company has had in the past decade and the data that it already has on the majority of internet users, some see that a 'Google Identity' service or similar that allows us as customers to consolidate all our personal data in one place for sharing with whoever needs access to it to validate who we are could well be in common usage by 2020.

Whatever organisation makes this happen, many believe that in the course of the next decade the business models that create an efficient and global centralised source of (non-government level) personal data, one that is open and accessible, with the right permissions, will have major impact. It would be a service that reveals only the relevant information needed to prove who you are, where you live or how old you are to the organisation that needs to know. Clearly, there are serious issues about privacy and trust that might jeopardise such an endeavour but the overriding benefit of having one central information point for all may well overcome this problem.

Related insights

Page 125

Page 175

Page 197

Page 235

Water management

Advanced water purification, irrigation and desalination technologies are used to help communities manage the growing supply–demand imbalance.

As highlighted in the key resource constraints chapter, water is the resource over which many governments, corporations and communities have greatest concern for the future. As populations increase and move to urban areas, and as consumption rises in line with economic growth, water stress will be the main challenge for many parts of the world.

At a basic level, many parts of Africa and Asia will suffer increased physical water stress as the available water per person falls below the UN minimum target of 50 litres per day. In many areas, sanitation, itself a UN Millennium Development goal, is increasingly seen as difficult to achieve. Today, around 2.5 billion people lack access to adequate sanitation and the aim of halving this figure by 2015 is likely to be missed by a considerable margin. In some parts of sub-Saharan Africa, achieving this goal even by 2050 is now considered to be an ambitious target.

From the US to Chile, southern England to Kenya and the greater parts of the Middle East to Southeast Asia, water scarcity is forecast to have a severe impact over the next decade. Indeed, economic water stress is expected to affect up to half of the global population by 2020. In many areas it is not that there is insufficient water over an annual cycle but that it comes in peaks and troughs: 'the wrong water at the wrong time in the wrong place'. This is increasingly occurring as, in one season, flooding

Economic water stress is expected to affect up to half of the global population by 2020.

encourages us to get rid of excess water as quickly as possible and, in another, drought leads us to try to catch every drop.

According to a recent World Bank/McKinsey report, 'by 2030, projected population and economic growth will lead to global water demand 40% in excess of current supply if no adequate action is taken in the coming years. This would leave one-third of the world's population with access to only half the water it needs.'

As governments develop national water strategies and both cooperate and compete to secure water supplies, companies will come under increasing pressure to make more effective use of water in their production processes. Some will follow the lead taken by the likes of SAB Miller, P&G and Dow in significantly reducing water consumption and the principle of water footprints will gain fast traction as media and governments seek to raise public awareness of the water challenge.

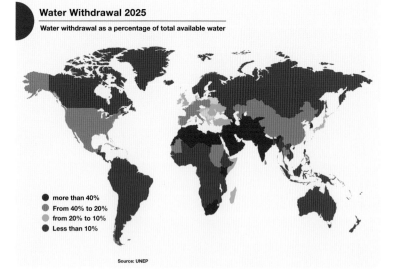

Water Withdrawal 2025

Water withdrawal as a percentage of total available water

- ● more than 40%
- ● From 40% to 20%
- ● from 20% to 10%
- ● Less than 10%

Source: UNEP

With momentum building up around the issue of water use, the impetus for improved water management will increase internationally. While major technological breakthroughs such as low-cost desalination will be sought and become major areas of investment over the next decade, the utopian vision of transforming sea water into fresh water available for all will not be realised. 'Desalination will remain a luxury for rich countries such as Israel, the UAE, Singapore and Saudi Arabia.' In addition, 'desal water' is too pure and so, in many countries, minerals need to be added to satisfy public health requirements.

Desalination will remain a luxury for rich countries.

Some argue that 'the water problem is not one of water scarcity but more of system management'. Therefore, in the next ten years, more pragmatic short-term solutions to help communities better manage the rising supply–demand imbalance will be implemented in such areas as water purification and irrigation. While the concept of a water grid, able to shift resources around regions and between buildings to balance supply and demand, is increasingly discussed, in many areas the next ten years will be more about driving consumption behaviour change. At the same time, the politics of water will continue to be a crucial issue. 'There are vested interests in the supply and management of water and the associated impact and influence of large-scale infrastructure. Most water infrastructures are managed both locally and regionally but are usually seen from a centralised perspective.'

Some say that the problem is one of consumer understanding and behaviour. In many regions where supply is not yet constrained, water is seen as having little value. People pay little attention to water because it is too cheap for them to care about. The view is that governments around the world should regulate such that everyone has a water meter and we can then build a wider public understanding of usage. In general, the privatisation of utilities such as water does not seem to have been effective and some companies are now proactively handing back the responsibility of running the infrastructure to non-profit public bodies and local authorities. Governance on catchment areas is key here. The UK system is the only one where the actual water supply has been privatised but it operates under government controls – and hence suffers from an inability to create value for the management companies.

'The water problem is not one of water scarcity but more of system management'.

The need to have an infrastructure that provides us all with water is the driving issue and we need to question whether large companies and organisations should be in control of this or whether it requires a local community focus. There was general agreement in the varied Future Agenda events that it really comes down to how you set up the institutions to achieve the aims and overcome the challenges at a local level. In urban environments, in addition to forcing us to reconsider certain lifestyles water scarcity could open up opportunities for innovation in areas such as water capture, treatment, conservation and efficiency. Changes in behaviour will require measuring our water consumption before we can manage it and solutions such as smart metering will find their way into our homes.

Community-driven mechanisms are particularly important in developing countries to ensure equity and effectiveness. One suggestion in India was to work more closely with women as, in the main, in many regions, it is they who fetch and carry water and therefore control access. There is also much to be gained from making the most of existing resources by reducing wastage, increasing water reuse, desalination and groundwater recharge. Simple but highly effective things like rain harvesting make a huge difference and, in the future, buildings will be better designed to align with this need.

The Economist is optimistic about the future and argues that change will happen where it is needed most: 'It will be in areas of high political, economic and social need that the key technological change in water will occur.' This is why Singapore is such a focus for water and its investment in low-cost desalination may be pivotal in the next decade. 'Both from government and companies such as Hyflux, many see that Singapore is a hub of water technology development.' Others are not quite so hopeful.

What everyone can agree on is that the issue is critical and that the right for all to have access to clean water is a priority. Therefore, a primary focus over the next decade will be to manage our supplies so as to enable this to happen.

Related insights

Page 87

Page 185

Page 219

Page 235

The future of locality

Finally we come to the future of all things local. With urbanisation an overarching mega-trend and so more of us, on average, living in urban environments in 2020 than do today, the increasing role of cities is another theme that drew a mass of comment and debate throughout the Future Agenda programme. From the design of future cities to the increasing political and economic influence of the world's mega-cities on the global stage, as well as how they compete, there is evidently change in the air. There are also related changes regarding the buildings in which we will live and work, and how we will get to and from them. In addition, within this cluster of topics linked to locality, we also cover such issues as future communities, feeding them and making more effective use of waste as a resource – all issues around which many have strong opinions for the future as well as some pretty clear directions already being established. The environments in which we live take time to change – urban planners often work in timeframes of decades. However, from the programme discussions, it is apparent that tangible change within the next ten years is both possible and probable in several areas and so these are the ones that we have highlighted here.

The topics covered in the following pages are:

Almost zero waste

Bridging the last mile

Community living

Dense cities

Intelligent buildings

Local foods

Mega-city states

Migration magnets

Almost zero waste

Escalating waste production and new attitudes, approaches, regulation and business models lead many to aim for an almost zero-waste society.

Some commentators predict that the amount of waste being generated will double over the next twenty years. This is due to increasing population, increasing urbanisation and increasing consumption. The problem is shared with energy, food and water supplies because the richer people get, the more they use. Waste is already the source of almost 4% of the world's greenhouse gases, mostly in the form of methane from rotting food. However, although great improvements have been made in dealing with it, the importance of waste management has been low on the collective agenda for too long.

The average American throws away over 700 kg of rubbish each year while, in Europe, each person produces over 500 kg of domestic waste and the developing nations are catching up fast. By 2030, Indians will be producing twice as much as they do now and Chinese people three times as much. On top of this, we generate huge quantities of construction debris, industrial effluent, mine tailings, sewage residue and agricultural waste. Dealing with it all is a costly exercise: rich countries spend some $120 billion a year disposing of their municipal waste alone and another $150 billion on industrial waste.

In a number of countries, the primary means of waste disposal is landfill and many see that this cannot continue – aside from the associated risks to human health and the local environment, there simply isn't enough land to fill. Yet the main alternative, burning waste, can be just as bad, both for people and for the planet.

The problem is that, with current practices, the world just can't cope. Many workshop participants suggested that we need to decouple waste generation from economic growth. It's a challenge to change people's mindsets but some regions have already introduced major initiatives to both reduce the amount of waste produced and also increase the levels of recycling. At one extreme, in places like San Francisco, new technologies are being introduced to automatically sort domestic trash and so reduce landfill. In his initial view on the future of waste, Ian Williams suggested that, 'in Switzerland, the practice of domestic sorting of waste has become so culturally ingrained that the country achieves some of the highest recycling rates in the developed world'. However, several people question this as a model for others: 'I wonder how far this model is transferable to other economies and cultures?' 'I can see a North European adoption quicker than an Asian one and so question its overall impact.'

In other places, even higher levels are being achieved. For instance, some claim that in Mumbai the natural system of domestic sorting to rag-pickers on the city's dumps means that recycling rates top 80%. In one Mumbai workshop, it was claimed that this figure is actually nearer 95%. That said, no matter how good Mumbai is at collecting its rubbish, its record

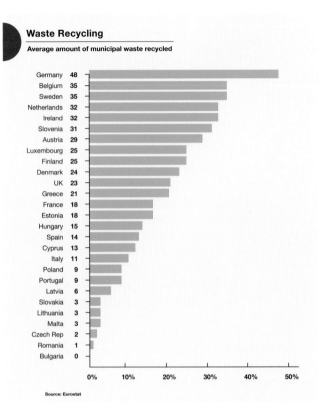

Waste Recycling

Average amount of municipal waste recycled

	%
Germany	48
Belgium	35
Sweden	35
Netherlands	32
Ireland	32
Slovenia	31
Austria	29
Luxembourg	25
Finland	25
Denmark	24
UK	23
Greece	21
France	18
Estonia	18
Hungary	15
Spain	14
Cyprus	13
Italy	11
Poland	9
Portugal	9
Latvia	6
Slovakia	3
Lithuania	3
Malta	3
Czech Rep	2
Romania	1
Bulgaria	0

Source: Eurostat

in disposing of it is poor. Dumps are unregulated so, for example, the city's biggest landfill site, Deonar, has no measures to control leaching, which means toxins are allowed to flow through the surrounding marshes and into the Arabian Sea.

Mumbai's waste collection process effectively works largely because there are enough poor people prepared to go through the cast-offs of the rich. Looking forward, it is argued, as individual wealth increases and the incentives change, the system will change and probably become less efficient. Certainly, few other countries would welcome the current Mumbai model of waste collection. Alternative approaches are needed.

A primary focus of regulatory and governmental attention in many countries has been on waste production by industry. Whether targeting waste discharge into rivers, recycling of key materials, design for disassembly practices or replacement of multiple plastic components with more sustainable options, industries around the world are being encouraged to improve production processes and reduce waste. However, in our workshops, it was emphasised that not enough progress has been made and that, to successfully tackle the waste challenge and move us to a more balanced system, three primary developments need to – and most likely will – take place over the next decade.

The first of these is improving consumer awareness. It is argued that, even in some leading European countries, our eco-literacy is still very low. Although places like Austria are seen to be well ahead in this respect, there is in general a lack of understanding of the impact that waste has on the environment and the economy, and the knock-on effects of transporting and burning waste. As such, we can expect a significant ramping up of school education, media campaigns and local council initiatives in the next ten years to nudge people towards behaviour change. 'A world where we focus as much on waste prevention as on waste treatment is essential.'

Secondly, the mindset of many in industry, as well as consumers, will need to shift towards waste being seen as a resource rather than a by-product. As the cost of dealing with waste escalates, new regulation around full cradle-to-grave product lifecycles comes into force and stories such as Nike's use of recycled

The mindset of many in industry, as well as consumers, will need to shift towards waste being seen as a resource rather than a by-product.

plastics for its 2010 World Cup shirts gain traction, many see that a fundamental re-think will occur as innovative businesses consider the possible opportunities presented by waste materials. While this may start with the more precious materials in short supply – and therefore be of particular interest to the electronics sector – it will quickly flow through into the mainstream world of plastic bottles, automotive components and food.

Food waste is increasingly an issue. In the UK today, over 35% of food is wasted; in the US, the figure is even higher. In a world where food security and supply are becoming key issues, many observers argue that a tipping point will be reached where attitudes to waste have to change. One suggestion in Mumbai was that we should learn from the past – why not return to the days where hawkers at the train station offer tea from clay cups rather than

polystyrene alternatives which are cast aside and scattered across the platform?

Thirdly, and arguably most critically, new business models for waste management will come into force over the next decade. In most countries, waste is seen from a centralised view with big investments in incinerators and the like. The trouble is that both the problem and the solution to better waste management is one that sits more comfortably in a small and distributed model. Local sorting and localised reuse are catalysts for major improvements in waste management, but the financial incentives are rarely there. Even where there are, in locations such as Mumbai, (allegedly) 'corrupt politicians are supporting the creation of large centralised mixed waste processing plants that will add complexity, increase cost and reduce the overall system efficiency.'

Around the world, we heard that this shift towards localised business models, ones in which we have 'a more intelligent way of managing resources on our overall balance sheets', is both essential and, if anything significant is to really change, highly probable. Governments and regulators should perhaps take note.

Related insights

Page 95

Page 159

Page 205

Page 213

Page 235

Bridging the last mile

Making public transport as flexible as private focuses attention on improving the last mile between multimodal hubs and the home/work destination.

The concept of 'the last mile' came into common language when telecommunications and cable television companies sought to deliver faster and better services to their customers. Although they can get data to hubs and exchanges quickly and cheaply, the challenge becomes far more complicated when it comes to reaching the final destinations and wires and cables have to fan out to multiple homes and offices. Not only is connecting the last mile more expensive than other parts of a network but it is also often in the last mile where loss of service quality occurs: reliability diminishes the farther you are away from the local exchange.

The same challenge occurs in the logistics sector as organisations increasingly offer their customers direct deliveries to home or office. Many firms have therefore been trying to optimise an increasingly complex system and smooth the supply chain. In addition, in many developing countries, the last mile has become a major problem for the distribution of healthcare services and medicines, especially ones such as vaccines that often require chilled environments. USAID, among other organisations, has responded by investing in the development of new tools and approaches to modify their supply chains in Africa and improve the final leg of delivery from urban depot to village health centre.

While these are all clearly major concerns, an issue raised in several of the workshops was that the last

This issue was seen to be just as significant in Delhi and Shanghai as it was in Brussels and Los Angeles.

mile is an equal if not greater challenge for people movement. Bridging the last mile (or first mile) at the start and end of the daily commute from home to work and back was seen as one way in which we can improve personal mobility and encourage people to make better use of public transport, and hence rely less on the car. Interestingly, this issue was seen to be just as significant in Delhi and Shanghai as it was in Brussels and Los Angeles. Although there are notable differences in the journey lengths and modes of transport, the principle is exactly the same: how do we better connect the home or workplace to an efficient transport hub? The concern here is that commuters seem disinclined to make better use of the public transport systems so, if the gap isn't bridged, they will find additional reasons for sticking to their cars. In many countries, a core problem with the first/last mile issue is that it induces people to use their vehicles for the whole journey and therefore bypass public transport completely. Many in our workshops agreed: 'Cars are used only because of a lack of better alternatives.'

Dealing with the logistics sector to begin with, where, according to the Council of Supply Chain

Cars are used only because of a lack of better alternatives.

Management Professionals, 28% of transportation costs are on average incurred in the last mile, there are lessons both good and bad to be learned.

Firstly, the argument that home delivery is both more convenient and more efficient has been gaining ground over recent years. Especially with the rise in internet shopping, the opportunities for individuals and businesses have been clear: customers can get exactly what they want, delivered directly to their doors, and so do not need to make a journey to a shop or supplier themselves. As a result, efficient distribution firms can build a healthy business fulfilling this need. In addition, the environmental advantages have been highlighted to support the cause: research in the UK, for example, has shown that a typical van-based home delivery service produces only 5% of the CO_2 emissions resulting from individuals' average trips to the shops by car. And the carbon footprint for a shopper going by bus is seven times greater than the home delivery option. On the downside, however, such has been the success of the home delivery model in many countries that it has attracted too many competitors and there is now increasing congestion as multiple deliveries are made to the same addresses each day. To counter such problems, organisations like SNCF are planning integrated freight deliveries that bring together multiple suppliers' consignments into single shipments per destination. Accompanied by more intelligent package-tracking technologies, companies such as UPS and FedEx similarly look to further optimise and consolidate the last mile.

For people movement, the future is less technology based but shares some core thinking with the logistics perspective: most significantly, the challenge is to provide seamless access and interaction with different transport systems at local hubs. For many would-be users of public transport, a fundamental issue is how they get to their nearest access point. While cycling is a common option worldwide, in many countries no provision is made either for allowing bicycles onto buses or trains, or for secure storage at the local hub, never mind providing cycles to rent at the other end. Investments are being made across many urban areas, from Paris and Amsterdam to London and San Francisco, to address this imbalance. Elsewhere, going on foot is an option but not for all: 'Cities in India have a very poor "walkability index". Walking is made impossible, not just because of harsh weather conditions (extreme heat, rain and cold) but also because of the absolutely atrocious state of footpaths in many Indian cities.' In other areas, the problem can be addressed by providing good car parking spaces at hubs such as bus depots and railway stations.

In a bid to offer practical solutions that will encourage greater use of public systems, some countries are building integrated transport hubs, following Tokyo and Munich as role models, to allow efficient multimodal public transport in Bogotá and Shanghai. In some places these are being funded by governments but in others large employers are paying for the infrastructure investment. Given the advantages to be gained in terms of reducing overall commuting time

Cities in India have a very poor "walkability index".

and providing less stressful travel, companies in several developing economies are placing an emphasis on this. Accompanied by more integrated communication and ticketing systems which allow easy switching from one mode of transport to another, many urban planners see that by the end of the decade people could be moving to and from, on and off efficient and flexible transport systems as smoothly as parcels through a logistics network.

Such is the variety of cityscapes around the world that there can be no ideal blueprint which will work everywhere but the common ambition of making

By the end of the decade people could be moving to and from, on and off efficient and flexible transport systems as smoothly as parcels through a logistics network.

public transport as flexible as individual transport is generating momentum globally. Bridging that last mile is key to this.

Related insights

Page 91

Page 159

Page 179

Page 231

Community living

In rural and urban environments, the community is a prized goal for the middle-aged middle classes as they seek to reconnect with 'people like us'.

In a number of the Future Agenda events, the increasing (not decreasing) desire among many of us to reconnect with others in deeper, closer and more localised communities came up as an issue. In discussions about the future of cities in Europe, 'village' communities within cities – where local facilities, local identities and closer connections all exist – were repeatedly highlighted as key ingredients for sustainable urban living: examples ranging from Greenwich Village to Hampstead to The Marais were given as role models. The need for a community to provide a common set of values and stability for people with increasingly complex lives was also recognised in a workshop held in an Oxfordshire village pub. In the USA, the rising popularity of gated communities, often marketed as places for 'people like us', was noted, not just in the fast-growing sprawls of Las Vegas and Houston but also in more established locations such as Washington and Chicago. Discussions in India identified the segregation of groups of people on a building-by-building basis as both notable and a growing trend – not just through an economic lens, but also by creed. All over the world, it seems that people are looking to reconnect with like-minded others, with common values or similar status, as part of a growing desire for community living.

On one level there is nothing new in this. In many places, ethnic groups already choose to live together within specific zones or areas: Chinatown is possibly the most visible manifestation of this in numerous cities, but think also of the Greek community within Melbourne, cities like Bradford in the UK where there is a high concentration of Pakistanis, gay centres in San Francisco, Rio and Sydney, and even the ex-pat groupings in many capitals from Delhi and Beijing to Bogotá and Ankara. Perhaps as exemplified by Jewish ghettos, people of similar background have always lived together. What is changing, however, is the nature of the groupings of 'people like us' and also the manifestation of community living.

At one extreme, we have the steady rise of gated communities which seek to isolate the rich or the upper classes. In Brazil 'condomínio fechado' are closed housing estates with their own power supply, sanitation and security to protect residents from the violent outside world. Similarly, in post-apartheid South Africa, 'security villages' or 'enclosed neighbourhoods' fulfil a similar function. In Argentina, 'barrios privados' have been seen as a symbol of wealth while in Saudi Arabia, gated communities exist to accommodate Westerners and their families. The suburb of Fairview in the TV show *Desperate Housewives* is a typical media view of an American gated community. At the other end of the scale, we can clearly see areas of cities that market themselves as having specific qualities in order to attract certain types of people and, in some cases, they compete with each other to attract specific groups. In London this is visible at many levels, with the competition between Chiswick, Hampstead and Barnes for

People are looking to reconnect with like-minded others, with common values or similar status.

young families being emulated by the Marylebone versus Kensington versus Islington competition for pre-family professionals. 'Village living' within cities around the world has become an important feature of the real estate business.

One commenter on the Future Agenda blog envisaged 'a rise in gated communities as the poor get poorer and the rich get richer. In fact, I see gated cities re-emerging. Not only will we have subdivisions of major fast-growing cities such as Las Vegas (with its imbalanced economic distribution) continuing to give rise to gated communities, but also I see that key Western cities will become electronically walled. Just as in medieval times, being inside rather than outside the wall at times of crisis will be pivotal.'

In the workshop discussions, the increasing significance of community living was signalled numerous times with several different underlying drivers. Foremost of these, and a shift from the past, is the practical freedom for some to select where to live and work, enabled by both new technologies and new ways of working. The roll-out of fixed as well as mobile high-speed broadband in many countries has given individuals the ability to connect with others anywhere in the world as efficiently as being in a corporate office. This means that people in the most remote of villages will soon be able to access and share data as effectively as those in the heart of the metropolis.

As urbanisation drives a growing exodus of populations from rural communities into cities, in some regions the countryside is gradually becoming a place where only the wealthy can live – effectively a playground for the rich. Accompanying this, the adoption of flexible working by corporate employers means that some employees can enjoy the benefit of this, particularly as the need to be at work, to be seen to have a 'proper' job, is on the decline and increasing numbers of knowledge workers decide to go freelance. Free agents already account for over 30% of workers in the US and this proportion is expected to exceed 50% in the next decade as more people choose to work outside the corporate norm.

As we look ahead, the potential for us not to have to commute on a daily basis is increasing. Rather than facing long journeys to and from work, as urban congestion increases and the financial cost of commuting grows, remote working and telepresence will enable more and more of us to avoid unproductive travel. By 2020, there is forecast to be an overall decline in the number of people in Europe commuting to an office. At the same time, within each local area, the rise of community hubs where people can connect both socially and for work is expected to increase. As the pervasive Starbucks option for the freelance worker becomes too great a compromise, many developers are now including

In some regions the countryside is gradually becoming a place where only the wealthy can live – effectively a playground for the rich.

dedicated flexible work spaces within new housing developments. In addition, as co-location of work and home becomes part of many urban planning scenarios, office space is increasingly being included in mixed developments so that the daily commute could become a thirty-second ride in a lift.

The challenge for many urban planners and social scientists is finding to what extent community living can be planned versus accommodated: how much is it about zoning and cul-de-sacs, as occurs in many new cities, rather than natural movement as districts build up new identities and so attract different groups of like-minded individuals? Of course, it could all go badly wrong. The author J.G. Ballard was especially interested in how people living together in artificial environments often become detached from the real world. Several of his later novels, such as *Super-Cannes, Cocaine Nights* and *Millennium People*, revisited the concept explored in his earlier *High-Rise* of how tribalism could re-emerge within planned communities. Neal Stephenson's science fiction novel *Snow Crash* highlights a future where mass-produced gated communities operate as independent sovereign city-states known as 'burbclaves'.

The challenge for many urban planners and social scientists is finding to what extent community living can be planned versus accommodated.

Although in many parts of the world, returning to the real village community (as preferred in Europe) is not an option and the rural-to-urban migration is definitely a one-way journey, the impulse for reconnecting with 'people like us' is a highly visible trend in an increasing number of cities. For example, in Mumbai this is illustrated by new apartment blocks being reserved for specific creeds and in Dubai by the division between nationals and ex-pats. Given all of this, it appears that, although cities are becoming more international and multicultural in their overall make-up, human nature continues to draw us towards those with similar mindsets and behaviours.

Related insights

Page 107

Page 117

Page 129

Dense cities

As urban migration increases, efficient, densely populated cities, not distributed options, are the blueprints for more sustainable places to live.

By 2025, nearly 2.5 billion Asians will live in cities. This urban growth is being fuelled by new levels of mobility and the migration of diverse populations within nations – especially in China, India and Brazil. These rural-to-urban migrants are attracted to live in cities by a number of factors – more opportunities, better jobs, better education and better healthcare. However, while a better quality of life is the aspiration, often the reality is very different. Especially in Africa, unemployed urban populations frequently congregate in squatter camps. Indeed, as they grow, most cities experience an equal growth in slums. Having 'two cities in one' is common and the frequent attempts to shift the slums to the periphery increases the rich–poor gap and makes cities less sustainable: low-wage populations in particular need to be near to their work so that they can spend more time earning and less time travelling.

According to the UN, one-fifth of all urban housing comprises temporary structures and a third of the world's urban population lives in slums. In sub-Saharan Africa, over 70% of people live in unplanned areas. 'One billion people live in disease-spreading slums characterised by inadequate housing, unsafe drinking water and open sewer systems. This makes the builders of informal housing the largest housing developers in the world and it is they who are creating the cities of tomorrow.'

However, as Ricky Burdett highlighted, with the right decisions we can address the problems: 'Take, for example, Ciudad Neza in Mexico City where, as hundreds of thousand immigrants arrive each year, an open-ended and networked community is succeeding in establishing a lively economy out of literally nothing.' Similarly, 'New Delhi holds 13 to 14 million people depending on the time of day. It used to have the highest pollution rates in the world but then overnight all the auto-rickshaws and the buses were made to change from diesel to natural gas. If you can use natural gas in New Delhi, then why can't you use it everywhere? Tokyo is the largest city in the world. Its transport system, integrated by overhead and underground rail systems, means that the average commute is around one hour. Compare that to Los Angeles, where the average commute is about two hours and at least 80% of the population takes the car to work. In Tokyo, 80% of the population uses public transport. There is little doubt that, seen through the lens of efficiency, more densely populated, compact cities are inherently more sustainable places to live than the likes of Houston and Mexico City.'

However, some see that while they attract a lot of attention for their efficiency, 'high-rise cities like Manhattan and Hong Kong are not the best models for every location. Low-rise, medium-density cities with between three and seven stories can also provide effective and efficient compact urban

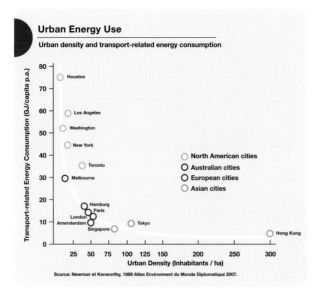

Urban Energy Use

Urban density and transport-related energy consumption

Transport-related Energy Consumption (GJ/capita p.a.)

Houston

Los Angeles

Washington

New York

Toronto

Melbourne

North American cities
Australian cities
European cities
Asian cities

Hamburg
Paris
London
Amersterdam
Singapore

Tokyo

Hong Kong

Urban Density (Inhabitants / ha)

Source: Newman et Kenworthy, 1989 Atlas Environment du Monde Diplomatique 2007.

environments – for example, look at Paris which is the third most densely packed city in the world.' Others disagree and point out that, 'Although Paris is a good example of a dense city without high-rise, it also has problems' because 'the centre of the city is frozen' and all the post-war growth has created ghettoisation which has resulted in increasing imbalance in social mobility.

Ninety-five per cent of urban growth in the next twenty years will be in the developing world and there, especially, dense cities are seen as the way forward: 'The future cities of Asia have to be dense rather than sprawls.' But, in this, people recognise that there is no single global solution, no silver bullet, for city design: 'Asia as a whole cannot have just one strategy. The solutions must be different for different countries.'

While the global mega-city is one extreme interpretation of a dense urban environment, others

see that groups of midi-cities are in many ways a better solution. 'A network of interlinked cities' with efficient transport systems operating between them can create a highly effective urban area without the challenge of scale in one place. Some commentators propose that the Netherlands, one of the most densely populated parts of Europe, is fast becoming a network of midi-cities. In an event held in Singapore, this view was endorsed, as 'new cities must follow a poly-centre model rather than having a single central business district. This will help cities cut down on travelling distances and transport demand.' And by another: 'There is no need to focus on building mega-cities. The more compact the city, the more sustainable it is. One possible solution is the creation of a mega-region which will consist of a number of small and mid-sized cities.' This is supported by a view from Saudi Arabia suggesting that, while it is easy to get excited about the global cities, local cities may have a greater overall impact, especially when connected to the global cities by effective transport networks. Equally 'actions such as decentralising schools or creating more local shops would decrease the need for people to drive, sometimes even long distances where people live outside of the city centre, and consequently reduce the congestion and pollution in cities.'

It is not all about urban expansion, however. Several experts pointed out that we must remember that in some parts of the world, cities are not getting larger: 'Global urbanisation in theory does not mean bigger cities in practice. In Europe declining populations in some countries means many of our cities are becoming less dense.' While from Singapore: 'Asia's experience of urbanisation is vastly removed from that of Europe. Europe's current challenge is that of regeneration. In Asia it is that plus the creation of brand-new cities that are economically and ecologically sustainable.'

Within the core idea of a dense city many people highlighted the need for 'quality open spaces' and better consideration of people: the comment that 'cities should be for people not cars' was widely endorsed. 'A primary focus for future cities must be to provide more quality open spaces – spaces that all can enjoy. For example we should free up as much public space for children. Parks are often so popular that they are too densely packed. Why not pedestrianise 50% of our streets as this would help to promote social interaction?' Green space per capita is one benchmark of quality of life and the WHO recommends at least 8m^2 per person. In London the average is 20m^2, in Shanghai it is 10 m^2 while in the sprawl of Los Angeles it is less than 7m^2. Gary Lawrence of Arup saw that 'much of what is generally discussed in relation to measuring urban environments addresses mobility, access, economic security, and so on – the cores of human urban systems. These are not, however, the cores of the human experience that were uncovered during a "choice to stay" discussion: peoples' choices to stay are rooted in non-monetary aspiration, fear and nostalgia, all issues difficult to quantify, but no less important for that.'

Another big concern raised by some about major future cities is that many of them are continuing to be built on the coast where better trade and communication with other countries has been a traditional rationale. With highly probable rises in sea levels caused by climate change over the next century, there is an emerging issue that most of the coastal cities in the world are not designed to float, or deal with floods. Recent research from

The future cities of Asia have to be dense rather than sprawls.

the Scientific Committee on Antarctic Research highlights that, 'on current projections, the average sea level will rise by 1.4m by the end of the century.' This would not only mean that the likes of Calcutta, Mumbai and Dhaka will be under water, but also, without considerable flood prevention investment, so will London, New York, Tokyo and Shanghai. Or, to put it another way, around 10% of the global population will be displaced. As many of 'the cities for the next decade have already been planned', this is worrying for some.

When we plan for the future, Ricky Burdett sees that 'Cities of the future have to be organic, flexible and versatile. As society and aspirations alter over time, the city has to adapt to change. Utopian cities have never worked. The people that created Rome, New York and London certainly didn't think of them as fixed artefacts that wouldn't change over time. We have to be clever enough as urban designers to design the city like a metabolism, like a body. When it gets older and weaker, you do corrective surgery. Cities need to be versatile; otherwise they atrophy and die. For example, many cities of the past fifty years have been designed around the needs of the car. But as oil costs soar, the city of the future will increasingly need to adapt to modes of transportation that are not petrol-dependent.' Others agree that future cities have to be more sustainable: ideally, they will 'produce more energy than they need, become net carbon absorbers, collect and process waste within city limits and collect and clean recycled water.'

Related insights

Page 107

Page 155

Page 179

Page 243

Page 247

Intelligent buildings

Smarter, better-connected, self-monitoring homes and offices provide safer, more secure, low-energy buildings able to self-manage utilities.

One of the much discussed, but yet to be realised, dreams for architects, engineers and progressive developers is the idea of the zero-waste, zero-energy building – one which, when in use, has zero net energy consumption and zero carbon emissions. As operation accounts for 85% of the total whole-life energy consumption of a building and buildings account for the majority of global CO_2 emissions, this would be an enormous step forward. Alongside the design of an office, home or factory, and the materials used in its construction, a key part of the process is to create 'intelligent' buildings – ones which adopt low- and high-tech methods to ensure optimum management of resources.

With the major technological advances taking place, increased integration of control systems and, in some markets, regulations for the rollout of smart meter systems, all the ingredients for the high-tech option are falling into place. With several countries such as South Korea taking the lead, smart homes that control energy, ventilation, communication services and so on are starting to be built. By 2020, many foresee that the majority of new buildings being constructed around the world, and many that are being refurbished, will be increasingly intelligent and so provide a big push towards the zero-energy building so avidly being striven for.

Today, 40% of the world's raw materials go into buildings and in the US they already represent 70%

Worldwide energy consumption for buildings over the next twenty years will grow by around 45%.

of total energy use, of which around half is wasted. In the EU, where air-conditioning is less prevalent and the average home is smaller, buildings currently account for 40% of energy end-use. A recent report from the SMART 2020 programme forecasts that, with increasing urbanisation, worldwide energy consumption for buildings over the next twenty years will grow by around 45%. The challenge is clear and action is finally being taken. While the concept of the intelligent building has been around for several years now, as we move towards delivering the reality, there is increasing alignment around what it is and what it can mean.

With a vast array of organisations from the EU and the city of New Delhi to IBM and Cisco all pushing towards the realisation of intelligent buildings, there is a growing wish-list of the capabilities that they will have. Most agree that, at the core, is a networked digital control system that will manage a host of services in the most sustainable and economical manner. On top of that backbone we have the ability to manage and control energy and water provision and consumption, heating and ventilation, lighting, building access as well as options such as

Smart buildings can reduce energy consumption and CO$_2$ emissions by 50% to 70% and save 30% to 50% in water usage.

surveillance and even tracking of people and things within the building. Some even see that, as part of new telecare and teleheath systems, buildings will soon have a major role to play in healthcare and be a key component to the rollout of automated people care.

As IBM views it, 'thousands of sensors can monitor everything from motion and temperature to humidity, precipitation, occupancy and light. The building doesn't just coexist with nature, it harnesses it. Smart buildings can reduce energy consumption and CO$_2$ emissions by 50% to 70% and save 30% to 50% in water usage.' The SMART 2020 programme, which looks at both technological and social change around carbon emissions, sees that smart buildings and accompanying smart grids will save around 4 gigatonnes of CO$_2$ equivalent emissions in 2020.

By bringing together ubiquitous computing and 'The Internet of Things' into the built environment, sensors and embedded micro- and nano-control systems can effectively make the intelligent building and all its services into a highly tuned machine, just like in a high-performance vehicle. The majority of energy, ventilation, access and water devices will have embedded RFID chips or SIM cards and so become intelligent objects within a wirelessly connected environment. Clearly the volume and complexity of all the information generated by the different

systems within each building will be significant, but with the ever increasing availability of cheap processing capability, most experts do not see this as a barrier. What does raise concern are issues such as conflicting standards in the construction industry, differing opinions of the best solutions, a lack of financial incentives for building owners to invest in smart technology and the generally slow response of the building sector to change. However, many commentators pointed out that progress is on the cards and momentum for change is itself building.

A critical element in all of this is the role of smart meters which will be introduced across many parts of the developed world over the next decade. In the EU, smart meters are seen as pivotal to meeting the energy consumption targets that have been agreed for 2020. Wirelessly connected to both utility suppliers and home management systems, these will not only measure instantaneous energy and water consumption but also be able to provide pricing information to help building owners and occupants tailor supply and demand. With their 'bi-directional communication capability' that will enable utility companies to undertake better demand side management, these smart meters also open the door to the idea of a smart grid where energy is sent to, from and between different locations. With each building effectively acting as an active node in a grid, local energy production and storage can become far more efficient and consumption peaks and troughs can be smoothed. Taken in conjunction with more distributed sources of renewable energy supply such as wind, solar and biomass, the smart grid and intelligent buildings can really make a difference in energy consumption and sustainable living. As part of the Future Agenda project, a team of postgraduate students at the Royal College of Art

A critical element in all of this is the role of smart meters which will be introduced across many parts of the developed world over the next decade.

the way that utilities, communications and access are managed. The challenge will be for us as individuals to both change our consumption behaviours, many of which conflict with improved efficiency, while at the same time preserving – and ideally enhancing – our ability to get the most out of our buildings.

designed a localised smart grid system, 'Just Energy', that showed how this concept may look and feel in reality by 2020.

On top of the functional side, many architects and engineers are very keen that future intelligent buildings are also better places to live and work in: they should be 'safe and secure' but also 'comfortable and make us feel happy and valued'. The regulatory actions already undertaken will ensure that, in many markets, the capability is there for more of the infrastructure to become increasingly 'intelligent' in

The average building is around for sixty years so whole-scale change to the zero-energy ambition will take far longer than the ten years currently under discussion but, through a combination of retrofit and new-build, over the next decade, many people are positive about progress in developed and developing markets. Indeed, some suggest that, linked to the rollout of high-speed broadband, developing countries could use intelligent buildings as another opportunity to leapfrog over the developed economies which have more of a legacy of infrastructure to deal with.

Related insights

Page 49

Page 87

Page 209

Page 213

Page 219

Local foods

Increased transparency on food availability and security, land use and eco-literacy accelerate mass consumption of locally grown and processed foods.

After nearly a century of interest in global foods sourced from different countries, some developed-world nations have seen a steadily growing middle-class focus on returning to locally produced foods: the organic movement, seasonal produce and 'locavores' are all now on the food industry radar. Across the globe, in the various workshops and discussions undertaken as part of the Future Agenda programme, we can see an alignment of multiple drivers of change around food, from GM crops and improved irrigation through to concerns about national food security and an increase in urban farming. Together these are leading many towards a global solution to food supply that is increasingly focused on the local. Although the approaches differ from region to region and state to state, it appears that the world of 2020 will be one in which more people are better fed through more intelligent use of resources.

Starting with the areas where there is not enough food to feed the local population, we can see that in recent years several factors have combined to make things worse – from imbalanced population growth to poor water management and the impact of global trading on the price of commodities. However, as one workshop participant highlighted, 'there is no such thing as a world food shortage; it is a supply and distribution problem and we therefore need to be better at managing this'.

Alongside better management of supply chains and more intelligent transportation of excess foods in some markets to areas of need, people point to major technological advances being made by some of the world's agribusinesses. For example, Monsanto and BASF have been working on drought-tolerant corn with modified genes. These and similar developments by other companies use new technologies to 'deliver yield improvements under water-stressed conditions'. Over the next decade they are destined to play an important role in the food supplies of Africa, India and parts of Asia as well as parts of the US and Europe as water stress increases. These crops can be grown locally, close to the population and so reduce dependency on long-distance aid and trade. As Jim Kirkwood highlighted in the initial perspective on the future of food, 'we need to significantly increase global research investment in biotechnology, genetics, food science and nutrition to reach the technical breakthroughs required for a second agricultural green revolution that will enable us to feed the world'.

For countries with enough food today, a rising future concern is that of food security and being able to guarantee adequate supply to feed growing populations in resource-constrained times. Especially as diets change and increasing numbers of us consume more meat, the knock-on effects on other foods as well as on water and farming mean that in many parts of the world there will be conflicting

Several workshop participants saw that, by 2020, GM crops will be accepted globally and that regulatory bodies such as the EU will have significantly loosened restrictions on them.

pressures around land use. Add in the possibility of 'peak fish' and 'peak grain' to go along with 'peak oil' and the continued impact of the growth in bio-fuels over the next few years, and even countries that are currently over-supplied with food will have to plan more carefully in the future. Whether it is food vs. fuel competition for land or simply more people consuming more, constraints on food supply are imminent. The World Summit on Food Security, organised by the Food and Agriculture Organisation of the United Nations (FAO) in Rome in 2009, highlighted that 'the global food security situation has worsened and continues to represent a serious threat'. At a national level, in India in 2008 the Ministry of Agriculture published a National Food Security Mission which included a plan to 'increase the production of rice by 10 million tonnes, wheat by 8 million tonnes and pulses by 2 million tonnes by the end of the Eleventh Plan in 2012'. In 2010, the UK announced a national food strategy, calling for a British farming 'revolution', with Hilary Benn, the then Environment Secretary, saying that: 'We need to produce more food. We need to do it sustainably. And we need to make sure that what we eat safeguards our health.' Across the world, countries are taking the food security issue very seriously and the goal of increasing the amount of locally produced food is a key component.

We also have the opportunity to develop more efficient farming methods. While organic food and the like is a suitable ideal for our gardens and the outlets serving wealthy consumers, some people assert that it cannot be a role model for feeding the mass population. Large-scale farming to feed the world's millions requires more refined crops and this implicitly means wider acceptance of GMO. Several workshop participants saw that, by 2020, GM crops will be accepted globally and that regulatory bodies such as the EU will have significantly loosened restrictions on them.

Another commonly agreed view is that we will see a rise in the number and size of urban farms. Both from a desire to keep some food production and processing as close to the market as possible and from the opportunity to make better use of our urban green spaces and roofs, many see urban faming taking off. At one level this will be encouraged by city planners and mayors keen to ensure local food security. According to Arup's Foresight team, 'half of Shanghai's pork and poultry, 60% of its vegetables and 90% of its milk and eggs come from the city and its outskirts'. Elsewhere in Asia, 80% of Hanoi's fresh vegetables come from farms within and around the city. In the developing world, local food supply has been a key concern for years and will continue to be a priority in the coming decade. In Europe and the US, however, there has been a shift to importing foods from half way around the world – lamb from New Zealand, asparagus from Kenya, kiwi fruits from Chile and so on.

But, with food security becoming a bigger issue, we can expect to see more urban farming occurring in the West. In cities where there are brown-field sites, people are already starting to use land for farming

We will see a rise in the number and size of urban farms.

rather than housing. Detroit is the prime example here: 'The amount of vacant and abandoned land in Detroit would roughly add up to the size of the city of San Francisco' and so, with urban land cheaper than arable land, John Hantz and his colleagues are leading programmes to grow fruits and vegetables for local consumption. Elsewhere, where land is more valuable, there are plans to make more use of flat roofs for agriculture and introduce vertical urban farms. From New York and London to Mexico City, highly efficient multi-storey vertical farms incorporating hydroponics and aeroponics are destined to become a common feature. One team in the Royal College of Art project conducted as part of the Future Agenda programme focused its attention on how innovative, sustainable building systems in unplanned ghettos of fast-growing cities could be used to provide vertical walls for growing crops for both home consumption and sale. Around the world, people and governments are starting to shift urban farming up the list of priorities to a point where it will have a significant impact on parts of the food system.

Lastly, we also have the increasing influence of the environmental and sustainable viewpoints. While workshop participants felt that 2020 is too soon for such developments as personal eco-footprints to take hold and drive consumer choice, several did feel that wider eco-literacy over the next decade will help people to explore alternative food options more intelligently. This will not just be simply about choosing not to eat products from certain locations as a consequence of 'food-miles', because the CO_2 savings of growing produce in greenhouses as opposed to air freighting them are sometimes marginal. Rather, it will be consumers choosing to consume more local, seasonal food; retailers choosing to steer choice by labelling and product selection, so 'nudging' their customers towards locally supplied and processed products; and more of us generally becoming aware of the overall environmental footprints of certain foods – in terms of water, waste and energy.

By itself, the eco-friendly view will take a long time to significantly shift the mainstream but, taken in conjunction with the other developments in food security, national food strategies, technology and commercial choices for food manufacturers and retailers, many see a world in 2020 where local foods will again become the global norm.

Related insights

Page 57

Page 95

Page 99

Page 185

Page 189

Mega-city-states

Increasing competition between cities overrides national priorities as mayors lead bold initiatives to place their cities at the forefront of the global stage.

In the Judge Dredd comic book series, Mega-City One is a huge fictional city-state covering much of the eastern United States, linking an urban corridor stretching from Atlanta to Quebec. With a population of over 400 million it is one of around thirty mega-cities that dominate the world, and outside which, in Cursed Earth, there is no law. It's true that this is an extreme view of life in the 22nd century, but some would say that the growth and importance of mega-cities is very much a 21st-century issue.

Today, many see that cities rather than nations are taking the big steps forward, introducing new approaches, adopting new strategies and generating more growth for the world. After a couple of centuries where nations drove the agenda, some people suggest that we are witnessing a rebirth of Roman, medieval and even 19th-century times, as cities become the centre of attention, exert influence and become magnets for innovation. By 2020, it is clear that the new mega-cities will not only be the beacons for the future but also that they will both cooperate and compete with one another.

City-states of the past have been the centres of power, of culture and of trade. From the ancient Greek cities of Athens, Sparta and Corinth, the Sumerian cities of Babylon and Ur, and Rome at the heart of the Roman Empire through to central Asian cities such as Samarkand and Bukhara, and the powerful Italian cities of the Middle Ages, city-states have had a central role in history. Largely independent entities with a focus on the urban centre, city-states have been run in the interests of their citizens rather than the wider regions within which they are situated. Cities such as Venice, Florence and Genoa defined their era and, in the 19th century, sovereign city-states in Germany and Switzerland including Geneva, Frankfurt, Bremen, Lubeck and Basel adopted a similar ambition. Although today we only have a few sovereign city-states left – namely, Singapore, the Vatican City and Monaco – we do have a number of urban areas that have a high degree of autonomy and essentially function as city-states within the nations they belong to: Canberra, Vienna, Brussels, Geneva, Hamburg, Moscow, Brasilia and Buenos Aires all come to mind. In addition, we have cities such as Washington DC, Mexico City, Islamabad, New Delhi and Kuala Lumpur that are federally administered as well as places like Hong Kong and Macau which operate as autonomous cities in China. Although arguably not yet as directly influential as the city-states of the past, many predict that some of these, and other notable additions, will become the natural drivers of change in the future.

In 1993, an article in *Foreign Affairs*, 'The Rise of the Region State', suggested that: 'The nation-state has become a dysfunctional unit for understanding and managing the flows of economic activity that dominate today's borderless world. Policymakers, politicians and corporate managers would benefit

Today, just forty city-regions account for two-thirds of the world economy and 90% of its innovation.

from looking at "region-states" – the globe's natural economic zones – whether they happen to fall within or across traditional political boundaries. With their efficient scales of consumption, infrastructure and professional services, region-states make ideal entryways into the global economy. If allowed to pursue their own economic interests without jealous government interference, the prosperity of these areas will eventually spill over.'

Sixteen years later, Parag Khanna, Director of the Global Governance Initiative at the New America Foundation, wrote an article for *Foreign Policy* entitled 'The Next Big Thing: Neomedievalism' in which he proposed that, 'as countries stumble to right the wrongs of the corporate masters of the universe, they are driving us right back to a future that looks like nothing more than a new Middle Ages, that centuries-long period of amorphous conflict from the 5th to the 15th century when city states mattered as much as countries. ... Today, just forty city-regions account for two-thirds of the world economy and 90% of its innovation. The mighty Hanseatic League, a constellation of well-armed North and Baltic Sea trading hubs in the late Middle Ages, will be reborn as cities such as Hamburg and Dubai form commercial alliances and operate "free zones" across Africa like the ones Dubai Ports World is building. Add in sovereign wealth funds and private military contractors, and you have the agile geopolitical units of a neomedieval world.'

In his seminal book, *City of Quartz*, Mike Davis saw that, in the future, Los Angeles will have become a concentration of competing smaller city-states. By contrast Paul Saffo has commented that 'our world is moving from one of nation-states to one of city-states. Rather than the future being one of the US versus China, it is going to be Silicon Valley vs. Beijing or Chicago vs. Paris. Each dominant city will define its region. With the "flattening" of the world, Chicago is no longer vying with US cities like New York for influence, commerce and jobs, but other major cities in the world.' The MIT 19.20.21 programme is just one of several research studies under way that are looking at future urban environments. Predicting that there will be nineteen cities with over 20 million populations in the 21st century, this sees that 'the rise of supercities is the defining megatrend of the 21st century'.

During the Future Agenda programme, the increasingly significant role of a group of elite cities was mentioned at a number of events. From trade to migration to innovation, the leadership of emerging mega-cities was rarely questioned. In some areas, we can already see examples of where cities are leading the way for change. For example, with the introduction of congestion zones in London and fat taxes in New York, cities are doing things that national governments will not. In the absence of agreement on climate change between the world's nations in Copenhagen in 2009, a number of the world's leading cities are taking action. The C40 cities see that they have a central role to play in tackling climate change and 'by fostering a sense of shared purpose, the C40 network offers cities an effective forum in which to work together, share information and demonstrate leadership'. The mayors, chief ministers and governors of these cities believe that with their Climate Change Action Plans they can collectively do something that nations seem to be unable to do.

Multinational businesses increasingly differentiate global urban markets from national ones and create specific products and services targeted on the common needs of rising mega-city populations. In terms of market focus, companies can see more in common between Shanghai, Mumbai and New York than they can between New York and Idaho. Mega-cities are already highly attractive markets in their own right and, as they grow, their influence will spread. As Neal Peirce of McKinsey has put it, 'National economies essentially are constellations of regional economies, each with a major city at the core.' In an event in Singapore it was highlighted that 'forty-five years ago, Singapore was not urbanised and there were slums around the city centre. However, being a city-state put Singapore in a unique position to tackle this challenge. The government from the very beginning took a great interest in how the city should urbanise – what policy frameworks should be adopted. Thus Singapore's urbanisation happened in a very planned manner.'

The phenomenon of the so-called 'endless city' has been explored in a number of areas, including the Urban Age project led by the London School of Economics. According to UN-Habitat, 'larger combinations of urban areas will be one of the most significant developments in the way people live and economies grow in the next fifty years'. The world's mega-cities are merging to form vast 'mega-regions' which may stretch hundreds of kilometres across countries and be home to more than 100 million people. The world's first mega-city, comprising Hong Kong, Shenzhen and Guangzhou, is already home to about 120 million people. Other mega-regions have formed in Japan and Brazil and are developing in India, West Africa and elsewhere. The top twenty-five cities in the world account for more than half of the world's wealth and the five largest cities in India and China now account for 50% of those countries' wealth. Nagoya-Osaka-Kyoto-Kobe is expected to have a population of 60 million by 2015 and will effectively be the powerhouse of Japan; a similar effect on an even larger scale is occurring in fast-growing 'urban corridors' such as that between Mumbai and Delhi.

By 2020, we can expect that, alongside a few select intergovernmental programmes and more regional economic partnerships, the catalysts for major change in the world will increasingly come from the forty or so mega-cities that drive the global economy, are home to many of its population and set the future agenda. Whether this will be a return to the role of city-states of the past or a version of the Judge Dredd future is, of course, open to question.

Related insights

Page 111

Page 231

Page 247

Migration magnets

Immigration is part of economic development strategies and, especially in low-fertility economies, nations position themselves to attract migrants.

Migration both within and between countries has been on the increase for many years and shows little sign of slowing as we move forward. As Professor Richard Black highlighted in the initial perspective on the topic:

"Although international migration has increased over the past few decades, it has done so slowly, rising from just 2% to around 3% of the world's population over the period from 1970 to 2005. It seems highly probable that this percentage will continue to rise slowly over the coming decade, or at least not fall, implying that by 2020 there will be more international migrants in the world than there are today.

"In addition, although it appears that new migration flows – in terms of origins and destinations – are emerging all the time, it also seems likely that the major 'channels' of international migration will be the same in 2020 as they are today, with few new major 'poles of attraction', and few new emerging countries of emigration – beyond the possibility of mass exodus associated with economic or political collapse in a small number of countries."

These so-called 'poles of attraction' have also been termed 'migration magnets' as they highlight where and why people want to move from one area to another. In many countries, the internal migration magnets are increasingly the cities where wealth generation is seen to occur, which in turn attracts the people who are able to move – generally the young. As mentioned by Ricky Burdett in the initial point of view on the future of cities:

"Urban growth is being fuelled by new levels of mobility and migration of diverse populations within and across nations, especially in China, Brazil and India. These rural-to-urban migrants are attracted by the tantalising prospects of jobs and opportunity and driven by the harsh realities of rural life. Cities like Mumbai experience forty-two people moving into the city per hour."

In several of the Future Agenda events, it was mentioned that, in the coming years, cities and city economies within countries will increasingly compete for the best talent. Just as in the past decade or so, as some regions have campaigned ferociously for direct investment and sought to attract companies to create jobs and stimulate economic growth, over the next ten years we can expect to see different cities within the same country competing with each other to attract the best people to help drive future growth. Whether this is by creating the best universities, hosting the best companies to attract top graduates or providing better housing and living conditions for families, the fast-growing urban environments and city-states in India and China – as well as in developed economies like Europe and the US – are all gearing up to market themselves

Some Important Current Migration Routes

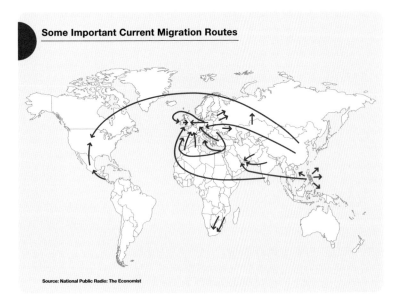

Source: National Public Radio: The Economist

as attractive growth magnets. Being the magnet that attracts the best talent will increasingly be seen as an economic and social priority by many a city mayor.

At a national level, as fertility rates continue to drop, dependency ratios accelerate and the desire for sustained economic growth continues in many developed countries, country-to-country migration will be increasingly seen in a positive economic light.

Over the next ten years we can expect to see different cities within the same country competing with each other to attract the best people to help drive future growth.

As such, countries will start to compete more for the migrants they need. Today, there are just a few nations such as Canada, Australia and New Zealand that are actively and openly seen to encourage skilled immigration. They all have a unique model aimed at building their populations with the best people and only accept skilled migrants that fill specific gaps as clearly laid out in their public policies. In New Zealand, 23% of the population are migrants, and, in Auckland, this figure is nearly 40%. In Canada, the government's immigration plan clearly sets out how and where another 250,000 immigrants who arrive annually will be integrated into the country and help to drive economic growth.

Following the lead of such countries as Canada, where immigration has clearly supported growth to such an extent that it has become multinational as well as multicultural, others will seek to selectively attract the best skill sets available. As one workshop participant highlighted, 'over the next decade, Canada, Australia and New Zealand will be joined by such countries as Japan, much of Western Europe and maybe even the US'. Japan and Western Europe especially are facing declining birth rates and rising pressures on their economies to sustain growth in the long term. As such, although in the past they have been accused of creating barriers to immigration, in the future they are expected to seek immigrants to provide specific skills. No longer satisfied with nominal net migration, at a country level they will all compete for the best doctors, nurses, engineers and teachers.

Consequently, as people like Peter McLeod have highlighted, 'Feeder countries will be specifically targeted in order to provide nations with the right skill and cultural mix and countries will promote themselves as ideal migration destinations.'

In many developed countries, country-to-country migration will be increasingly seen in a positive economic light.

New feeder countries will, in turn, evolve their emigration strategies. Whereas today there are just a few countries, such as the Philippines, that actively encourage skilled workers to emigrate to other countries to work and send back money to their families, as international remittances from migration scale up in their contribution to national economies, more and more countries will follow suit. This may be especially significant in areas such as sub-Saharan Africa and could place a major burden on the successful growth of the homeland. In addition, through tax incentives and the like, more countries

in Europe and beyond will seek to attract back the skilled workers that they may have lost in the past.

With this changing dynamic, migration may well cease to be seen in a negative light and couched as a cultural threat in the media. If they want to be top of the migration magnet league table, cities and countries will need to place greater emphasis on supporting a multicultural society, ensuring that migrants are welcomed and their skills put to good use.

Feeder countries will be specifically targeted in order to provide nations with the right skill and cultural mix and countries will promote themselves as ideal migration destinations.

Related insights

Page 107

Page 171

Page 231

Page 243

PART 3
Moderators of the future

Part 1 focused on the four macro-certainties, the things we see from the Future Agenda programme that are almost definitely going to occur over the next decade: imbalanced population growth, key resource constraints; the shift of economic power to Asia; and universal data access. In Part 2 we highlighted forty-eight probable futures that contributors to the programme suggest could happen, but which are dependent on contingencies, some of which are relevant to many of the issues discussed. These contingencies may accelerate, decelerate, postpone or even prevent the scenarios outlined in Part 2. Some are quite specific and relate to a technological advance (such as stem cells for halting Alzheimer's) or a regulatory change (such as allowing smart meters to enable dynamic pricing). Others have a more emotional relevance and relate to a societal change, such as the wider acceptance of euthanasia or a shift in behaviour so that in addition to acknowledging climate change, consumers go on to take action to mitigate its impact.

Alongside these contingencies, we can also see some general trends or umbrella themes. We see these as the main influences and suggest that they will shape a range of probable changes, again accelerating or decelerating their impact. In order to understand how these changes may happen, we have to understand what the influences are, how they will affect individual choice, social networks, organisations and institutions and, in turn, how these choices will affect others.

The way we behave and how we make decisions is, of course, immensely complicated and beyond the scope of this book, but to us and those who participated in the programme, there are three main influences that are worthy of discussion:

1   The impact that trust and privacy will have on society,

2   The role of global vs. local decisions, and

3   The nature of choice itself.

We need to consider how each will evolve in scope and scale and what their direct and indirect impact could be over the next ten years. We need to understand how they could influence some of the dilemmas we face and the potential trade-offs that need to be considered.

Will we, for example, more willingly take decisions that try to address short-term problems at the expense of the longer term? Will we favour the interests of individuals or small groups over those of the many? Will we put the growth of the economy ahead of protection of social values and of the environment? And should we drive change top-down with central control or bottom-up with distributed decision making?

Trust and privacy

Why worry about trust?

Trust can be defined as an individual's confidence in others to fulfil their promises or to be consistent in their policies, and their ethical codes and remain in line with the law. It is a measure of our belief in the fairness and honesty of others. It is important because it influences the way people and organisations cooperate and it is essential if social institutions such as governments, economies and communities are to function. Considering the key certainties and insights we have already discussed, it seems clear that who, – or what – we trust and how we are trusted will have even greater significance in the next decade than it has in the past.

Evidence suggests that a trusted community is one in which individuals, corporations and the state will prosper. Over the next ten years expect the need for individuals to place more trust in organisations to grow. Primarily this is because the challenges we face are growing too big to deal with effectively as individuals. For example, if we want to ensure there is enough food to feed the growing population, the use of 'pharma' or genetically modified foods and sources of alternative proteins may well need greater acceptance – particularly in Europe, which traditionally has been opposed to GMO. This means consumers will have to put their trust in the scientists and the government bodies that support and monitor the development and rollout of these products. Given the societal, historical and religious associations with food, this will be more acceptable to some than to others.

Understanding how and whom to trust is important because, when trust is broken or not established there are often negative consequences. This is true for all aspects of life, be they personal, corporate or regulatory. Sometimes the breakdown can be catastrophic – for example, some have suggested that a breakdown of trust between consumers, investors, banks, government, regulators and the media lies at the heart of the banking crisis that hit in 2008. Lapses in trust, particularly between different cultures, can also damage social cohesion – take for example the 2007 riots in Parisian suburbs which pitted disaffected Muslim youths against the French police. It can also play havoc with individuals. Public figures are perhaps particularly vulnerable, as ex-UK Prime Minister Gordon Brown so painfully discovered when he destroyed any hope of his re-election by accidentally making public his unflattering view of an elderly widow (and until that point a staunch supporter) in the 2010 campaign.

Trust in the state

Trust is necessary for good government. The core philosophy of democracy is based on trust as voters put the sovereignty of the nation-state in the hands of politicians. Trust gives legitimacy to regimes so there is greater willingness by citizens to comply with its rulings. A society that lacks trust in government often fails to comply with its rulings, resulting in strikes, demonstrations and other evidence of civil unrest. Lack of trust in state governance can also inhibit development and participation. In Mumbai, at a workshop on the future of cities, it was generally agreed that corruption at a city-state level was such that many capable people were disinclined to take part. 'There is an educated middle class who need to take some action and responsibility. They have dropped it these days. It is too corrupt here to get involved.' Lack of trust can also reduce the credibility of state information – even if it is independent and accurate. Take for example the UK public's disbelief upon the announcement that 'crime figures had reduced in the UK (falling by 8%) in July 2010'. Sixty-six per cent of people believed instead that crime levels had risen and dismissed the figures published by the Home Office.

Lack of trust in the institutions of the state can also provide a fertile ground for the growth of radical or extreme ideologies. In some cases, disenfranchised individuals turn to other places for structure. Consider for example the gang culture of South London, Rio and Moscow. This can be attributed to an underclass of young people who do not feel part of the mainstream, and so have created an alternative society with very complex societal rules and regulations of their own.

As the concept of government has evolved, we no longer feel comfortable depending on the actions of one organisation to ensure good government. Discussions within the workshops suggested that governments which partner with third parties such as NGOs to address the challenges of the day are likely to be better trusted than if they do not. This point of view was also clearly reflected in Edelman's Trust Barometer for 2010, which stated that NGOs are considered to be most trusted as institutions and that trust in their ability to deliver is on the increase. This is specifically evident in China where trust in NGOs has soared by 25% since 2004, a reflection perhaps on China's growing openness and wealth and the resulting demand for environmental responsibility, education and public health.

Francis Fukuyama, among others, argues that trust boosts economic efficiency. In his book *Trust: The Social Virtues and the Creation of Prosperity* he points out that:

"People who do not trust one another will end up cooperating only under a system of formal rules and regulations, which have been negotiated, agreed to, litigated, and enforced, sometimes by coercive means … Widespread distrust in a society, in other words, imposes a kind of tax on all forms of economic activity, a tax that high-trust societies do not have to pay."

He suggests that those countries with strong economies, such as Germany, are also those that have exhibited strong elements of trust. He goes on to argue that it is easier to trust those who share similar experiences and values, as this reduces potential conflicts of interest. If this argument is correct, as society becomes increasingly global in nature, the ability to identify these areas of common interest trust will become more difficult.

Trust in business

Trust and an understanding of its importance in the commercial world is gradually climbing up the corporate agenda, despite the fact that corporations in recent years have been driven primarily by competition, profit, cost minimisation and the efficient use of resources. The Edelman Barometer shows, for the first time in the ten years the report has been running, that trust and transparency are as important to a company's reputation as the quality of products and services it provides. Furthermore, in the US and much of Western Europe, trust and transparency are now ranked as more important than product quality, and by far outrank financial returns.

Alongside this, consumers are becoming more attuned to the value of the non-financial responsibilities of commercial organisations. There are now many examples of companies which have profited by fostering customer goodwill, handling risk responsibly and motivating their employees while also managing costs and driving innovation. In the UK, John Lewis and the Co-operative Bank are good examples of this approach; indeed, in 2009, the Co-op saw a 70% increase in profits in its financial division despite a 60% increase in write-downs, and in 2010 all John Lewis employees (or 'partners') were able to benefit from a 15% bonus.

Although this focus on the non-commercial elements of business may well be a straightforward response to the damaging effect of the credit crunch, it is becoming particularly important for individual CEOs to actively build trust. Generally speaking, they are the human face of the organisation so their behaviour both in and outside the boardroom is a reflection of the companies they represent. As Anthony Seldon in his book on trust points out: 'the demand for CEOs to have a vision beyond mere profit maximisation is likely to persist as the recession continues to be felt'. Furthermore, trust in CEOs can be dramatically affected by public perception, particularly if they are caught out in their unguarded moments. BP's CEO Tony Hayward was reminded of this when his wish to 'get my life back' was broadcast around the world, much to the disgust of many Americans whose livelihoods and lifestyles had been devastated by the oil spill from the Deepwater Horizon explosion in the Gulf of Mexico.

Trust in information

Traditional news sources currently face an unprecedented challenge in terms of both credibility and competition. This was discussed at length in one workshop where it was agreed that something is changing around the way people trust the media, given that more people turn to Wikipedia for information than to CNN. 'They represent different organisations – Wikipedia is open, amateur and democratic, while CNN is supported by professional media who have a different agenda', said one participant. Whatever the reason, instead of listening to the likes of CNN or Al Jazeera programmes, some people who wish to stay informed are building their opinions on the views of uncredentialled 'experts', often via Wikipedia. They are also turning towards the blogosphere where they can more easily identify and team up with people who have a similar viewpoint. The desire to counter this goes some way to explain why in recent times there seems to have been a substantial increase in the number of academics and industry experts in the traditional media, tv, radio and print, news channels.

As highlighted in Part 2, the fact that there are multiple ways to access the opinions of credible experts suggests that, in the future, there will have to be a visible shift in the role of many players in the media industry, from being choice editors to choice curators. In order to survive, news channels will have to reposition themselves not only as credible sources of information, but also as ones that have filtered out inaccuracies and put the news in a wider context. Faced with ever more information and more ways in which to access it, people will increasingly focus on content from believable sources. They will therefore turn to organisations they trust to provide a clear analysis of what it all means. Whether the original information comes from a corporate press release or the mobile phone of a passer-by, consumers will be looking for short cuts to deciding what to pay attention to, what to watch and what to ignore. Key media brands will become shorthand ways of guiding choice; simple heuristics in an overwhelming world.

Of course, in the end we will all play in both camps, partly drawn to the mass appeal of shared media language and stories to build community and common reference points, and another part drawn to finding out our own specific niche. 'Multi-media tasking' is becoming the norm – for example, following the news on a Twitter feed, while logging in to a news wire, watching the story develop on TV, and messaging a friend about it. In the future, the virtual sharing of events (particularly live TV, where the drama unfolds) linking in multiple media sources to create the feel of the community, the feel of participation, will become commonplace.

Trust in the community

Trust makes us happier and healthier as a community; indeed there is a distinct correlation between trust and well-being. A good way of building trust in small, local communities is for the people to get to know each other. Although the prospect of 'more working from home' has been discussed for many years, it does now seem that improved connectivity and increased dependence on knowledge workers will mean that, over the next ten years, a growing proportion of professionals should be able to spend more time at home – or at least outside the traditional office.

Many rural and suburban communities are currently sparsely populated during the day; with many of working age leaving home early to get to their jobs and coming back late at night, the streets are left to mothers with very young children and the elderly. This can lead to a sense of isolation among many, alongside a decline in community services such as youth clubs, lunch groups for the elderly and so on. Looking forward, the trend towards home-working could produce communities that are more vibrant throughout the week. People working from home will have more time to get involved with their local areas and provide support for others. This raises the genuine possibility of community life being rebuilt in many areas over the next decade.

Add in the establishment of local shared office spaces within villages and suburbs and so increased support of, and interaction between, more viable local businesses and we could see a reduction in isolation and the expansion of communities around new social and economic networks and areas of common interest and services.

That said, a significant issue arising from the remote working scenario is the erosion of trust – or at least the shifting paradigm for trust. Many of the contributions to the Future Agenda debate have highlighted the increasing use of, and dependence on virtual relationships among today's teenagers. As the 15-year-olds of today become the 25-year-olds of 2020, how important will real relationships be within the local community versus online interactions with like-minded individuals around the world? Bringing this into the local community context, the issue of who people will trust and why may become more significant. The ability to physically interact with others at a local level provides the foundation of relationships which some see as far stronger than virtual ones. Despite the evidently growing global and personal benefits of online social networks, some do not see them as a substitute for the grounding providing by the community school and wider local life.

The online world aside it is certainly easier to make decisions around trust in smaller communities. Indeed, smaller groups tend to engender greater trust and therefore a high level of support and understanding. The challenge is in recognising the tipping point in terms of the size where trust in the whole starts to diminish and subgroups form, as occurs in larger communities.

Trust and the individual

The argument goes that, although it is possible to live a life with low levels of trust, it will not necessarily be a happy one. It will certainly be time-consuming as we endlessly have to check and double check other people's work or do everything for ourselves. If we trust someone enough, we are happy to cooperate with them and let them make decisions on our behalf. In part, the reason for this is that the ability to trust others can free us up to do the things we really want to do. It can also allow us to hand over decisions or actions that we feel poorly equipped for to other people or organisations.

Given the challenges and dilemmas that we all face, ranging from local issues such as rubbish collection and noise pollution to larger societal issues such as climate change, disease prevention and so on, the majority of us often express concern but then pass on the responsibility for making decisions to those that we trust – believing that they are more capable of sorting out our problems – so we do not have to take any further action. In many instances this can lead to a lack of individual action to address the problem. As Yale University psychologist Stanley Migram described in his article 'The Perils of Obedience', 'in a complex society it is easy to ignore responsibility when one is only an intermediate link in a chain'.

Delegating responsibility because we trust others to do a better job than we would is all very well, but when community-based actions are needed as part of the solution to specific problems (such as climate change), trusting others to take the necessary action is not enough. Small wonder that a recent Accenture report suggests that 'In the future, consumers will need to understand the trade-offs and competing objectives in energy policy to provide suitable support to political officials and regulators to educate and include the public in choices for the longer term changes. It is critical that consumers be aware that there are no simple solutions and that any choice will have direct implications. This awareness will allow policymakers to begin a more informed debate.'

A decline in trust?

In recent times, the economic downturn, endemic corruption and mismanagement on an unprecedented scale has meant that trust in traditional institutions, be they corporations, government, or even the family unit, appears to be on a gradual decline (although the Edelman Trust Barometer has shown a tentative global rise for 2010).The specific reasons for this are manifold: the perceived greed and financial mismanagement of banks, the failure of governments to prevent the economic downturn, government corruption, involvement in unpopular wars, disputes in the church around homosexuals and female clergy, discovery of long-term child abuse by members of the Catholic Church, and disillusion with the institution of marriage (running at about 40% in the US). These are just some examples that seemingly signal that traditional institutions are failing to live up to expectations. Indeed, one workshop participant suggested that 'the recent global financial crisis has been so fundamental that in some cases it has shaken trust in the capitalist model itself'. Belief in previously held convictions has been questioned and many people are looking for new terms of reference and new organisations to trust.This might explain why so many people are now turning (or returning) to religion for help in facing the challenges in their lives.

Trust in faith?

With the glaring exception of Europeans, people everywhere are turning to religion for answers.This means that, alongside economic growth, religious growth seems to be taking place. In 1900, 80% of the world's Christians lived in Europe and the US – today, 60% live in the developing world. America is

the only developed country that still takes religion seriously. Looking at the 2008 Pew Global Attitudes survey, we can see that 55% of people in the US consider religion very important – and that figure jumps to 82% if you amend it to say 'somewhat important' – but even that compares poorly to the religious intensity of Pakistanis, 95% of whom say religion is very important and 98% say it is somewhat important. Even in China, a state historically tied to secularism, religious belief is gaining traction, with 31% of the population regarding it as very or somewhat important in their lives and only 11% stating that it is not at all important. By comparison, in France, the most secular of all the countries Pew surveyed, only 10% stated that religion was very important. Indeed, most European countries with a Christian heritage have seen a decline in traditional religious observance at the same time as they have seen an increase in Muslim immigration. A stark contrast results between the secular establishment and religious values.This is perhaps at its most extreme when you consider difference between the Muslim faith, with its strict rules on alcohol and dress, and the freedom offered by the West. This growth in faith and lack of trust in the existing systems is having interesting consequences – take for example the growth of interest-free, risk-averse Shariah banking, which has been gaining ground quietly since before the banking collapse.

Trading trust

Trust is becoming increasingly important when we consider the amount of personal data now held by governments and large organisations. Primarily this is because of the way in which it is being used, sometimes without our permission. Often we provide personal information freely for the purpose of a transaction, and it is a breach of our trust if this information is passed on without our knowledge or, more likely, without our understanding that the information will be shared more widely. For example, with computer data tracking, it is possible to follow a credit or loyalty cardholder's purchases and from this information target marketing towards an individual's spending habits. The sharing of data among organisations means that it is also possible for others to 'mine' data together so that eventually a picture can be built up showing who you are, where you live, what you buy, if you've ever defaulted on a payment, ever had parking tickets, who your friends are and so on. As consumers gradually understand the implications of this, and if organisations do not manage to hold information securely and responsibly, trust inevitably will decline.

Why does privacy matter?

In a way, the flipside of trust is privacy, a subject which is increasingly under the spotlight. Until recently the right to privacy was not considered of particular importance – mainly because it was relatively difficult to gain a full picture of an individual's habits and activities. The internet, mobile telephones and an increased concern about national safety have changed all that. Some argue that, after all, we are living in a society that is under threat and we have to accept that our right to personal privacy should be set aside for the greater good. This is why we queue up without protest and allow complete strangers to go through our hand luggage at airports. Alternatively, others say although there is a vast amount of personal electronic information available, there is no justification for simply accepting a decline

in personal privacy as a necessary precaution against terrorist attacks.

Given this, it is worthwhile stopping to consider the scope and scale of the surveillance society many of us now live in. The issue is not new. In 2007, *The Economist* pointed out: 'These days, data about people's whereabouts, purchases, behaviour and personal lives are gathered, stored and shared on a massive scale. Most of the time, there is nothing obviously malign about this. Governments say they need to gather data to ward off terrorism or protect public health; corporations say they do it to deliver goods and services more efficiently. But the ubiquity of electronic data-gathering and processing – and above all, its acceptance by the public – is still astonishing, even compared with a decade ago. Nor is it confined to one region or political system.'

This matters because the protection of personal data is fraught with problems. Data is both easy to lose and also easy to exploit. Worse, many people are only vaguely aware of the implications that loss of personal data can have. In the same article, a Cambridge University professor, Ross Anderson, offered a vivid analogy comparing the current situation to a 'boiled frog' – the frog fails to jump out of a saucepan as the water inside gradually heats up. The analogy is clear. If our right to privacy is gradually eroded over the years its loss will hardly be felt. But in the end, as a society, we might find ourselves in the same position as the frog. This might sound melodramatic – and, to be fair, Anderson went on say that this is not an inevitability – but the point is made.

A workshop we held on the future of privacy in Washington DC concurred with Anderson's theory. It was universally agreed that governance in the US makes it unlikely that there will be a major regulatory change in favour of increasing the individual right to privacy, without a significant catalyst – by which we mean a huge breach such as the loss of public tax or bank account records, the publication of sensitive patient records, identity theft on a large scale or some other revelation around the use of personal data for unlawful transactions.

The challenge is that many consumers are unaware of the extent of their own data trail left on multiple systems and are completely oblivious to the daily round of potentially useful information they can provide. Consider a day in the life of London's citizens: they will leave their apartment monitored by CCTV, stand at a bus stop again monitored by CCTV, use electronic payment to board a bus or a train, go through security and clock in at work, sign onto their laptop, make a few phone calls either by mobile or land-line, pay for something with a credit card etc. In so doing, they allow someone to monitor their every movement and activity. This whole process is repeated on the way home most days of the week. Furthermore, the information is gathered indiscriminately about everyone – there is one CCTV camera for every ten people in the UK – rather than in previous times where surveillance of an individual was targeted and necessitated considerable effort.

DNA has also become an increasingly popular surveillance tool but, despite its high profile and beloved as it is of police dramas, it is not always accurate. Despite this, 4.4 million people, 7% of the British population, are now on the national database, which was set up in 1995. Most other EU countries have no more than 100,000 profiles on theirs. This difference is because, in Britain, DNA has been taken from anyone arrested for a 'recordable' offence, such as being drunk and disorderly. It is then stored for life, even if that person is never charged or is later acquitted. As the *Economist* points out, no other democracy does this.

In many democracies, electronic surveillance has not yet had a big impact on most people's lives, but as the amount of data collected and stored about us increases, so does the risk of abuse. Perhaps that's all very well in the West, but consider the potential impact of this in countries where hard-fought personal freedom and civil liberty is in its infancy. What if things go wrong there?

Privacy, trust and technology

With technological innovation and economic opportunity, many of us live in a much more interconnected world than our parents and more people than ever now live in cities far away from the communities in which they were born. The internet has certainly widened our circle, giving access to a global community in a way that was never available to previous generations. The effect of all this is that we now have far more interactions of all kinds with a range of organisations and individuals, many of whom we have not met, or with whom we have a very tenuous relationship. This has provided us with a wealth of information delivering both social and economic benefit – for example, research has shown that there is a clear correlation between mobile penetration and GDP growth in emerging markets – but at the same time, the ability to be globally interconnected has amplified questions of reliability, veracity and privacy. The problem is not a new one – we have always had to work out who and what to trust – but, as Diane Coyle eloquently put it in her initial point of view for the Future Agenda programme, 'the skill of verification has become fundamental'.

Electronic communications and access to data have also thrown up a new challenge and that is, quite simply, how do we manage the amount of information currently available? There is a clear trend towards increasing volumes of data being shared, stored, accessed and mined – and much of this will be personal data relating to individuals. All indicators show a steady growth in pervasive user-generated content, ever-expanding data collection by governments and corporations (for example, in social networks), increased collection of transactional data, improved decision-support algorithms, new and ubiquitous wireless technologies and connectivity, and new types of data from an ever-widening range of next-generation sensors. This is all adding to the collective store of information being created and made available for use. At the same time, the cost of data storage will continue to fall and in the end, be reduced to almost nothing.

Over the next decade, as data collection grows exponentially, so will the value of the information. Therefore, it will become increasingly important to identify who we trust to have access to it. Consumers will become aware of both the worth of their personal information and the damage that can be caused by abuse of it. This is likely to occur at the same time as organisations recognise this value and create the market mechanisms and vehicles through which it can be monetised – at its most simple, this will be in the form of more sophisticated, targeted advertising. Governments will also seek to improve the integration and intelligence that can be gained in order to deliver a smarter and safer planet.

As a consequence, in many countries, the burgeoning share of the population who care about their data will become increasingly concerned and want to better control access to their personal information. They may well also turn to collective information sharing in some instances such as health. Expect a flurry of personalised technologies to come to the fore which will help improve monitoring, diagnosis and treatment as the effects of genomic knowledge start to have impact. Tackling diabetes and other chronic diseases through collective information sharing requires individuals to trust a system in which patients are willing to share medical diary data. The challenge will be to foster trust in the organisations that hold the data. Expect new, specific protections to be provided to the users – but not necessarily all users and probably not in all locations. In other areas, where the benefits of sharing data are less clear, there may be a greater reluctance to participate.

As a result of all the technilogical innovations, it is becoming more and more difficult to manage personal information. There are numerous reasons for this: the increasing decentralisation of services and storage will make control and clear responsibility for data protection an open issue; the international nature of information will present greater challenges relating to how we consider and manage where it should be located; changes to current telecom structures and interoperability between different technologies will present a range of new issues for us to master; and, at the same time, consumers will become increasingly aware of more local, individualised online communities. The proper management of this through individual actions, government regulation and corporate governance is a tough challenge as we head into the next decade.

In order to be successfull, all those involved, technologists, regulators and, to a lesser extent, consumers, need to understand the innovations taking place. This is not straightforward given the current rate of change. In particular, they will have to grapple with the concept of the 'right to forget' given that data communications are increasingly being archived. Erasing our digital footprint is already difficult but in the future expect it to become even harder to do and increasingly important as the Facebook generation grows up and has to deal with the consequences of potentially embarrassing or damaging memories from the past.

Sharing information

The internet, with its philosophy of openness, quite literally created a World Wide Web of trusted and trusting users. Until recently, that is. New issues to do with security, banking scams and identity theft have all put our trust in the system to the test. This means that the information people are willing to share is changing and there are shifts in how they share it. As recent controversies around Google Buzz and Facebook's privacy settings engender wider public reaction, individuals may want to share less, or at least hold back information.

At the core of this, people will increasingly come to realise the fundamental issues involved with sharing their data. Some may question the cost/benefit ratio in terms of what are, or are not, the immediate paybacks to be gained from sharing. While it is possible that a national or, more likely, an international 'Privacy Chernobyl' will be needed for major regulatory change, for individuals the consistent drip-feed of breaches of trust might

have a similar effect and could change behaviour and attitudes. Perhaps, despite our overwhelming willingness to communicate, ongoing lapses in privacy by corporate and government organisations, widely reported in the media, will motivate individuals to limit their online profiles and choose not to share personal data electronically. It might be this lack of trust in the system rather than public regulation which will act as the online policeman of the future.

This scenario is all the more likely when you consider that information is increasingly global and therefore beyond the reach of national regulation and protection. Will people continue to share information as routinely as they do now? There are obvious benefits, including convenience, speed and access to associated but relevant information, but equally there are disadvantages, particularly if trust in the system fails.

Consumer privacy

Privacy anxieties and a growing lack of trust in large online organisations could be mitigated by open, interoperable networks that give users control over their own information in the future. This would meant that people could then choose who to share their information with, decide to remove it from one organisation and transfer it to another, and, most importantly, they would be able to delete it altogether without concern that it will be cached somewhere to resurface later. Here there is an opportunity for a trusted intermediary who can facilitate this interface – a 'data bank', for example, or a way for companies to lend their algorithms and their technologies to users who keep control of their information rather than giving it to companies to process within their own technological domain. There are already shifts in, for example, the financial services industry to provide or create new trusted intermediaries to hold and share private data about customers. These may, within certain constraints, lead to changes in consumer-focused data use. Some participants in the programme see that in future we should advocate an ownership model where the user and the company collecting the user's information are joint custodians of that data.

Greater transparency may also have an impact on consumer attitudes. If, for instance, companies had to disclose how much the information they have is actually worth to them in business terms, individuals may recognise more readily the balance of the cost–benefit equation and make conscious choices about what to share and with whom. In a health infrastructure based on mobile phone technology, it was found to be a more effective form of transparency to authorise wide access to patient records among healthcare providers, but notify the patient when a record had been accessed, rather than control and pre-approve viewers of information. In healthcare, particularly, wider use of consumer data is clearly seen by many as a benefit, but one with the potential for great individual costs given the complexities of reimbursement of healthcare costs from insurance companies in some economies. In areas where the potential is great for harm to individual consumers from misuse of data, we should not take this for granted. We must be careful not to give an illusion of control – ineffective controls that let users think they have complete control over their data when they do not.

For many services, it is difficult to move, correct or erase data, so privacy must be a priority feature.

People must clearly see the benefits of sharing their information. Current legal structures designed to protect privacy may not actually serve as a catalyst for this: privacy as a legal compliance issue is a cost, not a feature, and legal compliance does not spur privacy innovations. In addition, most of the discussion today considers only current technologies – instead we need to recognise that someone might be able to protect their privacy or breach such protection using a totally different technology. Even if competition did spur innovation, we may see a 'dancing partner' effect, since it is the intent of all companies to maximise the value of data.

Systemic privacy

Although much attention is focused on the privacy relationship between the individual and companies, we should also recognise the shift in the citizen–government data relationship. While there is widespread acceptance of increased government surveillance to counter national security threats from terrorism and so on, in some countries there is resistance to overt rather than covert personal information collection. Data collection can provide societal benefits in areas beyond national security – public health, for example. To help manage the rising societal/financial burdens of chronic diseases, for example, some governments are making use of connections between areas such as individual health costs, food preferences and behaviours.

Equally, the advent of smart meters as part of the wider smart grid is prompting discussion about the introduction of flexible, dynamic pricing of energy and water that will influence patterns of consumption. Although benefits can be shown, a balance must be struck between those benefits and the invasiveness of the data collection and the costs or harm to citizens. Negative reactions may arise with an approach that relies purely on the 'stick', but such an approach may be more effective initially. Well-focused incentives – the 'carrots' – must also play a part. Discounts to incentivise sharing of data may well be introduced and pricing policies will change so, for example, we pay per mile travelled rather than per gallon of gasoline or per year of car insurance. However, in all this we must keep in mind there are various values at play here.

The next generation

As members of the next generation live ever more virtual lives, the amount and value of their data is on the rise. One common assumption is that today's children and teenagers don't care about their privacy and are not fully aware of the availability of their data. That is not strictly true and is a view increasingly being challenged. Studies such as those by the Pew Research Center are showing a much more nuanced approach, highlighting that youngsters do want control over their data, but who they trust and who they want to keep information from is completely contextual. University students, for instance, care less about government or corporate access to their information than they do about the university itself (which, in their lives, really plays the role of both government and corporation). We should not be surprised that attitudes to privacy and trust amongst young people are a function of age and experience, not a generational shift. With maturity comes an understanding of the consequences of sharing data, and behaviour change is evident amongst some. Already today, many kids are taking information off their Facebook and MySpace profiles and restricting what data are open to the public. Looking ahead, we can only expect this trend to increase as the private data/public data balance changes. Later generations are likely to find the negotiation between public and private online lives much easier.

Global versus local

Global or local?

Alongside getting to grips with the balance between trust and privacy over the next ten years, we need to consider how change happens. To what extent, for example, do things develop because of cooperation between individuals, companies and governments as opposed to people, companies or nations doing their own thing? An important issue today is the role of global organisations, their influence upon individual states and, indeed, the impact that state will have on communities and ultimately individuals. As highlighted by the discussions around global pandemics, electric mobility, a third global reserve currency, local foods and migration magnets, decisions will have to be taken on the basis of the balance between global versus local needs and priorities. Will we, for instance, increasingly 'think global and act local' or will we be able to effect change at a global level in concert with others? In many ways the balance between these two is the basis of all human behaviour and so can be seen as a moderator of the future and a catalyst for change.

In his book *The World is Flat,* Thomas Friedman argues that the 'biggest source of friction is the nation-state'. Certainly, looking around the globe at the current areas of conflict, it is difficult to argue against this. The problem is, as humans, we like to belong to a group. Hence we crave a sense of identity to bind us together and for many years a sense of nationalism provided the glue. Times are changing, however.

Mike Hardy suggested in his initial perspective on the future of identity that, 'as our world becomes smaller through migration and mobility, both virtual and real, it may be that people and groups will express themselves most insistently though multiple rather than single identities'. The question is how this will affect the way we deal with the challenges ahead. Will the interconnected generation collectively take responsibility for global change or will it simply re-align behind new groupings of self-interest?

The current world order, especially its institutions such as NATO and the UN, was established after World War II and was created to deal with the limitations of nation-states endeavouring to stop wars between countries and provide a platform for dialogue. Not surprisingly, the priority was world peace. Given there has been a significant increase in the number of nation-states (the UN began with 51 members and it now has 192), the fact that a third global war has been avoided is evidence that the overall strategy has worked. That said, this success has been tempered by the failure of the UN to intervene to stop some of the worst atrocities in our recent history, most noticeably the genocides in Rwanda and Bosnia.

Recently there has been a change of emphasis. Not only has anxiety around security become of more international concern but the shift in the economic balance of power has meant that America and Europe can no longer set the global agenda without the involvement of China, India, South Africa, Brazil and others. What started out in 1975 as the G6 and then became the G7, and then the G8 when Russia joined in 1997, is now the G20. Its members represent 85% of global gross national product, 80% of world trade (including intra-EU trade) and two-thirds of the world population. As it stands, alongside other institutions such as the IMF and the World Bank, the G20 is increasingly responsible for managing global financial systems. After the economic crisis hit in 2008, the G20 grew in stature and the debates that take place when the group now meets shape national agendas on various policies relating to trade, exchange rates and financial sector regulation.

In addition to economic and security issues, the world also faces global challenges that transcend national boundaries in ways which could hardly have been anticipated in the immediate post-war era. Climate change, health security, water management and organised crime are now high on the agenda and need to be addressed by international collaboration on an unprecedented scale.

Global collaboration

Global collaboration seems to work most effectively when there is a clear problem to address. Take for example the issue of conflict and 'blood diamonds'. The trade in these illicit stones has fuelled decades of bloodshed and devastation in countries such as Angola, Côte d'Ivoire, the Democratic Republic of the Congo and Sierra Leone. The Kimberley Process, led by the diamond-producing African countries themselves, is a joint government, industry and civil society initiative to stem the flow of these diamonds. It imposes extensive requirements on its members to enable them to certify shipments of rough diamonds

as 'conflict-free'. The Kimberley Process now has forty-nine members, representing seventy-five countries, with the European Union and its Member States counting as an individual participant. No one would say that the process is perfect but diamond experts estimate that conflict diamonds now represent a fraction of 1% of the international trade in diamonds, compared with estimates of up to 15% in the 1990s.

Global technology networks are agnostic so in addition to offering great opportunities for legitimate business they also provide great opportunities for crime – money laundering and drug trafficking, for example. Money laundering is a particularly tricky problem. Some suggest laundered money amounts to between $800 billion and $2 trillion a year; others suggest it could represent as much as 10% of global GDP. Whatever the real figure, it seems one reason that we are failing to address the problem in any significant way is because global collaboration on crime has not been effective and regional laws are allowing the bad guys to get away with it.

Turning to health, a key priority for global collaboration is the need to manage and control disease outbreaks. We have already discussed how increased trade and travel spread disease with extraordinary speed – at the time of writing this book (August 2010) around 620 million passengers have taken a flight this year alone. On top of this, the poor quality of healthcare services in some regions means that the risk of the spread of infectious diseases is growing. Pandemic outbreaks of disease are becoming more common. These need not necessarily be new diseases – many of the 'traditional' killers have grown resistant to existing treatments. The World Health Organization states that, in some places, one in four people with tuberculosis (TB) becomes ill with a strain that can no longer be treated with standard drug regimes.

Individual states can do little on their own to cope with problems such as this and there is a risk that richer countries may ignore fundamental deficiencies in health infrastructures in their poorer neighbours – the very places where outbreaks can occur. As highlighted by the earlier insights on global pandemics and bio-surveillance, a priority for the WHO is therefore to gather and share disease information, statistics and policy on a global basis. We also need to develop and implement strategies for containing outbreaks and sharing best practice around the globe. The SARS outbreak in 2003 clearly demonstrated that failure to act swiftly to contain the spread of disease can have both societal and economic implications; the estimates of business and spending loss are around $60 million. Building on the improved response to H1N1 in 2009, we can expect the work of the WHO to play an even more prominent role on the world stage in the next ten years.

In the water arena, there has been increasing concern in recent years over the likelihood of water wars. As water-stressed regions in the Middle East, Africa and Asia have started to try to secure new supplies of fresh water, some commentators predicted the return of conflict over water as a shift from oil. 'Is water the new oil?' has been a popular phrase. The reality, so we heard in the Oxford workshop in the UK, is that there are many examples of countries cooperating over water supplies, even if some of them are in dispute over land and other resources: for example, countries in the Congo river basin are working together to ensure trans-border water management based on joint strategies and principles. The Democratic Republic of the Congo, Cameroon, Republic of the Congo and Central African Republic have also been working together on issues such as decreasing pollution and improving access to water sources.

Climate change is another area where national boundaries have little relevance and where many see that Copenhagen failed to generate meaningful agreement. By contrast, the Montreal Protocol on substances that deplete the ozone layer is a good example of how international action has had marked success. Indeed, it has been hailed as an example of exceptional international cooperation, with Kofi Annan quoted as saying that it is 'perhaps the single most successful international agreement to date'. The Montreal Protocol worked because there was compelling scientific data, an agreed answer on the way forward and an iconic public impression of the hole in the ozone layer above the Antarctic.

However, unlike the hole in the ozone layer which offered a wealth of clear data to support the need for multilateral action, climate change is a much more subjective process with insufficient consensus on the extent of its impact. For example, the Intergovernmental Panel on Climate Change predicts a wide range of outcomes from a mildly warming global temperature increase of 1.1°C by the end of the century to a hothouse of 6.4°C. This uncertainty – the time lag between initiatives to reduce climate change and a noticeable decline in temperature – makes it difficult, particularly for politicians driven as they are by electoral cycles, to deliver change on any significant scale. Added to this, the immediate economic expediencies of the global recession could, in some way, explain the reasons behind the failure of the Copenhagen Summit to achieve what was originally planned.

Although not as influential as they could be, given the challenges outlined above, it is clear that there is still a role for global institutions. Some have already changed the lives of millions of the most needy – take, for example, the work of the World Health Organization, the United Nations Children's Fund (UNICEF) which focuses on the rights of the child or the UN Development Programme with its work on poverty reduction. These organisations are testament to the effectiveness of international collaboration. That said, organisations such as these tend to be bureaucratic and slow and, given some of the challenges we now face, it is clear that we have a long way to go to achieve change. Lack of progress on the big issues – poverty, sanitation, climate change – has led some to question whether implementation of solutions at a global level is the best way to drive this change. Clearly there is a role for global organisations to analyse, quantify and monitor activities, share best practice even, but as they are not held directly accountable, they have to work within confines and are therefore limited in the way they can act and operate. They can set an ambition and direction but rarely, it seems, execute actions to hit the targets successfully. As we look to the future, the issues we face are too significant and too global to deal with without them but global initiatives are only effective with national and local support.

Global markets

Thomas Friedman argues that globalisation in the 21st century is built on the power of the individual to collaborate and compete on a world wide basis. He stated that, 'because the world is flattening and shrinking, Globalisation 3.0 is going to be more and more driven not only by individuals but also by a much more diverse – non Western, non white – group of individuals'. In the years to come it will be increasingly difficult to differentiate between organisations, large or small, on the basis of location.

This flattening out of business processes has led to growing pressure to break down trade barriers and we now see nations around the globe keen to liberalise trade regionally, bilaterally and unilaterally. The growing acceptance of free trade and trade groups such as NAFTA (North America Free Trade Agreement), the EU and, in particular bilateral trade agreements (especially with China and other countries) has accelerated country-to-country trading, making it easier for multinationals and smaller companies to do business internationally.

Although there is hope that the reduction of trade barriers will have significant benefits in the long term, there is still a long way to go. The world trade system is currently labouring under a massive proliferation of regional trade agreements. Richard Baldwin, Professor of International Economics at the Graduate Institute, Geneva, said: 'This tangle of trade deals is a bad way to organise world trade. The discrimination inherent in regionalism is already economically inefficient but its costs are rising rapidly as manufacturing becomes ever more internationalised. Stages of manufacturing that used to be performed in a single nation are now often geographically unbundled in an effort to boost efficiency. Supply chains spread across many borders. Unbundling, which accelerated since the 1990s, is the most important new element in the regionalism debate. It is the reason why business is pushing so many nations to "tame the tangle"'.

This complex regulatory model is having a particularly negative effect on poor nations, as it is prohibitively expensive for them to compete. Development aid to emerging economies is one way of addressing the gap between the rich and poor nations but history has shown that, despite significant investment, it is difficult to ensure that money is well spent or even arrives at its intended destination. An alternative solution is to remove trade tariffs from products made in poorer countries by, for example, extending schemes like the 'Everything but Arms' initiative.

Working locally across the world

Open access to information in the workplace is now becoming commonplace for many organisations. Chris Meyer's view of 'Enterprise 2.0', with its 'porous boundaries, shared responsibilities, greater transparencies and fewer mandatory rules and practices' is enabling many, particularly perhaps in the West, to find jobs which are more diverse and stimulating whilst at the same time enjoying the comfort of our own home. High-speed internet connections mean that many of us can now live locally but work globally, spanning continents at the click of a button. This ability to connect world-wide will offer some the luxury of being able to spend more time at home and participate more in local activities. It also means that the way we live and work could change, reducing the need to travel to and from office locations and increasing the need for localised hubs where like-minded people from different walks of life can enjoy a sense of togetherness. In this light some see globalisation as a potential saviour of community living.

Although it is possible for some to use 'Enterprise 2.0' as a means of staying in touch while eschewing the need to travel, for many others the requirement to find work has meant an enforced displacement from family and friends. Some fear that increasing migration will lead to the 'McDonald's effect', the 'Westernisation' of culture, yet the ability to keep in touch may well mean that cultural diversity will enjoy a renaissance as migrants are able to access a wealth of information from their country of origin. Diaspora communities around the world can use today's global media networks to maintain contact with their communities. For example, it is perfectly possible for anyone living in New York to go online to listen to Chinese music, watch an Indian news channel or look up a Sri Lankan recipe. Whatever their nationality, access to connectivity allows people to maintain and share links with their traditions.

At the same time, the fact that people in emerging economies are able to innovate without having to emigrate means that local cultures have a better chance of survival. It is no longer the case that an MBA graduate from Delhi has to move to London or New York to get a good job – he or she is equally likely to want to go to Bangalore or Mumbai.

Joel Cawley, VP of Corporate Strategy at IBM, talks about 'localising the global', where companies which understand the emerging global infrastructure then adapt all the new tools it offers to local needs. This applies just as much to the multinational as the self-employed car mechanic who uses the internet to source cheaper spare parts from foreign suppliers.

Link of local to global

James Gleick was one of the authors who brought chaos theory to the mainstream. One of the issues highlighted in this was the butterfly effect where, due to the interconnection of the world's weather systems, 'a butterfly fluttering its wings in Brazil could cause a tornado in Texas', or a typhoon in Asia. The global economy is itself now a set of interconnected local and regional economies and man-made systems where actions in one area can have an impact on another. Some of this we understand, but not all. We are only just starting to recognise how some of the systems we have created actually work and how they are interdependent. While the links between US sub-prime mortgages and Greece's public debt have recently become apparent, many observers expect that such causal relationships will multiply in the coming decade. This will be not only in financial systems but also across public healthcare, nutrition and information.

In an always-connected world, the speed at which events amplify across systems seems to be increasing steadily and leading, in some places and some parts of society, to feelings of being out of control. Just as we thought we knew how the global financial system worked, and then had some nasty shocks, we can expect to experience new changes in the future. What is important here is that we recognise how a local event can change global attitudes.

Some of the most notable changes in public policy over recent years have come from actions that others have copied. Take for example the introduction of the congestion charge in London and the smoking ban in New York: both were local moves to address local issues and both have since been adopted and adapted in many other nations. With groups like the C40 in operation to share experience between cities, we can expect to see more new approaches and a faster migration of ideas. So, for example, how quickly will the world adopt a fat tax on high-calorie foods to try to halt the obesity epidemic? Will New York introducing a 'soda tax' on cola act as a catalyst for change as other cities, rather than nations, take the initiative? While the 20th century was characterised by a drive towards global platforms and standard products, maybe the 21st century will witness a much more varied world with locally appropriate solutions implemented using local resources and so increasing the resilience of the systems to shocks and surprises.

Global and local

What, we hope, this illustrates is that global change can occur both from globally agreed courses of action and from local initiatives. The Kimberley Process and the Montreal Protocol have worked because of global agreements just as much as congestion charging and smoking bans in public areas have worked from action taken at a local level. Although we live in an increasingly globalised world, we need to also recognise that globalisation does not in itself cause the changes to happen. Certainly the more connected systems within which we now operate can significantly accelerate and amplify a change, but it is the difference between global and local which is most significant.

What we also need to recognise is that while many, including the Future Agenda team, have used the term 'global/local' to capture this relationship, in reality global is often not global at all but instead national or regional. The EU, for instance, is a regional body that at one level is just a local player on the world's stage with the ability to pass regulation on say, smart meters, that could have a global impact just as its policies against GM food have not. At the same time, as a cross-government body, the EU often fails to get things done at a regional level which individual countries or cities within its footprint can do. Equally, in the US there have been many instances on issues as varied as stem cell research and environmental controls when individual states such as California have been able to make a change that is way beyond what the US government at a federal level can get agreement for. And, while being the world's leading superpower, there have been several examples – from the invasion of Iraq to the adoption of GM food – where the US has been unable to take the world with it.

Global/local as a driver of future change is an important issue that matters as much at an individual/village level as it does at a national/world level. Sometimes things happen because everyone agrees that it is the right thing to do, and so get on with it. Sometime things happen because someone just does it and others copy.

Choice

The nature of choice

Alongside the global/local, top-down versus bottom-up view of change, it is important to recognise that, while the way decisions are made can differ widely, how we as individuals make choices is also a major influence on how the future will roll out. But making decisions is not easy, especially when the emotional and political may be as strong as the rational. In education, business and government circles, people have to make conscious choices that are highly influenced by what they feel. What we believe may be less dependent on hard data and instead more influenced by our perceptions of how others will view us, our understanding of social norms, the incentives and penalties that we think will accrue to us and our memories of how similar experiences have made us feel.

Back in the 1960s, the aforementioned Yale psychologist Stanley Milgram undertook some research on obedience and willingness to obey authority figures. His findings led to two theories. The first, the theory of conformism, suggested: 'A subject who has neither ability nor expertise to make decisions, especially in a crisis, will leave decision making to a group and its hierarchy.' The second, the agent state theory, outlined that: 'The essence of obedience consists in the fact that a person comes to view himself as the instrument for carrying out another person's wishes, and therefore no longer sees himself as responsible for his actions. Once this critical shift of viewpoint has occurred in the person, all of the essential features of obedience follow.' So, it seems, for big decisions, many in the world will agree with what is said by authority figures through delegation or recognition of responsibility. This is supported, fifty years later, by Accenture research on energy choices which concludes that 'while concerns over energy-related issues are high, consumers are unwilling to do significantly more themselves but are happy for action such as developing low-carbon sources of power to be taken by the energy supply side'. When faced with difficult choices, we like to take the easy option – and often the easiest option is to let others make the choice for us. Encouraging the public to get involved in long-term decision making is therefore a big hurdle for many governments.

In the world of simpler choices, such as what products to buy, we are generally happier making decisions, but here also there are some interesting issues. In his original view on the future of choice for the programme, Professor Jose Luis Nueno of IESE shared some insights from some recent research: 'It may seem counter-intuitive but fewer choices provide higher levels of satisfaction: people like to have lots of variety, but when faced with too many choices, we tend to vacillate and delay decisions. We may want thirty-one options instead of six, but we find it easier to choose one of six than one of thirty-one. In a series of experiments with men and women from a range of different cultures we found that the greatest level of satisfaction, both with the final choice and the decision-making process, was reached when people chose from an intermediate number of alternatives as opposed to large or small choice sets. These findings have practical implications for people offering many choices to customers, consumers and employees today.' Professor Nueno and others' views are that, even for relatively easy decisions, in the future we may increasingly be offered fewer choices and be happier with that. However, the question then is: who will decide which options we are given?

The 2008 book *Nudge* by Richard Thaler and Cass Sunstein has been credited with changing the way many politicians around the world are looking at how to get things done. Anecdotally on the reading list of many EU ministers, it explores how coherent choices can be made by presenting decisions differently and proposes that 'default outcomes of a situation can be arranged to be the outcome desired by the person or organisation presenting the choice'. According to the authors this is an underused method and has many areas of application such as financial planning, sustainable consumption and healthcare. For example, as highlighted by success in Spain and Belgium, a greater supply of transplant organs can be created by using a system of presumed consent followed by an opt-out rather than opt-in process: the default is that we are all organ donors and have to choose not to be, as opposed to us proactively making the decision to be a donor. As such, the number of hearts, kidneys and other organs available has risen significantly in Spain and Belgium. This is the concept of 'choice architecture', which is how the options available for us to choose from are laid out. Looking ahead to the world of 2020, some see that this will be hugely influential in determining how, for example, fat taxes, carbon credits, personal healthcare budgets and pay-per-mile transportation will be shaped and adopted in different countries. Real-time data, and even predictive analysis, will enable individual people, companies and government departments to make better decisions, but key to this is how the options are presented.

There are also decisions that are made for us that we are rarely aware of. For many of us, global standards are not something we think of on a day-to-day basis yet they shape much of what we do and determine some of the choices available to us. Whether the standards and protocols that make the internet function, the standards that have been defined so that DVDs all work the same way, health standards that set out how drugs should be tested or standards around time, finance and labour, these global agreements influence us greatly. Although often considered a bit dull, institutions such as the ISO have been pivotal in working with competing companies across different sectors to set down the way things will operate and work together to make things simpler and more efficient. Standards are choices that have been made for us at a global level just as much as tax levels are set nationally or regionally.

Looking forward, as China increasingly sets the standards that others will follow, questions are being raised about which institutions will be the most influential and what customs will be reflected in the rules of interoperability that result. As the main producer and consumer of most of the world's products, China will have the lead and, if companies in other countries wish to trade with China they will have to follow Chinese standards for manufacture and operation. While the ISO may still have a guiding role, some see that its rudder will be very much steered by China.

While some issues in the past may have been too difficult for us to make choices on, as we become more aware of them and thus feel better able to take a view, we become more confident in our decision making. For example, many commentators believe that over the next decade we will increasingly make choices about the environment based on a global view. The Worldwide Fund for Nature (WWF) published the influential Living Planet report in 2008 which showed that wild species and natural ecosystems are under pressure around the world. All areas that they detailed, from pollution and over-exploitation to climate change and habitat loss, 'stem ultimately from human demands on the biosphere'.

The Global Footprint Network has presented this in a highly tangible way by looking at how many planets' worth of resources we are currently consuming: 'Today, humanity uses the equivalent of 1.4 planets to provide the resources we use and absorb our waste. This means that it now takes the earth one year and five months to regenerate what we use in a year.' Many people feel that this 'number of planets' view is far easier to understand than carbon footprints, food miles, embedded water and the like and will become a major datum by which we measure activity going forward. As a globally relevant reference, some are putting their weight behind it becoming a core metric by which alternatives are compared and thereby allow more informed choices to be made. As environmental concerns become more influential than economic ones in some regions, this could be a major influencer of choice.

Common causes and global champions

Another element in how change happens is when there is a global cause to support, and how it is supported. Those such as the eradication of global poverty and hunger, reducing child mortality, improving sanitation and combating AIDS are part of the UN's Millennium Development Goals and therefore steer policy and resources. Equally, there are causes such as ending whaling and preserving free speech that are more effectively led and championed by NGOs such as Greenpeace and Amnesty International. At the same time there are causes that are taken up by philanthropic ventures such as the Clinton Foundation, which is working with the C40 cities to reduce greenhouse gas emissions, and the Gates Foundation, which is well on the way to helping eradicate polio and improving access to vaccines. In addition, there is the catalytic role played by celebrities, from George Harrison in raising funds for Bangladeshi refugees, to Bob Geldof with Live Aid to provide famine relief, to Bono and the Red brand that supports the Global Fund to Fight AIDS, TB and Malaria.

All of these, and more, are examples of how momentum around an issue can be built up in a way that connects people and organisations around the world to fight a common enemy. They are often different from government agendas, or cut across them, and are too big to be dealt with in local isolation. What they create are common causes that we can all understand but then use a global champion as the catalyst for change. Whether an NGO, a foundation or a rock star, these global champions help to bring issues to our attention and provide a conduit for action, and so help us make choices to get involved in change that is often global in scale and impact.

The next decade

As highlighted by many of the views gained from the Future Agenda programme, over the next decade we have some major challenges to face and some big decisions to make. Dealing with the implications of just the four issues detailed as certainties in Part 1 will be a major test. Providing accommodation, food and employment for another billion people at the same time as many of the key resources on which we depend for our livelihoods or just to live are running out could be seen as an impossible task; however, with global connectivity, universal access to information and the massive growth in economic power that is taking place in Asia and other developing economies around the world, the talents, technologies and finance that we need to use are arguably becoming available. When we look at some of the other issues discussed in Part 2, from electric mobility and almost zero waste to halting Alzheimer's, reducing the rich–poor gap and better managing our water supplies, there are a host of decisions to be taken and choices to be made.

We all live in local communities making decisions and choices on a day-to-day basis that may seem far removed from global concerns such as climate change, resource shortages, poverty and the future of currency. However, in this connected world, as more are recognising, the collective decisions that we take over the next few years will have a significant impact in the long term. Some observers even predict that the nature of the infrastructure, climate and economic growth for the 21st century and beyond will be shaped by pivotal decisions that are taken between now and 2020. 'The impact of the choices and trade-offs we make over the next few years will be felt for decades to come.' How we make those choices will be heavily influenced by what we have outlined so far in Part 3 and so we need to understand potential linkages between and across these issues.

Dimensions for change

Bringing all this together, we can see that in discussing the issues of trust and privacy, global/local and choice, some of the topics evidently overlap. If, for instance, we have more trust in an organisation then we are less likely to be as concerned about privacy: if, as a patient, I have great confidence in the healthcare system that I use, I will willingly give them access to as much of my personal data as they can make use of; I am more likely to give them information about myself because I trust them to make better decisions on my behalf and provide me with the best support. The converse is also true. If you have low trust in an institution, you will be more cautious about sharing data and hence privacy will be a bigger issue for you. So, one way of looking at the first two issues is to view them as part of a single dimension of how things can change. The way we interact with institutions, governments, companies and individuals lies on a spectrum. One end is characterised by 'strong collaboration' with high trust and low concerns for privacy while the other end can be seen as 'independent action' with low trust and hence high concern for privacy.

Turning to the global/local discussion, some of our examples illustrate that many of the big decisions being made around the world are having an impact on issues that are often initially left to global decision-makers but, in the end, are pre-empted by local actions. While many agree that high-calorie food is bad for us, we recognise that most governments and major companies will not proactively decide to ban them. In most countries, the big top-down decisions take time to make and so it is more practical for a chain of supermarkets to decide to, for example, put high-calorie foods in a separate 'indulgent' aisle and so present customers with easier health-related choices. There are exceptions though, such as in Finland, where the highly consensual population embraced wide-ranging government action to change national diets in order to reduce the high Finnish mortality rates associated with cardiovascular disease; the measures included not having high-fat milk available in shops. However, in general, local seems quicker than global.

While globalisation has increased our ability to exchange ideas across geographical boundaries and the systems now in place accelerate and amplify this communication, the nature of how change happens still very much revolves around whether people, companies or governments agree to do something together as a collective or in isolation. A common way of looking at this is that change can happen in the top-down 'centralised' manner where all sign up to the change and act on it, or it can occur in the bottom-up decentralised manner where decisions and actions are 'distributed' by design or consequence. Sometimes, action that might be considered better undertaken in a centralised manner can have higher success when dispersed: a World Bank study in 2006 highlighted that 'decentralisation in the form of moving government closer to the people

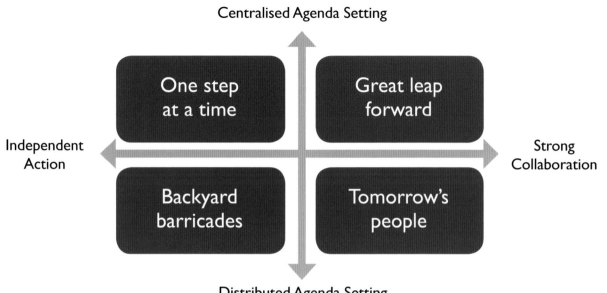

by empowering local governments helps to reduce corruption due to increased accountability'. Although there are many issues that require centralized decision making, for others the distributed approach may be more effective.

Add in to this the apparent desire for us as individuals to make easy rather than difficult choices (or at least choose from a limited portfolio of options), then tackling some of the big issues for the next decade becomes even more of a challenge. If we consider future changes that could occur, such as those detailed as outcomes of the Future Agenda programme in the preceding parts of this book, we can see that we need to accommodate numerous different possible contexts within which that change will happen.

We have two dimensions to consider – one of strong collaboration (with high trust and low privacy) versus independent action (with low trust and high privacy) and one of centralised versus distributed agenda setting. Putting these together we can see four different possible worlds in which change may occur. These could be seen as four scenarios within which the future may develop and we all need to be cognisant of them. None of them is certain and none can be selected as a preferred route by a government, a company or an individual. While some are potentially more linked to specific topics than others, they are all possible ways of something taking place and are therefore all credible worlds in which the future can unfold.

Great leap forward

In a world of centralised agenda setting and strong collaboration, we can rely on high levels of institutional influence and clear common global aims while at the same time having good partnerships between organisations willing to trust each other and openly share information. This is the world Copenhagen was aiming at, but missed, and is also the one that will best enable us to deal with global pandemics, use less energy and reduce the gap between rich and poor. It is how a third global currency will most likely come into being. This is where the 'great leap forward' can happen but it is also where enormous effort is required to get everybody not only to agree on the issues, the ambition and the direction, but also to agree to pull together to make it happen. This is about working for the greater long-term good where short-term sacrifices may need to be made by some but where all agree on the need to do something significant for the collective benefit.

Tomorrow's people

By contrast, in a world of strong collaboration but distributed agenda setting, decisions will be taken locally but individual organisations, cities and nations will openly share their experience and insights. While the actions that occur are primarily locally focused and driven by individual views on the right way forward, open innovation and knowledge transfer is rampant. Individuals still share and collaborate even if they are deciding what to do separately. This is the world of city-states doing their own thing but being part of a club; it is a world in which mobile money can have an impact as each region adopts its own version but they are interoperable and share

platforms; it is where 'tomorrow's people' take the decisions that are right for them but do so by sharing and learning from others such that all can progress, even if not following the same path. For many, this is the way most things in the past have happened and so is a default setting for the future.

Backyard barricades

The world of independent action and decentralised agenda setting is one in which, as Leo Roodhart put it in the initial view on the future of energy, 'nations will rush to secure energy resources, fearing that energy security is a zero-sum game, with clear winners and losers'. This is where 'backyard barricades' are erected as each individual, village or country does its own thing and seeks to serve and secure their own agendas without reference to others. This is where all-out competition is the name of the game, where the short term is probably more important than the long term and where economic growth is prized above all else. It is a world of self-interest and protection with high suspicion of change, slow innovation and bilateral deals rather than global agreements. Regulatory hurdles are erected to protect intellectual property and keep things close. Ironically this is a world that could accelerate trends towards local foods, local currency and water management, as looking after your own is the priority, but is also a world more likely to move towards more drone wars and increasing reinvention, less migration and more waste.

One step at a time

Lastly, we have to consider the world of independent action but centralised agenda setting. This is a world in which we move incrementally towards a better future 'one step at a time', where all agree on the big picture but deal with it in their own way. It is where all share a common ambition but no one can agree the right way to act on it and we don't trust each other enough to want to cooperate. People and organisations have a global view, but, with all the best intentions, place their own needs ahead of the collective good. This is where, for example, all recognise key resources demands but manage their own resources within that context. It is a world that favours different regions all supporting electric mobility by creating the right solutions for their needs but without sharing technology platforms. It is where competition increases but within a global context and so issues such as mass medical tourism and migration magnets come to the fore ahead of others.

All four of these are credible worlds in which different ways of making changes take priority. They share some common features but are also distinct in how change will play out. Unfortunately, we cannot choose which one to follow because all are possible. At times and in certain locations around different topics, some may be more probable than others but they are all still credible and therefore have to be accommodated. We cannot choose to go for one scenario and ignore the other three and must plan for all options. How we all make choices and influence the future will be as an amalgam of multiple technological, social and economic issues, but how we deliver those choices will probably need to be in reaction to the way our world moves.

In the final part of this book, we shall look at some of the implications of all this for governments, organisations and individuals.

PART 4
Innovating the future

Having explored the certain and probable changes for the next decade, including the drivers and moderators of these changes, Part 4 draws some conclusions and raises a series of key considerations for governments, organisations and individuals. Governments need to address these questions so they can make the right policy decisions and enact effective regulation. The questions for organisations are aimed at stimulating innovation and provoking responsiveness to change. For us as individuals, we need to understand what our roles will be by 2020 and identify how and where we can exert our influence in the decade to come.

Innovation as well as foresight

The rationale behind the Future Agenda project was twofold: open foresight and stimulating innovation. We all need to be more informed about the big issues and challenges we face, so a primary focus has been to obtain a better impression of what the world will look like in 2020. To do this we have combined different perspectives and cut across different sectors to create a richer, deeper picture of the future. This has allowed us to have a clearer view of the probable versus the possible and make connections between different events that may occur in order to help us to make more informed decisions.

While this has been the central theme of the programme to date, it was always intended that the insights that make up the majority of this book should act as stepping-stones to additional activity. We want to encourage people to think about the 'so what?' in order to help companies, governments and individuals build strategies to prepare for the future. This is why we decided to make the information we collated as widely available as possible so that everyone could have immediate access and use it to stimulate their thinking.

One notion that we all seem to agree on is that 'business as usual' isn't an option and therefore something has to change. In addition, it seems clear that the choices we make in the next few years will greatly define not just the world in 2020 but also the shape of the world that our grandchildren will inherit. This is why we believe that, when thinking about the future, it is important to be open to different approaches and consider the opportunities presented by different industries and seemingly unrelated initiatives. After all, real innovation often occurs at the intersection of disciplines and the cross-over between sectors as technologies and business models jump from one area to another.

It is also worth considering the possibility that change could emerge from unlikely places, stimulated by unexpected events rather than being driven from a top-down global initiative. Policymakers, businesses and key influencers can often take advantage of this and have a significant role in amplifying and accelerating the pace and scope of change by investing in supporting infrastructure, encouraging the 'right' habits and choices through education, information and incentives, developing reinforcement policies and bringing to market new products and services.

Throughout all our discussions, there was general agreement that if we are to deal with some of the major challenges that evidently face us over the next decade we need to innovate across the board. We need new policies and regulations to both accommodate and moderate some of the events that we can now see on the horizon, and we also need to create new products, services and business models that will both create value as well as change the rules of the game so that, as an increasingly global society, we can make tangible, sustainable and positive progress.

Seeing the bigger picture

If progress is to be made from innovation at a higher, broader level, then it is necessary to take a view beyond the usual horizons. This is not just about seeing further into the future in your own sector but also means better understanding forthcoming developments in other areas and recognising how they could have an impact on your future.

Previous initiatives have demonstrated that before you can start to take decisions on your potential future focus, you first need to gain a clear overview, which should be a combination of what you know from within your industry and what you can learn from outside your industry that could potentially have implications for you.

Matching the 'inside-out' and the 'outside-in' views enables organisations to identify a host of innovation opportunities beyond an internal extrapolation of today. This is an approach that was initiated by Shell and has been widely adopted by others, ranging from P&G and Mars in the private sector to government bodies from Ireland to Singapore in the public arena. Understanding the bigger global picture ahead of making decisions on the 'so what?' has helped them all see emerging opportunities ahead of their peers.

Challenging existing views

For many organisations, making use of credible foresight to validate existing thinking is top of the agenda. Many a company and many a government have strong views built up from years of experience and these often form the basis of their core strategic assumptions. As most organisations seek to have differentiated and robust growth strategies for the future, we hope the Future Agenda insights will be used to challenge and then support their existing perspectives. Governments will, for example, have validated perspectives and policies that they may already have in place around issues as varied as food and energy security, migration, privacy and healthcare costs. Equally companies may have been able to verify existing views on the demographic shifts around an ageing and an increasingly urban population; the challenges of operating in a networked world where capabilities are temporary; the opportunities available in better managing increasingly scarce resources; or the potential that lies in rethinking and reinventing business models.

While this is very useful in areas such as economic planning and government research funding prioritisation, other organisations also see value in using new insights to challenge and change their existing views. As well as picking the elements that map onto the 'organisational mindset', some will use the Future Agenda insights to see how they could change the status quo and undermine the assumptions that have been made in the past. As GE has termed it, seeking to 'destroy your own business' is a highly effective way of identifying your weaknesses and gaps in strategy. Rather than using new insights to prop up current views, having them challenge these perspectives and see how a challenger brand or nation could usurp the current leadership is a great way to spot the issues that may need attention.

Accommodating wild cards

Within this context, it is often easy to focus only on the high-impact, high-probability futures. While these are clearly important, focusing solely on these can be problematic. High-impact, low-probability events can also be the source of major change and, if they occur, can significantly undermine a government's or company's growth strategies.

To address this, companies such as Nokia complement what they know and believe with consideration of 'what if?' scenarios. As Nassim Nicholas Taleb describes in his book *The Black Swan*, this is a way of understanding the possible effects of high-impact, low-probability events. Recent cases would include, for example, the volcanic ash cloud. In the main, these events are ignored by governments and companies alike because the minute likelihood of their occurrence – perhaps a one in a million chance – makes them almost impossible to plan for. They are therefore not automatically resourced but, when they do happen, their impact is significant.

We suggest that pragmatic organisations need to focus just as much on the possibilities as on the probabilities as they plan for the future. By gaining a view of what might potentially have an impact on their plans and what the implications could be, they can then decide where to make the necessary investments. For some organisations, the answer is to direct the majority of attention towards scoping and delivering the big deals for the future but, at the same time, ensure there is a dedicated team in place to look at the potential wild cards. By setting up an 'early warning system' that tracks identified high-impact, low-probability events, such as, for example, the 'Privacy Chernobyl' discussed earlier in this book, organisations, be they government or corporate, can then have a richer picture of the opportunities and threats ahead of them.

Building scenarios

As Peter Schwartz, co-founder of GBN, recently outlined, 'Scenario planning is a methodology designed to help guide groups and individuals through exactly this creative process. The process begins by identifying potential forces of change, then combines them in different ways to create a set of diverse stories – or scenarios – about how the future could evolve. Scenarios are designed to stretch our thinking about both the opportunities and obstacles that the future might hold. They explore the dynamics that might alter, inhibit, or enhance current trends, often in surprising ways. Together, a set of scenarios captures a range of future possibilities, good and bad, expected and surprising – but always plausible. Importantly, scenarios are not predictions. Rather, they are thoughtful hypotheses that allow us to imagine, and then to rehearse, different strategies for how to be more prepared for the future – or, more ambitiously, how to help shape better futures ourselves.'

Creating such views of the future as clear stories has been part of the strategic process in companies and countries for a number of years. Looking ahead, as the global interconnection between events grows and the speed at which change occurs accelerates, we can already see many more organisations adopting this process. However, in doing so, there is a risk that some will use scenarios simply to explain the development of their market or region within the known/known boundaries. We think this is a mistake and has led to identikit growth scenarios in numerous corporations where a technology-enabled future is believed to be inevitable, which means the only questions that are raised are around priority and speed of application. In the cosmetics sector, different organisations have similar views on the future impact of wellness and the cross-over with healthcare. In the world of food, many companies have scenarios around the impact of convenience and nutrition, but not so many also consider security-of-supply issues or the acceptance of GM and pharma foods.

Going back to the comments in Part 1 about the need to also explore the unknowns, accommodating the broader view is critical. Rather than keeping the scope close to the core, the leaders in scenario development look at the big picture beyond their specific area of interest and then filter out the implications for their own activities and interests afterwards.

Identifying growth opportunities

By using the insights from the Future Agenda programme that apply within and around an area of focus, and combining them with existing internal views of how the future may unfold, we hope organisations will be able to build different pictures of the future that can be used to stimulate new thinking. Sometimes these organisations may include the perspectives on trust, cooperation and centralised versus distributed agenda-setting outlined in Part 3

as an integral part of this. On other occasions, this will be a secondary layer that fits alongside more regional- or sector-based scenarios.

As the Future Agenda programme has progressed, we see some signals of change that organisations may want to consider. For example:

- Due to a perceived lack of success from centralised action on global issues, people are again coming together at the community level to do practical things that are within their control.

- New institutions, from the C40 to locavores, are developing to support these initiatives and share stories and best practices.

- There is significant potential for behavioural change around, for example, energy use to make a difference whilst we await global deployment of new technologies.

- Many institutions are developing a better understanding of how to 'nudge' choices to help people make better decisions and to change the nature of demand.

- Technology can be used to help shift demand – as everything becomes 'smart', it becomes easier for us to make the right choices.

- But there is also concern around gaps in understanding that consumers and policymakers have about many of the issues and challenges.

At a time when others may be more focused on the predictable, shorter term, having a strong, longer term perspective is essential. From government departments and intergovernmental institutions such as the IEA to multinationals such as Ericsson, Ford and PepsiCo, major organisations around the world are looking for the future view to drive innovation. Implicit within this is the need to explore key options and implications. The questions to ask include: What are the consequences to us if X happens? If we bet on alternative A, what are the chances that B, C and D could occur and with what impact? How can we use our capabilities to enable a wider change? These are all questions to ask.

By beginning with informed and credible views from across different areas, the Future Agenda programme is designed to act as a catalyst to emphasise new issues at a level deeper than would otherwise be the case. Just as has already happened in a number of areas with organisations from the healthcare and media sectors through to transport and energy, we hope that the insights will be used to highlight a number of major new growth platforms.

Questions

Given the breadth of the insights summarised in this book, you might have had numerous questions come to mind already.

Some of the salient issues that deserve further consideration could include the impact of public debt in the West; the rise of the Asian consumer; concerns over security of supply of key materials and their associated prices; the need to shift to a low-carbon economy; the possible split of the developed world into a two-speed grouping; increasing security; societal shifts around privacy; the interconnectedness of global systems; fragmented organisational structures and new alliances; the impact of new technologies; advances in medicine; the role of the elderly in society; the shift from ownership to access; or the impact of growing unemployment in mega-cities.

While each organisation and individual will have a different understanding of the specific impacts and implications of many of the issues discussed, it is clear from this project and many of the subsequent programmes already under way that there are some common questions that many participants are seeking to answer. Some of these can be seen at a government/regulatory level, others at more of a company/organisational level and still more at an individual/personal level. To help start additional conversations and stimulate some thoughts, in the following pages we have outlined ten questions for each of these levels that we hope will be useful.

Ten questions for governments

Are we really focusing on the big issues for the next decade?

We know about climate change and the energy crisis, but are health, food and water as high as they should be on our agenda? Are we making assumptions about citizens' willingness to share data?

Do we share the big challenges we all face with the right people and organisations?

How many of us are being straight with the public on the likely impact of a 4°C rise in temperature, the increasing cost of healthcare for the ageing and those with chronic disease, and how to pay for it all?

To what extent can we really use taxation and policy to change behaviour?

Can we nudge people to adapt to a new world, eat less meat and use less energy or will we have to ban certain products and, if that doesn't work, how effective will the tax lever be?

Which new areas of the economy should we be investing in for the future?

Will our current local strengths be long-term global successes? Should we stop supporting legacy industry and shift to a new world and, if so, where can we have the greatest effect?

What new skills will we need to have access to in order to support higher growth?

Does our population have the capabilities best suited to the challenges ahead? How quickly can we re-equip our workforces with the right skills? Should we start attracting the best migrants ahead of others?

Which regions of the world will we need to cooperate more effectively with?

Will our current trading partners be the best ones in 2020? As the centre of power shifts to Asia, should we forge new bilateral agreements or can we all act together as a coherent bloc?

Which currency should we be saving and trading in?

Do we have the right balance of foreign reserves? Are we too dependent on the US dollar or the euro? How prepared are we to trade in alternative currencies and change our reserve mix?

What is the balance between providing education and providing pensions?

Should we invest more in the next generation than we did the last? Can we rely on their income tax to pay for the rising cost of the elderly or should we put money aside to get us through?

How well are we prepared to deal with inevitable surprises?

Do we have the right bio-surveillance in place to protect our nation's health? Are we over-dependent on the wrong sorts of food? How good is our data security and can we be self-sufficient in energy by 2020?

Will we tackle the big challenges in isolation or will we collaborate?

How well aligned are we with other countries on the pivotal issues? Will we all agree on the right path and work in unison or are there areas where we will go our own way and, if so, where?

Ten questions for organisations

How well do we recognise the big issues on the horizon?

Are we really challenging ourselves to look beyond the status quo, to understand how changes outside our control will impinge on our sector and to plan for a different future?

How well do we understand the full implications of resource constraints?

Will we face problems from water shortages? How will we cope with less energy? How will we secure access to the materials that are running out and what options do we have for change?

Where can we use existing capabilities to create new sources of value?

As the world changes, what new activities will come to the fore where our skills and experience can be more effectively deployed and how can we best take advantage of the opportunities?

To what extent do we expect to have influence over our human resources?

If the world is getting smaller and flatter and the best talent is mobile, how can we attract the key people we need for the future to work with us, how can we stimulate them and how will they be rewarded?

What will we be required to report to stakeholders in 2020?

Will water footprints and carbon footprints become compulsory and what about energy use? Will intangibles be more important than fixed assets and what levels of risk will be acceptable to the market?

Is our understanding of future areas of opportunity better than that of our peers?

Are we paying enough attention to what we don't know? Do we understand the future any better than others? How vulnerable are we to change from outside and how and where can we best understand this?

How well equipped are we to respond to adjacent sector changes?

If new technology developments or changes in customer relationships occur in other areas, how can we best take early advantage of these in our own space and do we know how they could threaten our current activities?

How well are we tracking the possible future risks and challenges?

Are we paying enough attention to monitoring threats to both our core and potential new areas of activity? Can we create competitive advantage by spotting new opportunities earlier than others?

How will we manage our reputation in the future?

Will we be able to communicate with stakeholders in 2020? Will we be in control of our brand or will consumers have more influence? Are we prepared to change the way we act?

Are we sufficiently influential in new regulatory change?

Where will the new international standards emerge from and how can we be involved? Are we able to match our global and local operations to changing legal frameworks?

Ten questions for individuals

How can I play a part in changing the status quo?

How and where can I, as one person, make the greatest impact? What issue is most relevant to me? Who will I trust to give me accurate information?

How can I better live within the means of the planet?

Will technology allow me to do everything I want or will I have to use fewer resources? What sacrifices may I need to make? Should I judge wealth in the same way as my parents?

Which of my daily choices will have greatest influence over the future?

Should I walk to work or buy a bike? Will an electronic car be affordable? Should I become a part-time vegetarian? Is living in the city the best option for me and should I have a smaller apartment?

Am I prepared to pay the full cost for things in the future?
Will I pay $10 a gallon for fuel, €2 a litre for milk or £5 for a loaf of bread? Will I pay my carbon tax and fat tax on each purchase or against my monthly personal allowance? What am I willing to do without?

To what extent should I openly share information about myself?
How will I make and maintain friendships in the future? Will my virtual networks be as important as the people I meet in the 'real' world? Will I only share my personal information with my closest friends but be prepared to give all my health data to the government?

Where in the world will I find the greatest opportunities?
If I stay here, will there be enough for me to do or will I need to move? Do national boundaries matter? Should I consider moving to another country or continent or just be willing to travel further to work?

What professions will exist in 2020?
What should I learn? How will I manage and plan for a changing career portfolio? Should I become a bio-informationist, a privacy officer, a reputation enhancer, or an urban farmer? Or am I better off as a teacher, a doctor or a lawyer?

How can I best plan for retirement?
Can I afford to live to be 100? Shall I expect to work beyond 75? How will I keep myself healthy and active? What foods should I eat and where should I live?

How should I raise my children to prepare them for their future?
What is the best way to educate them? How do I ensure they have the right expectations and values?

What will I believe in?
How will I know what I should believe in? What and who will I trust? Should I consider the opportunities offered by religion?

Resources and references

I THE FOUR CERTAINTIES

Institute for the Future: http://www.iftf.org

IBM Global Innovation Outlook: http://www.ibm.com/ibm/gio/us/en/

Rumsfeld, NATO speech of 2002: http://www.nato.int/docu/speech/2002/s020606g.htm

UN Population Division Facts: http://www.un.org/esa/population/publications/popfacts/popfacts_2010-1.pdf

UN Population to 2300 Forecast: http://www.un.org/esa/population/publications/longrange2/WorldPop2300final.pdf

OECD Factbook 2010: http://www.oecd.org/document/62/0,3343,en_21571361_34374092_34420734_1_1_1_1,00.html

UN Population Division World Mortality Summary 2009: http://www.un.org/esa/population/publications/worldmortality/WMR2009.htm

UN Population Division World Fertility Patterns Summary 2009: http://www.un.org/esa/population/publications/worldfertility2009/worldfertility2009.htm

Economist Special Report on Fertility 2009: http://www.economist.com/node/14744915

UN Population Division International Migration Summary 2009: http://www.un.org/esa/population/publications/2009Migration_Chart/2009IttMig_chart.htm

Institute for German Economy Report (2007) on engineer shortage: http://www.euractiv.com/en/socialeurope/eu-labour-shortage-time-bomb/article-164261

UN Population Division Ageing Summary 2009: http://www.un.org/esa/population/publications/WPA2009/WPA2009_WorkingPaper.pdf

UN Population Division Urbanisation Summary 2009: http://esa.un.org/unpd/wup/wall-chart_1.htm

IEA Key Energy Statistics 2009: http://www.iea.org/textbase/nppdf/free/2009/key_stats_2009.pdf

IEA Energy Scenarios to 2050: http://www.iea.org/textbase/nppdf/free/2000/2050_2003.pdf

'How Many Years Left?' – *New Scientist* (2009): http://www.newscientist.com/data/images/archive/2605/26051202.jpg

IBM GIO Water Report: http://www.ibm.com/ibm/gio/media/pdf/ibm_gio_water_report.pdf

UNESCO World Water Development Report – Water in a Changing World: http://www.unesco.org/water/wwap/wwdr/wwdr3/

IFPRI data on farming efficiency: http://www.businessworld.in/index.php/Economy-and-Banking/From-Plough-To-Plate.html

CIA Factbook: https://www.cia.gov/library/publications/the-world-factbook/

Niall Ferguson, *The End of Chimerica* (2009): http://hbswk.hbs.edu/item/6094.html

Goldman Sachs – Long Term Outlook for BRICS: http://www2.goldmansachs.com/ideas/brics/long-term-outlook.html

Goldman Sachs – Is this the BRICS Decade? http://www2.goldmansachs.com/ideas/brics/brics-decade.html

East or Famine – *The Economist* (February 2010): http://www.economist.com/node/15579727

Accenture/Vodafone Carbon Connections Report (2009): http://www.vodafone.com/etc/medialib/cr_09/carbon.Par.76396.File.dat/carbon_web_2009.pdf

ICRIER/Vodafone – Impact of Mobile Phones Report (2009): http://www.icrier.org/pdf/public_policy19jan09.pdf

2 DRIVERS OF CHANGE: KEY INSIGHTS

The future of health

Automated people-care

Assisted living technologies for older and disabled people in 2030: http://www.fastuk.org/pagedocuments/file/Ofcom%20assisted%20living%20services%20report.pdf

iRobot Future of Robotics in Healthcare: http://www.irobot.com/sp.cfm?pageid=86&id=521&referrer=85

UK Personal Care at Home Bill 2010: http://www.dh.gov.uk/en/Publicationsandstatistics/Legislation/Actsandbills/DH_110405

Clinical enhancement

Darpa exoskeletons: http://www.howstuffworks.com/exoskeleton.htm

Soldier of the future: http://www.nypost.com/p/news/opinion/opedcolumnists/item_cRlyg3lsJH4jTFhCA3XFKM;jsessionid=6B52435CD7B0315F980280937DC216F5

Raytheon exoskeleton: http://www.raytheon.com/newsroom/technology/rtn08_exoskeleton/

Helicon: http://www.helicontherapeutics.com/cgi-bin/main.pl?section=Scientific

Turbo-charging the brain: http://www.scientificamerican.com/articlecfm?id=turbocharging-the-brain

Diabesity

Diabetes: the price of increasing prosperity – Deutsche Bank Research (2009): http://www.dbresearch.com/PROD/DBR_INTERNET_EN-PROD/PROD0000000000245092.pdf

'Epidemiologic and economic consequences of the global epidemics of obesity and diabetes' – *Nature* (January 2006): http://users.ox.ac.uk/~chri3110/details/NatureMed_01_06.pdf

Tackling Obesities: Future Choices – Project Report, UK Government Office for Science 2008: http://www.foresight.gov.uk/Obesity/14.pdf

World Diabetes Foundation: http://www.worlddiabetesfoundation.org/

Bloomberg Says a Soda Tax 'Makes Sense': http://www.nytimes.com/2010/03/08/nyregion/08soda.html

Global pandemics

World Health Organization – Pandemic Response: http://www.who.int/csr/disease/influenza/pandemic/en/

'Pandemic Hot Spots Map a Path to Prevention' – *Scientific American*: http://www.scientificamerican.com/article.cfm?id=pandemic-hot-spots-map

Singapore flu pandemic guides: http://app.crisis.gov.sg/Data/Documents/Resources/FluPandemicGuides/FluPandemicGuides/FLU_PANDEMIC_GUIDE_ENGLISH_LOW_RES.pdf

Halting Alzheimer's

Alzheimer's Association Facts and Figures: http://www.alz.org/documents_custom/report_alzfactsfigures2010.pdf

'Alzheimer's Disease — How Long Before We Find a Cure?': http://www.berkeleydailyplanet.com/issue/2010-02-25/article/34707?headline=Alzheimer-s-Disease-How-Long-Before-We-Find-a-Cure-

'Stem cells can rescue the memory from Alzheimer's disease' – *Daily Telegraph* (2009): http://www.telegraph.co.uk/science/science-news/5873215/Stem-cells-can-rescue-the-memory-from-Alzheimers-disease-claim-scientists.html

'Alzheimer's: Forestalling the Darkness with New Approaches' – *Scientific American*: http://www.scientificamerican.com/article.cfm?id=alzheimers-forestalling-the-darkness

Lund University Stem Cell Center: http://www.med.lu.se/stemcellcenter

Stem cells to aid study of Parkinson's: http://www.ox.ac.uk/media/news_stories/2010/100715.html

Mass medical tourism

Cosmetic Surgery Statistics: http://www.cosmeticplasticsurgerystatistics.com/statistics.html

Aravind Eye Hospitals: http://www.aravind.org/

Narayana Hospital – International Patients: http://www.narayanahospitals.com/internationaldivision.html

Narayana Hospital – Model for Affordable Care: http://knowledge.wharton.upenn.edu/india/article.cfm?articleid=4493

'Henry Ford of Heart Surgery' – *Wall Street Journal:* http://online.wsj.com/article/NA_WSJ_PUB:SB125875892887958111.html

Deloitte Medical Tourism Update: http://www.deloitte.com/assets/Dcom-UnitedStates/Local%20Assets/Documents/us_chs_MedicalTourism_111209_web.pdf

Pharma foods

UN FAO Health and Nutritional Properties of Probiotics: http://www.who.int/foodsafety/publications/fs_management/en/probiotics.pdf

Next Generation Nutraceuticals Report (2006): http://www.globalbusinessinsights.com/content/rbhc0172t.pdf

Biotechnology Industry Organization FAQ: Transgenic Animals: http://www.bio.org/animals/faq.asp

Golden Rice: http://www.goldenrice.org/

Systemic euthanasia

Brazil healthcare costs: http://www.scielosp.org/pdf/rpsp/v24n2/a06v24n2.pdf

End-of-life warning – Bloomberg: http://www.bloomberg.com/apps/news?pid=20601087&sid=avRFGNF6Qw_w

BBC report on euthanasia: http://www.bbc.co.uk/blogs/theeditors/2010/02/euthanasia_debate.html

Terry Pratchett lecture on assisted suicide: http://news.bbc.co.uk/1/hi/uk/8490062.stm

'Assisted suicide legal changes' – *Guardian* (UK): http://www.guardian.co.uk/society/assisted-suicide

Dignitas: http://www.dignitas.ch

EXIT: http://www.exitinternational.net/page/Home

The future of wealth

Differentiated commoditised knowledge

Thomas Friedman: http://www.thomaslfriedman.com/

Work Foundation report on Innovation, Creativity and Entrepreneurship in 2020: http://www.thework foundation.com/research/publications/publicationdetail.aspx?oItemId=241&parentPageID=102&PubType=

Gary Hamel on non-standard knowledge: http://blogs.wsj.com/management/2009/12/16/management's-dirty-little-secret/

Maven Research: http://www.mavenresearch.com/

MIT OpenCourseWare: http://ocw.mit.edu/OcwWeb/web/home/home/index.htm

Dynamic pricing

EU smart meter rollout: http://www.greenbang.com/smart-meter-rollout-to-reach-25bn-in-europe-by-2020-says-greenbang_14899.html

Airsage: http://www.airsage.com

Sense Networks: http://www.sensenetworks.com/

Lease everything

Zipcar: http://www.zipcar.com/

Spotify: http://www.spotify.com/

Bicycle rental in Paris: http://www.velib.paris.fr/

Renault Twingo recyclability: http://www.renault.com/en/capeco2/les-criteres-renault-eco2/pages/renault-eco2-champions.aspx

Less energy

IEA World Energy Factsheet 2009: http://www.iea.org/weo/docs/weo2009/fact_sheets_WEO_2009.pdf

E.On Use Less Energy: http://www.eontalkingenergy.com/

McKinsey US Energy Efficiency Report 2009: http://www.mckinsey.com/clientservice/
electricpowernaturalgas/downloads/us_energy_efficiency_full_report.pdf

Local currency

Brixton pound: http://brixtonpound.org/what/

Uganda Mobile Airtime: http://mmublog.org/africa-east/mtn-mobile-money-spotlight-on-uganda/

Mobile money

Wizzit: http://www.wizzit.co.za/

M-PESA: http://www.safaricom.co.ke/index.php?id=745

Globe GCash: http://site.globe.com.ph/

Digital Money Forum: http://digitaldebateblogs.typepad.com/digital_money/

Juniper Research on m-payments: http://juniperresearch.com/viewpressrelease.php?pr=173

Ernst & Young Mobile Money Report: http://www.ey.com/Publication/vwLUAssets/Mobile_Money/$File/
Mobile_Money.pdf

Richer poorer

OECD Growing Unequal Report 2008: http://www.oecd.org/document/4/0,3343,en_2649_33933_414609
17_1_1_1_1,00.html

LSE Report – An Anatomy of Economic Inequality in the UK: http://sticerd.lse.ac.uk/dps/case/cr/
CASEreport60.pdf

UN Habitat – State of the World's Cities 2010/2011 – Cities for All: Bridging the Urban Divide: http://www.
unhabitat.org/pmss/listItemDetails.aspx?publicationID=2917

Third global currency

Robert Zoellick: U.S. Dollar's Primacy Not a Certainty – Bloomberg (2009): http://www.bloomberg.com/
apps/news?pid=newsarchive&sid=aj_IWM84rMQ8

Niall Ferguson, *The End of Chimerica* (2009): http://hbswk.hbs.edu/item/6094.html

China currency decision boosts risk sentiment – *Financial Times* (2010): http://www.ft.com/cms/s/0/e3bc5b30-7d7a-11df-a0f5-00144feabdc0.html

ICRIER – Feasibility of an Asian Currency Unit: http://ideas.repec.org/p/ind/icrier/208.html

Is the renminbi the next global currency? – *McKinsey Quarterly*: http://www.mckinseyquarterly.com/Is_the_renminbi_the_next_global_currency_2532

The future of happiness

Active elderly

Yourencore: http://www.yourencore.com/

Retirement ages: http://www.ageuk.org.uk/latest-news/german-retirement-age-should-be-70/

Omkari Panwar – world's oldest mother: http://www.timesonline.co.uk/tol/news/world/asia/article4543797.ece

Choosing God

God is Back: http://us.penguingroup.com/nf/Book/BookDisplay/0,,9781594202131,00.html?God_Is_Back_John_Micklethwait

Pews Global Attitudes Survey: http://pewglobal.org/

'Market Economies with Churches and Market Economies without churches', Professor of International Business Economics at Beijing University, Zhao Xiao: http://www.danwei.org/business/churches_and_the_market_econom.php

Cocktail identities

Facebook Connect: http://developers.facebook.com/blog/post/108

Facebook Opengraph: http://developers.facebook.com/docs/opengraph

Guinness Book of World Records: http://www.guinnessworldrecords.com/

Enjoying the ordinary

Glam camping: http://goglamping.net/

Slow luxury: http://www.msnbc.msn.com/id/18561238/site/newsweek/

Lagom: http://www.treehugger.com/files/2008/04/word_of_the_yea_1.php

Less variety

IESE – Choice: How Much Is Too Much? http://insight.iese.edu/doc.aspx?id=1002&ar=12

Rhapsody: http://www.rhapsody.com/welcome.html

Live experiences

AEG: http://www.aegworldwide.com/03_music/music.html

LiveNation: http://www.livenation.com/

Seamless media consumption

Wired magazine iPad app: http://www.wired.com/magazine/2010/05/mag_editors_letter/

MIT Media Lab: http://www.media.mit.edu/

Switching off

OECD Korea Worklife: http://www.oecd.org/dataoecd/38/58/39696376.pdf

EU Working Time Directive: http://ec.europa.eu/social/main.jsp?catId=706&langId=en&intPageId=205

Nielsen US Internet Use Analysis: http://blog.nielsen.com/nielsenwire/online_mobile/facebook-users-average-7-hrs-a-month-in-january-as-digital-universe-expands/

The future of mobility

Asian aviation

IATA – State of Industry 2010: http://www.iata.org/pressroom/speeches/Pages/2010-06-07-01.aspx

Airbus Global Market Forecast 2009: http://www.airbus.com/en/corporate/gmf2009/

Boeing Current Market Outlook 2010: http://www.boeing.com/commercial/cmo/

New Airports for China: http://www.chinadaily.com.cn/business/2008-01/27/content_6423580.htm

World Tourism Association – Tourism 2020: http://www.unwto.org/facts/eng/vision.htm

Chinese trains

HSBC – China Railways Expansion: http://www.hsbcnet.com/solutions/emerging-markets/china_express.html

'Engines of Growth', Austin Ramsey, *Time* (2010): http://www.time.com/time/magazine/article/0,9171,2008791,00.html

US Strategic Plan for High-Speed Rail: http://www.whitehouse.gov/blog/09/04/16/A-Vision-for-High-Speed-Rail/

Clean shipping

International Maritime Organization: http://www.imo.org/

MacKay, David, *Sustainability Without the Hot Air*: http://www.withouthotair.com

Clean Shipping Organization: http://www.cleanshipping.org/

Seas at Risk – Clean Shipping: http://www.seas-at-risk.org/n3.php?page=67

Electric mobility

Tesla Motors: http://www.teslamotors.com/

Renault Zero-Emission Vehicles: http://www.renault-ze.com/

Better Place: http://www.betterplace.com/global-progress

'China and the US: The Potential of a Clean Tech Partnership' – *McKinsey Quarterly* (2009): http://www.mckinseyquarterly.com/Automotive/Strategy_Analysis/China_and_the_US_The_potential_of_a_clean-tech_partnership_2419

German National Platform for Electric Mobility: http://www.volkswagenag.com/vwag/vwcorp/info_center/en/news/2010/05/Volkswagen_AG_Invites_German_Chancellor_to_Journey_to_the_Future.html

Intelligent highways

DARPA Grand Challenge: http://www.darpa.mil/grandchallenge/index.asp

San Diego Automated Highway PATH project: http://www.path.berkeley.edu/nahsc/

FROG project Netherlands: http://faculty.washington.edu/jbs/itrans/parkshut.htm

Volvo 2020 safety aim: http://www.volvocars.com/uk/top/about/news-events/pages/default.aspx?itemid=5

Booz & Co – The Intelligent Highway: A Smart Idea? http://www.strategy-business.com/article/li00064?gko=9148d

EU eCall Programme: http://ec.europa.eu/information_society/activities/esafety/index_en.htm

Muslim Europe

Eurostat: http://epp.eurostat.ec.europa.eu/portal/page/portal/eurostat/home

Europe: Integrating Islam – Council on Foreign Relations (2009): http://www.cfr.org/publication/8252/europe.html

Demographic Challenges for Europe (2008): http://ec.europa.eu/regional_policy/sources/docoffic/working/regions2020/pdf/regions2020_demographic.pdf

'The Changing Face of Europe', David Coleman, University of Oxford: http://www.oeaw.ac.at/vid/empse/download/empse08_01_1.pdf

People tracking

iPhone location services: http://support.apple.com/kb/HT1975

Google Latitude: http://www.google.com/intl/en_us/latitude/intro.html

Google Goggles: http://www.google.com/support/mobile/bin/answer.py?hl=en&answer=166331

Face.com: http://face.com/

Facebook Places: http://blog.facebook.com/blog.php?post=418175202130

Urban (im)mobility

TRL/Shell: City Blueprints – Pathways to Sustainable Mobility: http://www.trl.co.uk/downloads/general/City%20Blueprints%20Pathways%20to%20Sustainable%20Mobility.pdf

Professor Jeff Kenworthy, 'Transport Heaven and Hell' – ITS (2008): http://www.fh-frankfurt.de/de/.media/fb1/Studiengaenge/Urban_Agglomerations/research/its_focus_411_final1.pdf

The future of security

Alternative proteins

International Food Policy Research Institute – Fish to 2020: http://www.ifpri.org/publication/fish-2020

China Corn, Soybean Demand to Climb – *Business Week* (2010): http://www.businessweek.com/news/2010-05-20/china-corn-soybean-demand-to-climb-executive-says-correct-.html

Depleted fish stocks: http://www.euractiv.com/en/cap/fish-farming-seen-driving-food-security/article-187688?Ref=RSS

Meat tax: http://www.foodnavigator-usa.com/Financial-Industry/Bioethics-professor-argues-for-meat-tax

In vitro meat: http://www.invitromeatfoundation.eu/home_en.html

Meat Free Mondays: http://www.supportmfm.org/index.cfm

Synthetic Genomics: http://www.syntheticgenomics.com/

Bio-surveillance

Biosense: http://www.cdc.gov/biosense/

WHO Integrated Disease Surveillance Programme: http://www.afro.who.int/en/clusters-a-programmes/dpc/integrated-disease-surveillance.html

Chatham House Centre on Global Health Security: http://www.chathamhouse.org.uk/research/global_health/

Corporate LEGO

The Management Lab: http://www.managementlab.org/

Funky Business: http://old.funkybusiness.com/funky/

Credible sources

Semantic Web: http://www.w3.org/2001/sw/

Drone wars

'Drones Are Weapons of Choice in Fighting Al Qaeda' – *New York Times* (2009): http://www.nytimes.com/2009/03/17/business/17uav.html

BAe Taranis: http://www.baesystems.com/Sites/Taranis/index.htm

General Atomics: http://www.ga-asi.com/

Solar sunrise

Michael Moyer, 'Climate Change May Mean Slower Winds': http://www.scientificamerican.com/article.cfm?id=climate-change-may-mean-slower-winds

Sustainability Without the Hot Air, David MacKay: http://www.withouthotair.com

Solar America Initiative (US DOE reports): http://www1.eere.energy.gov/library/default.aspx?page=7

Shell Technology Futures: http://www.shell.com/home/content/innovation/news/technology_futures/

Carol Sue Tombari, *Power of the People*: http://www.amazon.com/Power-People-Americas-Electricity-Speakers/dp/1555916260/ref=sr_1_2?ie=UTF8&s=books&qid=1280393014&sr=8-2

Virtual authenticity

Open ID: http://openid.net/

Know Your Customer Process: http://www.complinet.com/connected/solutions/global-screening/sanctions-enforcements/

Google boss warns on social use of media: http://www.bbc.co.uk/news/technology-11009700

Water management

World Bank/McKinsey – Charting Our Water Future: http://www.mckinsey.com/App_Media/Reports/Water/Charting_Our_Water_Future_Full_Report_001.pdf

WBCSD H20 Scenarios: http://www.wbcsd.org/DocRoot/6lpXteuAUNqxK50GOKNZ/h20-scenarios.pdf

SAB Miller Water Footprinting Report: http://www.sabmiller.com/files/reports/water_footprinting_report.pdf

Water Report – *Economist* (2010): http://www.economist.com/node/16136302

The future of locality

Almost zero waste

Waste Report – *Economist* (2009): http://www.economist.com/node/13135349

EU WEEE initiative: http://ec.europa.eu/environment/waste/weee/index_en.htm

Bridging the last mile

Council of Supply Chain Management Professionals: http://cscmp.org/

Logistics Research Centre, Heriot-Watt University – Carbon Auditing the 'Last Mile': http://www.imrg.org/80257418006E81C9/(httpInfoFiles)/484AE15036BC4CF18025757D00344948/$file/Online-Conventional%20Comparison%20Heriot%20Watt%20180309.pdf

Community living

Cisco Telepresence: http://www.cisco.com/en/US/netsol/ns669/networking_solutions_solution_segment_home.html

J.G. Ballard: http://www.ballardian.com/

Dense cities

Urban Age Project – LSE: http://www.urban-age.net/

WHO Global Age Friendly Cities: http://www.who.int/ageing/publications/Global_age_friendly_cities_Guide_English.pdf

Climate Change and the Environment – Scientific Committee on Antarctic Research: http://www.scar.org/publications/occasionals/acce.html

UN Habitat: http://www.unhabitat.org/

Intelligent buildings

NREL Zero Energy Buildings: http://www.nrel.gov/docs/fy06osti/39833.pdf

SMART 2020 programme: http://www.smart2020.org/

IBM Smarter Buildings: http://www.ibm.com/smarterplanet/uk/en/green_buildings/visions/index.html

Cisco Intelligent Buildings: http://www.cisco.com/web/strategy/docs/trec/GruppoRETI.pdf

Local foods

World Summit on Food Security (2009): http://www.fao.org/wsfs/world-summit/en/

India National Food Security Mission: http://nfsm.gov.in/

UK National Food Strategy: http://www.foodvision.gov.uk/pages/food-strategy

Hantz Farms Detroit: http://www.hantzfarmsdetroit.com/

Mega-city states

C40 Cities: http://www.c40cities.org/

Rise of the region-state: http://www.foreignaffairs.com/articles/48759/kenichi-ohmae/the-rise-of-the-region-state

The Next Big Thing: Neomedievalism, Parag Khanna: http://www.paragkhanna.com/?p=154

MIT 19.20.21 Programme: http://www.192021.org/

Urban Age Project – LSE: http://www.urban-age.net/

Migration magnets

Migration Development Research Centre: http://www.migrationdrc.org/index.html

Canada Immigration Plan 2010: http://www.cic.gc.ca/english/department/media/releases/2009/2009-10-30.asp

Peter McLeod on Canada Immigration: http://itunes.apple.com/us/podcast/german-marshall-fund-podcast/id203080872

3   MODERATORS OF THE FUTURE

Chris Patten, *What Next? Surviving the Twenty-first Century*: http://www.amazon.co.uk/What-Next-Surviving-Twenty-first-Century/dp/0713998563

Thomas Friedman, *The World is Flat: The Globalized World in the Twenty-first Century*: http://www.amazon.co.uk/gp/product/0141034890/ref=oss_product

Thomas Friedman, *Hot Flat and Crowded: Why The World Needs A Green Revolution – and How We Can Renew Our Global Future*: http://www.amazon.co.uk/Hot-Flat-Crowded-Revolution-Global/dp/0141036664/ref=ntt_at_ep_dpt_2

Edelman Trust Barometer 2010: http://www.edelman.co.uk/trustbarometer/

Anthony Seldon, *Trust: How We Lost it and How to Get it Back:* http://www.amazon.co.uk/gp/product/1849540012/ref=oss_product

Russell Hardin, *Trust*: http://www.amazon.co.uk/gp/product/0745624650/ref=oss_product

Marek Kohn, *Trust: Self-Interest and the Common Good*: http://www.amazon.co.uk/gp/product/0199217920/ref=oss_product

Richard Dawkins, *The God Delusion*: http://www.amazon.co.uk/God-Delusion-Richard-Dawkins/dp/055277331X/ref=sr_1_1?s=books&ie=UTF8&qid=1282731131&sr=1-1

John Micklethwait and Adrian Wooldridge, *God is Back: How the Global Rise of Faith is Changing the World*: http://www.amazon.co.uk/God-Back-Global-Faith-Changing/dp/0141024747/ref=sr_1_1?s=books&ie=UTF8&qid=1282731164&sr=1-1

Richard Thaler and Cass Sunstein, *Nudge: Improving Decisions About Health, Wealth and Happiness*: http://www.amazon.co.uk/Nudge-Improving-Decisions-Health-Happiness/dp/0141040017/ref=sr_1_1?ie=UTF8&s=books&qid=1282730867&sr=8-1

Malcolm Gladwell, *The Tipping Point: How Little Things Can Make a Big Difference*: http://www.amazon.co.uk/Tipping-Point-Little-Things-Difference/dp/0349113467/ref=pd_sim_b_4

Stanley Migram, *The Perils of Obedience*: http://www.grossmont.edu/bertdill/docs/perilsobed.pdf

Accenture, *The New Energy World – The Consumer Perspective*: http://www.accenture.com/Global/Services/By_Industry/Utilities/R_and_I/Energy-Consumer.htm

Pew Research Centre (2007), *Teens, Privacy and Online Social Networks*: http://pewresearch.org/pubs/454/teens-privacy–online-social-networks

The Economist, 'Legal confusion on Internet privacy: The clash of data civilizations': http://www.economist.com/node/16377097

The Economist, 'A survey of mobility: A world of witnesses': http://www.economist.com/node/10950499

The Economist, 'Civil liberties – surveillance and privacy: Learning to live with Big Brother': http://www.economist.com/node/9867324

Richard Baldwin, 'Multilateralising regionalism: The WTO's next challenge': http://www.voxeu.org/index.php?q=node/959

Francis Fukuyama, *Trust: The Social Virtues and the Creation of Prosperity*: http://www.amazon.co.uk/Trust-Social-Virtues-Creation-Prosperity/dp/0684825252

James Gleick, *Chaos – Making a New Science*: http://www.amazon.co.uk/Chaos-Making-Science-James-Gleick/dp/0749386061

4 INNOVATING THE FUTURE

GBN/The Rockefeller Foundation – Scenarios for the Future of Technology and International Development: http://www.rockefellerfoundation.org/news/publications/scenarios-future-technology

About the team

The Future Agenda programme was undertaken by an international team working together to design, deliver and synthesise the fifty workshops, numerous online discussions and additional dialogues with organisations around the world.

The team was led by Dr Tim Jones who originally conceived the programme, ran the majority of the workshops and undertook much of the synthesis. Tim has supported a wide range of government and corporate organisations in identifying future growth platforms over the past decade and is a regular speaker at international conferences on this topic. He can be contacted on tim.jones@futureagenda.org

Caroline Dewing led the Future Agenda programme within Vodafone, organised many of the workshops and took the lead role in the collation of all insights. Caroline can be contacted on caroline.dewing@vodafone.com

Supporting Tim and Caroline was a host of forward-looking people who gave their time and ideas to the programme. These included:

- Don Abraham at the Futures Company in New York
- Jacqui Allen at the British Council in Washington DC
- Elif Arslan at Vodafone Turkey in Istanbul
- Nicky Chambers of Best Foot Forward in Oxford
- Kasey Chappelle, Karl Slootweg and Binaya Neupane at Vodafone Group in London
- Tom Chignall at Vodafone New Zealand in Auckland
- Nuri Colakoglu at Dogan Media International in Istanbul
- Cornelia Daheim and team at Z_Punkt – The Foresight Company in Germany
- Madvendra Das and Prema Shrikrishana at Vodafone India in Mumbai
- Roger Dennis at Innovation Matters in New Zealand
- Will Gagley and Andrew Curry at the Futures Company in London
- Wendy Jordan at the British Council in London
- Themba Kinane and Leverne Cass at Vodacom in Johannesburg
- Andy Lewis, an independent consultant in the UK
- Dave McCormick, an independent consultant based in London
- Adam Newton at Royal Dutch Shell in The Hague
- Ian Noble at PepsiCo International
- Rachel Philips at Oracle UK
- Julia Rawlins at the British Council in Germany
- Tobias Rooney and Atif Sheikh at ?WhatIf! in London
- Dr Wendy Schultz at Infinite Futures in Oxford
- Anupam Yog and Sumati Nagrath at Mirabilis Advisory in New Delhi
- Eirini Zafeiratou and Cindy de Koninck at Vodafone Group in Brussels

In addition, there were sixteen people who provided the initial personal perspectives upon which the programme dialogue was built. These were:

- Dave Birch at Consult Hyperion in Surrey
- Professor Richard Black at the University of Sussex
- Professor Stewart Burn at CSIRO in Melbourne
- Professor Richard Burdett at the London School of Economics
- D J Collins at Google in London
- Diane Coyle OBE of Enlightenment Economics and the BBC Trust in London
- Jan Farjh at Ericsson Research in Stockholm
- Professor Mike Hardy OBE at the British Council in London
- Jim Kirkwood at General Mills Inc in Minneapolis
- Dr Ravij Kumar at ICRIER in New Delhi

- Dr Jack Lord at Navigenics Inc in California
- Chris Meyer at Monitor Networks in Boston
- Professor Jose Luis Nueno at IESE in Barcelona
- Mark Philips at Jaguar Land Rover in Coventry
- Leo Roodhart at Royal Dutch Shell in The Hague
- Professor Ian Williams at the University of Southampton

The fifty workshops that formed the core of the programme dialogue were undertaken by the team around the world. The locations of these workshops included Auckland, Bangalore, Barcelona, Berlin, Brightwell-cum-Sotwell, Brussels, Chicago, Christchurch, Eindhoven, Istanbul, Johannesburg, London, Los Angeles, Madrid, Melbourne, Mumbai, New Delhi, New York, Oxford, Rome, Shanghai, Singapore, Tallinn, Washington DC and Wellington.

The ultimate success of the Future Agenda programme is dependent on the enthusiastic support and participation of people who want to help shape the future, who have generously shared their expertise and been prepared to challenge the status quo. We would like to thank everyone who has contributed either online, though workshops, by participating in discussions or commenting on the outputs. We hope we have provided an accurate reflection of the views expressed and take full responsibility for any mistakes.

Index

First published in 2011 by
Infinite Ideas Limited
36 St Giles
Oxford
OX1 3LD
United Kingdom
www.infideas.com

A CIP catalogue record for this book is available from the British Library

ISBN 978–1–906821–57–9

All images © istockphoto.com
Except page 260, Mega-city-states and page 256, Local foods © Tom Fecht / Royal College of Art; page 218 Drone wars © BAE Systems.
Cover image, The world resized by population in 2020: www.worldmapper.org © Copyright SASI Group (University of Sheffield) and Mark Newman (University of Michigan).

Text designed and typeset by Nicki Averill
Printed and bound in Great Britain by Bell & Bain Ltd, Glasgow